What people are say

Muslim Mecha

It reveals and explains what is common among Jews, Christians, and Muslims. But its greatest gift is that it is a primer for Christians about Muslims. Unlike many items written by Christians, this is not an attack on Islam. It discusses Islam on an equal plain as Christianity while providing a focus on Sharia Law, something eerily strange to followers of Christ and members of a Democracy. The text is based on history and well researched. It uncovers Sharia Law not as a code for interaction but a way to exist with God.
Jamie Clary, Mayor, Hendersonville, TN

Eminently worth reading... I have read a number of books on as well as served in the Middle East; none lay out the similarities and contrast on Muslim and Islamic culture and Christian beliefs as well as Charles Brewton's book *Muslim Mechanics*. Few writers capture the depth of his analysis and understanding. After reading this book I believe you will agree with me, it is a "must read" for those wishing to step up their foundational knowledge of world religious dynamics.
Lieutenant General Dennis D. Cavin, US Army (Retired)

Whether you have a grasp on Islam or are a novice, *Muslim Mechanics* will improve your understanding. In a readable study, Charles gives insight on the beliefs and rules that Muslims follow, the actions they take, and where they are headed. If you are looking to get a handle on Islam, this is a read for you.
Reverend Don Hutchinson, Lead Pastor, Hendersonville First United Methodist Church

What part does religion play in the government of man? For Muslims quite a lot. As our United States enhances her diversity by welcoming those who follow the teachings of Allah we must try to understand the whys and wherefores of the interconnectivity of the Muslim faith and government. Dr. Brewton presents an in-depth analysis of historical research and current-day practices that reveal concepts of the Muslim faith that are at odds with the advancement of democratic and technological progress. It ignites an interest in learning more as we live and work together in a progressive society.

Betty Gallina, Retired Educator, Pinellas County Schools, Pinellas County, Florida

Muslim Mechanics

The View from
Behind the Curtain

Muslim Mechanics

The View from
Behind the Curtain

Charles H. Brewton

Winchester, UK
Washington, USA

JOHN HUNT PUBLISHING

First published by O-Books, 2023
O-Books is an imprint of John Hunt Publishing Ltd., 3 East St., Alresford,
Hampshire SO24 9EE, UK
office@jhpbooks.com
www.johnhuntpublishing.com
www.o-books.com

For distributor details and how to order please visit the 'Ordering' section on our website.

Design: Matthew Greenfield

UK: Printed and bound by CPI Group (UK) Ltd, Croydon, CR0 4YY
Printed in North America by CPI GPS partners

We operate a distinctive and ethical publishing philosophy in
all areas of our business, from our global network of authors to
production and worldwide distribution.

Contents

Preface

Mechanics

This book is not about Muslim mechanics who work on automobiles, although some good ones undoubtedly do. This book is about the study of Islam as a religion, as an organization, as a social institution, and the rules that make it unique. If you look up the term "mechanics," depending on the source, you will find descriptions like this:[1]

Pronounced m*uh*-**kan**-iks, noun
1. The branch of physics that deals with the action of forces on bodies and with motion, comprised of kinetics, statics, and kinematics.
2. The theoretical and practical application of this science to machinery, mechanical appliances, etc.
3. The technical aspect or working part; mechanism; structure.
4. Routine or basic methods, procedures, techniques, or details: the mechanics of running an office; the mechanics of baseball.

A basic mechanics textbook covers force and motion, work and energy, and fluid mechanics applied in industrial operations. It explains operation principles for simple machines, such as the lever, inclined plane, wheel and axle, pulley, and screw. Consider *Muslim Mechanics* as a necessary examination of the rules and principles that guide our understanding of Islam. I propose the following descriptions:

1. A branch of social science that explains how energy and forces affect populations and organizations.
2. The practical application of mechanics to the design,

construction, or operation of organizations and institutions.

3. The functional and technical aspects of an activity, like the study of classical mechanics but on an organizational and institutional level.

The purpose of this text is to understand why Muslims do what they do. What rules do imams and jihadists follow? Why do Sunni Muslims and Shiite Muslims have a history of animosity? To paraphrase an old term, up until now, "it's been Greek to me." This text tries to explore the rules and governing laws that Muslims follow. It has helped me immensely, and I strongly recommend it to anyone interested in knowing what the rules are.

Introduction

What do Christians, Jews, and Muslims have in common? They all believe in one God, angels, the Day of Judgment, and the afterlife that follows. In summary, when believers of these faiths die, they think they will be judged by God and hopefully experience eternity from God's purview. The significant issues that Muslims and Christians differ upon are the rules and criteria by which their God judges them. These criteria are a big deal. Each religion believes that they possess the proper knowledge, which their adherents must follow to be accepted and loved by the deity they believe in.

The average American does not understand much about Islam and its customs and beliefs. While not as prevalent with current-day Christians or Jewish believers, disrespect of Islamic beliefs can inspire some of their adherents to kill for religious purposes:

> Lack of knowledge about Islam and the Middle East ensured that twentieth-century media coverage of major news events involving U.S. interests in the region portrayed the Muslim world as the inevitable adversary of the West. These include the 1973 oil embargo; the 1979-80 Iranian Revolution and seizure of American hostages; the 1983 car bombing of the U.S. embassy in Beirut with the death of hundreds of Marines; the (1985) hijacking of a T.W.A. flight to Beirut, the murder of a Jewish passenger during the (1985) seizure of the *Achille Lauro* cruise ship; and the First Gulf War of 1990-91.[1]

The terrorist group, the Islamic State, or ISIS, is a microorganism of fundamentalist Islam. This quote by Major General Michael K. Nagata, special operations commander for U.S. Central Command in late December 2014, is even more to the point: "We do not understand the movement [i.e., the Islamic State], and until we do, we are not going to defeat it." Of the group's ideology, he said: "We have not defeated the idea. We do not even understand the idea."[2]

This ambiguity is partly true because Islam is a closed religion. For the most part, Muslims do not feel the need to share their beliefs with Christians for several reasons. Muslims believe that Christians have maligned their religion to make it easier to convert people to their faith. Muslims also believe that Christians are blind and intolerant to a religion whose logic seems unassailable.[3] That puts Christians at a disadvantage in dealing with Muslims. That fact came out during the trial for the so-called "Blind Sheik" following the 1992 World Trade Center bombing and again during the Fort Hood shooter's judicial proceedings in 2001.[4] Polling data suggests Americans have a poor understanding of essential elements of Islam but growing anxiety about Islam's (specifically Islamic fundamentalism's) compatibility with Western values of tolerance, acceptance, and civility.[5] This book is being written for that reason, to explain to the Christian community why Muslims do what they do.

Islam has a history of persecuting and killing "heretics" and "apostates" – those alleged to have departed from the correct path of faith in either word or deed. (Sadly, Christianity has a similarly dark history.) In many Muslim countries, crimes such as "heresy" are still punishable by death. We will look at what constitutes this blasphemy; it is not far different from the Bible.

Practically all the information I have found is available to the public. However, it is not in one source nor one location. I have gleaned information from scores of books and hundreds of journals. I have gone to the Library of Congress to look at Thomas Jefferson's copy of the Qur'an as well as other manuscripts. It is like a finely woven fabric, with each thread representing a piece of knowledge integral to an Islamic tapestry. If you understand the "why," the "who," and the "what," the rest of the puzzle begins to make sense.

To make a long story short, why do Muslims do what they do? The sole purpose of the Muslim religion is to establish Sharia[a] Islamic Law.[6] A prominent Muslim educator in the United States, Sharifa Alkhateeb, addressing a Muslim conference identifies the same objective but less concisely:

> our final objective is to create our own Islamic Systems and not only create Islamic systems for Muslims but to look at all the other people who are sharing this country with us as potential Muslims and if we look at them as potential Muslims and feel that we have the obligation which Allah has told us to try to bring them into the same style of thinking into the same way of behaving into the same objectives that we have then we have to have some way that we can communicate with them in some way we can work with them and in that long-range process of making America, Muslim, all of America, Muslim, then we have to have some actual short-range goals, we have to have some way of dealing with them and know how we're going to deal with them and in which ways and be very calculated about it, or else we will not accomplish our goals.[7] [Wording comes from the closed caption feature on the video clip.]

Since you now know how the plot unwinds, why read the book that follows? The old saying goes, "the devil is in the details," and many details go into this story. Most people do not understand what sharia law is. As research indicates, many jihadis fighting for the Islamic State caliphate only had a shallow awareness of how comprehensive it was.[8] Sharia law is a detailed outlook on how to live your life. It is inclusive and affects everything a Muslim does. If you understand sharia, you will better understand the Muslim mind.

One thought that stuck with me in my research is that Muslims are more structured than spiritual. They are bound by tradition – in that they follow theological rules, laws, and customs in making decisions. One branch of Islam called Sufism is very mystical and, as such, did seem to have a spiritual nature, but Sufism represents a minority view in Islam. Sunnism, the majority branch of Islam, expresses spirituality by believing that there is something greater than oneself. Still, Sunnis are expected to be subservient to their religious laws without hesitation, without thought, without disagreement. Two incidents stood out in my readings that supported this theory. In one instance, potential terrorists in Indonesia disbanded their activities after one influential Saudi scholar concluded they had strayed from their original purpose.[9] In another incident, representatives from the Islamic State caliphate removed a provincial commander in Somalia from command.[10] The regional commander had taken it upon himself to kidnap dozens of Muslim schoolgirls for ransom. The commander was relieved of duty because no religious precedents called for such action (the abducted girls were Muslim). It was acceptable to kidnap "unbelievers" such as Christian girls, which was not the case.

It can be hard to believe that it was the Islamic State which made this decision. The same organization that slit the throats of hundreds of orange jumpsuit-clad prisoners in Palmira, burned a Jordanian air force pilot in a cage and captured hundreds of Yazidi women in Iraq as sex slaves. That they would relieve a military commander because of religious malpractice makes a point where their values lie.

One key trend that I explore in this text is the growth and exposure of all the most significant world religions. Since my background is business strategy in an international arena, I used two common business concepts, the Product Life Cycle and the Growth-Share Matrix, to determine where Islam stands vis-à-vis other world religions. This analysis also reveals the types of strategies that work best in expanding influence.

One of the best sources of information that I found

originated with our military. During college, I remember a story from World War II concerning Germany's U-boats. There was not much information on how to hunt and destroy enemy submarines. U-boats were a relatively new technology and a considerable menace to domestic shipping at the beginning of the war; they sank millions of tons of war supplies in transit from the United States to England. By the end of the war, the U-boats' effectiveness was dismal as Allied military engineers had developed and refined tools, munitions, and processes to find and destroy them. They did this within a relatively short time of two to three years by applying operational research sciences.[11] I bring this up because, after the attacks on 9/11, the U.S. intelligence community pivoted quickly to become more knowledgeable about the country's new adversary. U.S. military scholars have studied Islamic fundamentalist organizational structures, networks, infiltration patterns, modes of operations, how they move money and resources, and their thought processes. The impact of their terrorism is slowly diminishing, albeit at a cost. Low casualties on American soil indeed indicate that intelligence and law enforcement agencies have performed well. You can find this unclassified information in scholarly journals such as the *CTC Sentinel*, published by the Combating Terrorism Center at West Point.

While exploring Islam, I have found many misperceptions about Judaism and my faith, Christianity. Islam claims many of the same prophets and the same stories, as seen in the Bible. Their stories, if correct, would change and challenge our beliefs in our faith. For that reason alone, I began this journey to find out what is real and what is not. After studying the Islamic religion, I am still an American Christian with a jaundiced eye for what is valid and not valid in our own beliefs.

One last thought I share with the reader is that fundamentalist or progressive Muslims do not fully share the American values of liberal democracy and free-market capitalism. First, a century ago, in 1905, Max Weber, a renowned German sociologist, argued that Christianity, after the Reformation, helped spur capitalism's rise.[12] Capitalism is the best economic means for allocating resources in a society, and it needs liberal democracy, free speech, and unregulated markets to work effectively. Second, there is statistical evidence that Protestant missions and missionaries were the most significant and best source of liberal democracy worldwide.[13] These freedoms are the source of American exceptionalism.

Most Islamic countries do not have and do not want institutions that focus on the individual's rights. As I shall explain in forthcoming chapters, Islam is a community-based religion. The needs of society are placed ahead of the needs of the individual. At the time that Jefferson was studying his Qur'an, he was unaware of this dichotomy in values.

Jefferson Must Be Spinning in His Grave

The idiom "spinning in his grave" originates in the late 1800s and refers to a deceased person to imply that some recent development would have caused them to be extremely upset if they were alive.[14]

In the U.S. Presidential election of 1800, Thomas Jefferson was the first American politician to incur accusations of being a Muslim from his political opponents. It would be two centuries later before that accusation was made against another presidential candidate, President Obama, in 2009. When John Quincy Adams, the son of the second President, John Adams, called Jefferson a "Muslim," it was the biggest insult a person could be labeled at that time. The Prophet Muhammad's negative caricatures had circulated in the press in America since the seventeenth century, and early Reformation preachers had cast Islam as the Devil's partner. Jefferson was known for promoting individual human rights, allowing Muslims, Jews, and even Catholics to have political rights equal to Protestants.

Jefferson won the election, but his understanding of Muslims turned out to be shallow.

As a Deist, Jefferson found that his opinions about the Trinity and the humanness of Jesus were parallel in Islam. Still, Jefferson subscribed to the anti-Islamic views of most of his contemporaries.[15] According to Jefferson, the Islamic laws that dealt with women, war, and Jews were not par for an advanced culture. During that period, most information about Islam originated from stories about the unfair patriarchal gender systems of the Middle East and North Africa regions. Most scholars now see Islam as no more inherently misogynist than the other major monotheistic traditions. While America had slaves, using war to encapsulate more slaves was unacceptable. Of course, the Muslim disparagement of the Jews was unsuitable for a Christian nation whose religious founder, Jesus Christ, was a Jew. For the last few years of his life, he continued to write about the Qur'an and the Prophet in disparaging terms.[16] In his view, "Islam was 'an improvement over the pagan religions yet fell short of the belief system Christianity represented.'"[17]

So, what might have caused Jefferson to be upset? There are three ways in which Muslim doctrines violate Jefferson's philosophy for a free and fair government. First, Jefferson penned the line "all men are created equal," found in the second paragraph of the Declaration of Independence.[18] Overall, this book will show that Muslims do have a degree of racial equality but not equality based on gender, sexual preference, or religion.

Second, Jefferson believed that the state should not prefer one religion over another. In other words, the state should not fiscally sponsor – through tax collections, tax revenues, or enforce laws of attendance or laws of tithes – one religion at others' expense. Islam is a way of life. Muslims believe that their faith should be the foundation of the way they live, their government. In Islamic majority countries, like Iran or Saudi Arabia, Muslims tolerate other religions but generally restrict their ability to grow, proselytize, or do missionary work. In those countries where Islam is dominant, principles of the Qur'an are in their constitution. For example, in Saudi Arabia, their Constitution is the Qur'an and the sunna of the Prophet Muhammad.

Third, Jefferson was a student of the law. He believed in democracy. He worked on drafting the United States Constitution so that this new country would have a system of rules that could adapt to its citizens' needs. The reader will soon see that the Muslims think democracy is secular; they believe that governing by man cannot stand up to governing by God. However, Muslims do like democracy in democratic countries as it allows their followers to run for office and pass laws that restrain individual rights and liberal democracy.

Yes, Jefferson knew a little about Muslim laws; after all, that is why he bought his two-volume copy of the Qur'an. However, with a few exceptions regarding Islamic law over 60 years of legal practice, Jefferson never had anything positive to say about Islam.[19] If he knew what we know now, he would be spinning in his grave.

Overview of the Book

In Chapter 1, "Links to the Bible," I trace both the shared and divergent histories of Christianity and Islam. The Prophet Muhammad is an assumed descendant of Abraham; thus, the story starts with him. The story of Abraham, the father of three world religions, is reviewed from both Biblical and Islamic perspectives. The latter part of this chapter explores Bible verses explained as the Muslim prophecy of the forthcoming Prophet.

Chapter 2, "The Qur'an," is a review of the origin of the Qur'an and most of the Islamic sacred rituals and beliefs. A short review of the Satanic verses, the Doctrine of Abrogation, and Thomas Jefferson's Qur'an fall at the end of this chapter.

In Chapter 3, "Islamic Beliefs," I devote some space to the

sovereignty of Allah. I discuss the corruption of the Bible and Muslim beliefs about the crucifixion of Jesus, the Gospel of Barnabas, the confusion of the Trinity, and how original sin does not fit into the Muslim religion.

Chapter 4, "Islamic Fundamentals," explains how violation of basic issues like kufr, shirk, idolatry, blasphemy, and heresy can lead to takfir, excommunication from the faith, which, in some countries, and territories, can lead to execution.

"Where Islamic Fundamentalists Stand on Select Issues," Chapter 5, explores where Islam stands on six issues: conversion to other faiths; abortion; honor killings; child marriage; homosexuality; and Dhimmitude.

In Chapter 6, "Sharia Law," we find that the Qur'an is less a law book than a guide on how to approach nonbelievers. Most Islamic law comes from hadith and consensus, reasoning by analogy, public interest, and critical personal rationale.

Chapter 7, "American Islam," is a short history lesson. American Islam had growing pains in the Civil Rights era of the early 20th century. The Nation of Islam (NOI) was the beneficiary that copied Islamic rituals while skipping Islamic principles. Even today, there is no love lost between fundamentalist Muslims and the NOI.

Chapter 8, "Sharia Finance," discusses the impact that distributive justice and commutative justice have on Islam's economic beliefs. Consequently, usurious interest and high-risk speculative behaviors are forbidden.

In Chapter 9, "Islamic Democracy," most Muslims believe that democratic law is secular and considered human-made law. Islamic law (the Qur'an and sunna), on the other hand, comes from Allah through the mouth of his Prophet, Muhammad.

In Chapter 10, "Growth & Market Share," there are two business concepts that every businessperson is familiar with, The Product Life Cycle (PLC) and the Growth-Share Matrix, and I use these to compare Islam with Christianity.

Chapter 11, "Muslim-Jewish Enmity," tries to identify all the reasons why some Islamic nations have an undying hatred for Israel. This chapter attempts to identify the causes.

There are approximately 1.8 billion Muslims on the planet, and they are divided into five categories: mainstream Muslims, Islamists, Salafis, Jihadis, and the Ulama. In Chapter 12, "Who are the Players?" we discuss each category's characteristics.

Chapter 13 addresses the problems in Islam's path. "Where is Islam Headed?" looks at four situations. We examine the steady population growth, radical Islamic extremism, socialist tendencies, and the disallowance of critical thinking.

Transliteration

For transliteration of Arabic terms, given this book is primarily meant for nonspecialists, I have adopted a simple system. I have avoided the use of diacritics (accents and other symbols) on Arabic words, though, in some words, such as Qur'an, I do use the single quote mark to separate the syllables.

An additional topic I list here is the name of the translator of the Qur'an that I refer to throughout this text. For my research, I used a translation called *The Meaning of the Glorious Koran* (New York: Alfred A. Knopf, Inc., 1930), by Muhammad Marmaduke William Pickthall. One source of this text is located on Quran Archive (www.quran-archive.org). While there are other sources of the Pickthall translation online, this website presents the best commentary.

Since I also refer to Bible scriptures frequently, let me acknowledge my source as the HOLY BIBLE, NEW INTERNATIONAL VERSION®. Copyright ©1973, 1978, 1984 by International Bible Society. Permission granted by Zondervan. All rights reserved. I used the Archaeological Study Bible version which provides excellent commentary about the time and conditions in which the scriptures occurred.

Dates

Some sources that I have pulled information from used the symbols BC to indicate the period Before Christ and AD to indicate the period after Christ. When I used their data, I also used their dating system. Other sources used BCE and CE for Before Common Era and Common Era. When I referenced their information, I also used their dating system. I did not try to convert data from one source to the timeframe of another source. For the twentieth century, I used CE only (for example, 1969). Whenever I mentioned a prominent Muslim, I listed the year of their death (for example, (d. 864)).

End-of-Chapter Notes and Endnotes

This manuscript employs both end-of-chapter notes and reference notes. Supplemental information relevant to the content of the chapter is listed at the end of the chapter. Source information is listed primarily in the reference notes.

Acknowledgments

I could not have completed this project or kept my day job without the patient, loving help from my wife, **Pat Brewton**. It is no exaggeration to add that Pat allowed me the privacy and time to research and write this text. Her knowledge of computers and how they work was a great help. Her wisdom and support on many other decisions are appreciated.

I am grateful to **Rebecca Lunsford**, an extraordinary grammarian whose history as an English teacher has helped many more than myself. Let me recognize two individuals from Hillsdale College in Michigan. First, **Peggy Youngs** is the Director of Lifelong Learning Seminars of Hillsdale's Center for Constructive Alternatives (CCA). CCA is the sponsor of one of the most extensive college lecture series in America. On occasion, Ms. Youngs provided me with material from some Islamic presenters, and I am grateful for that. Before I had written a single word, I attended a four-day seminar about Islam on the Hillsdale campus. One of the lecturers was Hillsdale's Assistant Professor of Religion, **Donald Westblade**. Professor Westblade made a lasting impression then and was kind enough to read the manuscript and offer his thoughts. While the Professor took issue with me on several topics, his insight was invaluable, and this project could not have concluded without him. Also, a hat tip to **Dr. Ron Callaway**, Professor of Intercultural Studies for Welch College, for providing critical information about Christianity's contribution to democracy and capitalism.

I want to thank the beta readers who volunteered their time and patience to read and review this book's content. **Ben Duggan**, always on the lookout for conspiracy theories and hoaxes, was a big reader of the manuscript and my related website, MuslimMechanics.com. **Dr. Dwight Watt** and **Dr. Steve Holcombe** both provided inspirational opinions. **Dr. Clay Owens** was most helpful in printing out the entire manuscript, going through it line by line, and connecting me with Drs. Watt and Holcombe.

End-of-Chapter Notes

a. Known as sharia law, the term has had several methods of spelling, including but not limited to "shariah," "sharia," "shari a," and "syariah."

Chapter 1

Links to the Bible

This chapter looks at the early formation of the Abrahamic religions and specifically Islam. Since the Prophet Muhammad is the assumed descendant of Abraham, it seems obvious to start there. There are connections between Judaism, Christianity, and Islam, and it will be worthwhile to see how Muslim adherents perceive their legitimacy in the family of religions.

Regarding the environmental climate for the ancient Middle Eastern region, which encapsulates places we recognize in present-day Iraq, Syria, Jordan, Israel, Saudi Arabia, and Egypt, archaeology shows that the environment in these places was vastly different from what we recognize now. Ancient Saudi Arabia and the Sahara Desert in North Africa were lush and tropical as late as 6,000 years ago. Researchers and scientists have also uncovered 10,000 ancient lakes and riverbeds across the Arabian Peninsula.[1] There is a reason to believe that traditions and scriptures found in Genesis and Exodus, early chapters in the Old Testament Bible, occur when the whole desert and the Middle East's semi-arid region received more rainfall than now.[2] Archaeologist James Breasted referred to this area from southern Iraq to northern Egypt as the "Fertile Crescent."[3] This environment would help explain how tribal peoples, numbering in the tens of thousands, could maintain their sustenance during their desert wanderings, manna notwithstanding.

The person whom we are interested in during this period is Abraham. Abraham is considered the progenitor of three major world religions: Judaism, Christianity, and Islam. His recognition of one God during this period of history, where it was common to worship and recognize multiple deities, sets him apart. Preceding the chapter of Genesis in my *NIV Archaeological*

Study Bible is a section called "Introduction to Genesis." This source lists Abraham's life as somewhere between 2166-1991 BC, approximately 4,000 years ago.[4] Another Biblical scholar, Amy-Jill Levine, records the time frame as somewhere near 1750 BC.[5] In either case, this particular period is called the Bronze Age, where metal workers had learned that adding a little bit of tin to copper made a metal harder, hard enough to be shaped to fit one's needs. The significance of this discovery made it possible to replace chiseled stone tools and weapons with lighter, more durable, designer tools and armaments. Donkeys had been recently domesticated, and writing systems were in their infancy. Even though the wheel was new technology, war chariots were still on the drawing board for another three or four centuries.[6]

Muslim scholars, such as Ibn Ishaq (d. 767), claim the Prophet Muhammad has ancestral lineage to Abraham through Ishmael, his son. Therefore, we must follow Abraham's story of monotheism as it explains some of the origins of Islam's holiest religious sites. In the Bible, it's not until the eleventh chapter of Genesis that Abraham enters the narrative. As he's known at this stage, Abram is the son of Terah, the head of a small tribe composed of his extended family. As the story progresses, Terah decides to move with his family, servants, and flocks from the Sumerian city-state of "Ur of the Chaldees," located on the Euphrates River in current-day Iraq. The tribal lands of his son in Haran, Turkey, is Terah's destination. It is worth noting that this particular area of Iraq had some of the largest cities. If not the largest, Ur was undoubtedly close to it, with a population of approximately 65,000.[7] Archaeological research shows that during this time and in this place, civilization began to collapse: "People stopped paying taxes, armies melted away, and bandits seized entire cities. By 2150 BC, the Akkadian Empire and Old Kingdom Egypt, the two biggest states in history up to that point, had ceased to exist."[8]

Usury, the lending of money or commodities with repayment

in kind, along with interest, was typical. Frequent loans with interest existed as early as the third dynasty of Ur (2060-1950 BC). The Laws of Eshnunna found in an archaeological dig close to Ur, dated to 1930 BC, had the earliest laws governing the use and guidelines of usury.[9] Is it possible that Terah ran afoul of borrowing resources and had to move? This chaos was indicative of the political, economic, and religious environment in Mesopotamia (Iraq) and may have had something to do with Terah's decision to relocate.

Haran is in southeastern Turkey, about 1,200 miles to the northwest of Ur. A journey of similar length would be traveling on foot from Los Angeles, California, to Wichita, Kansas.[10] Fortunately for Terah, there was a well-established trade route in that day and time that they could follow parallel to the Euphrates River. After the trip, Terah dies in Haran, and the name change we witness in the Bible, Abram to Abraham (Genesis 17:5), indicates that he becomes the patriarch of the tribe. From Haran, the tribe moves to Damascus in present-day Syria and then to Shechem, located on the West Bank. The Biblical trade route known as the "Way of the Philistines" linked all of the cities that Abraham traveled from Damascus to Egypt.[11] The Bible lists 17 locations that Abraham would visit and inhabit while in Canaan or Egypt.[12]

Side Note: The land of Canaan, according to the Bible, was named after the grandson of Noah, who settled this area (Genesis 10). The territory was promised to Abraham (Genesis 15:18-21), subsequently to his son Isaac (Genesis 26:3), and finally to Jacob, Isaac's son, and (Genesis 28:13) Abraham's grandson. According to Exodus 23:31, the Promised Land was from the Red Sea/Reed Sea[b] to the Mediterranean Sea and from the desert to the Euphrates River. Five hundred years later, Moses would be more specific. This time, the Lord reduces the size of the Promised

Land, as indicated in Numbers 34:1-12. Canaan includes the lands from the Mediterranean Sea to the Jordan River, from the slopes of Mount Hermon and the Golan Heights in the northeast to the Dead Sea in the south.

There is a familiar and extended dialogue between Abraham and his God beginning in the twelfth chapter of Genesis and subsequent chapters.

> "I will make you into a great nation, and I will bless you" (Genesis 12:2).
> "I will make your offspring like the dust of the earth, so that if anyone could count the dust, then your offspring could be counted" (Genesis 13:16).
> "... 'Look up at the heavens and count the stars! – if indeed you can count them.' Then he said to him, 'So shall your offspring be'" (Genesis 15:5).[13]

In the same chapter that Abram's name changes to Abraham (Chapter 17), the Lord God reiterates the boast to make nations out of Abraham's seed. His God was requesting a pledge of fidelity, and in return, God rewards Abraham and his descendants. This chapter has the first mention of a covenant between Abraham and God.

Side Note: As a matter of history, the concept of contracts had been around in ancient Mesopotamia well before Abraham's period. The earliest covenant between a god and his people is the Stele of the Vultures, written before 2500 BC.[14]

However, it was evident to Abraham and his wife Sarah that there was an inheritance issue. There were no heirs, and Sarah was past childbearing fertility. The Bible (Genesis 16:2) indicates that Sarah suggested that Abraham sleep with an Egyptian maidservant named Hagar. Abraham did so, and Hagar bears a son that Abraham names Ishmael.

Thirteen years later, the Lord returns to Abraham to reinforce his covenant for fidelity. By Abraham's monotheistic loyalty, the Lord strikes a covenant with Abraham that all male babies be circumcised eight days after their birth. On the day that Ishmael was circumcised, Abraham and all other male family members were circumcised (Genesis 17). It is a familiar custom to the Jewish and Christian community that all male babies are circumcised; it is not well known that all Muslim male babies are also circumcised. This fact is but one indication that remnants of Abraham's beliefs have filtered down into the religions of his progeny.

It is also at this time that Abraham hears of Sarah's impending pregnancy. Sarah gives birth to Isaac (Genesis 21), and two years later, Sarah weans the child. At that time, Sarah petitions Abraham to get rid of that slave woman and her son as she does not want Ishmael to share in Isaac's inheritance.

According to the Bible, Abraham gives Hagar and Ishmael food and water and sends them off. "She went on her way and wandered in the desert of Beersheba" (Genesis 21:14). The legal customs of that period suggest that Abraham was wrong to expel a female servant and her child from their camp. Research on the Code of Hammurabi in Babylonia (early eighteenth century BC) and Hurrian law from the Nuzi tablets (fourteenth century BC) excavated in northern Iraq provide a glimpse of family and administrative archives for that period. The Code of Hammurabi and the Nuzi tablets came from Mesopotamia (present-day Iraq), and their customs and arrangements were similar to the traditions in the land of Canaan.[15] One legal practice expressed in the Nuzi tablets prohibited the arbitrary expulsion of a servant girl's son. In essence, Abraham violated tribal customs to satisfy his wife. Because this action appears to contradict local tradition, it would seem that Abraham may have done more to improve

Hagar's ability to survive in the desert.

It is at this point those Biblical scriptures and Islamic traditions separate with different stories. The Bible suggests that Hagar and Ishmael wander in the desert and survive with divine intervention. Genesis 21:20 says, "God was with the boy as he grew up." Ishmael does grow up, marries an Egyptian woman, and sires 12 sons who become tribal rulers. Many years later, when Abraham dies, both Ishmael and Isaac participate in burying him with his predeceased wife, Sarah, in a cave near Hebron (Genesis 25).

According to the legend passed down by the Prophet Muhammad, Abraham accompanied Hagar and Ishmael through the wilderness to the location of Mecca, in current day Saudi Arabia, a distance less than 900 miles.[c] Genesis 21:21 says that Ishmael lived in the Desert of Paran, a location that traditional Islam refers to as the wilderness and mountains towards Mecca's location.[16] Islamic tradition holds that Abraham brought both Hagar and Ishmael to Mecca then returned to Canaan after leaving them in this uninhabited region of Arabia. He would later return when Isaac was older to build the Kaaba. The Islamic religion holds that Abraham and Ishmael built the Kaaba after hearing a direct revelation from Allah.[17] Some years after the "house of God" was erected, local Arabs corrupted the rituals that Abraham had set forth and set up idols in the structure, which then began a tradition of polytheism. This polytheism is what Muhammad encountered during his early years as the Prophet in Mecca (610-622 AD).

The Kaaba, sometimes referred to as a "cube," was a simple unroofed rectangular structure about 35 ft by 40 ft. It is 50 ft high.[18] One of the specific attributes of the Kaaba is a Black Stone, inset into the eastern corner of the building. In contrast to the pagan Arabs before them, Muslims do not worship the Black Stone, but they do highly revere it. It is unclear if Abraham and Ishmael put the Black Stone in the original construction or if the

Prophet Muhammad added it later. Some knowledgeable people believe it is a meteorite, while others believe it is a terrestrial stone. Over the centuries, the Kaaba has endured wars, fires, and floods. The authorities in charge have rebuilt it numerous times. The current day appearance is probably much different from its initial construction. It is considered the most sacred site in Islam. Muslims face in the direction of the Kaaba when performing their daily prayers.

Side Note: The use of "black stones" as a religious prop has many precedents. The Hindu god, Shiva, had black stones representing it in many temples in India circa 1000 BC.[19] The Roman emperor, Elagabalus, in AD 218, brought his religion and his black stone to Rome from his home in Syria. It was called the Black Stone of Emesa and believed to be a meteorite.[20] There were also sacred black stones found at Golgi in Cyprus, in the Phoenician temples at Malta, and the Mistress of Turquoise's shrine in Sinai.[21] One reference in the Bible describes some meteorites as being in such places of worship (Acts 19:35).[22]

No historical facts support the claims that Abraham and Ishmael built the Kaaba. Reports and surveys of western Arabia from historians, geographers, and cartographers from the fourth century BC to the fourth century AD indicate no signs of Mecca either as a trading post or a religious center.[23] There is no archeological evidence that Mecca was inhabited in the seventh century, either. The Saudi government's mortal dread of *shirk* (the worship of things in addition to God) has strictly prohibited the study of Mecca's archeological and historic sites. They are afraid that discovering actual relics and foundations of old Mecca will lead to relic worship, a form of shirk. The Saudis appear determined to obliterate the city's archeological record in their hurry to ring the Kaaba with skyscrapers. An estimated 95 percent of Mecca's historic buildings have already been demolished to permit this construction spree. Wary that they become shrines, the Saudi government treats the remaining historical sites with a combination of fear, contempt, and avoidance. One example of this fear and disdain is that the residence of Khadijah, Muhammad's first wife, was converted into a block of toilets. Likewise, radical clerics have repeatedly called for the demolition of a building in Mecca situated right above the site which scholars believe to be the Prophet's birthplace.[24]

Generally, Muslims believe that Abraham was the first monotheist mentioned in any historical record. Even the Qur'an refers to its beliefs as "it is the cult of your father Abraham (22:78)."[25] On this belief that Abraham and Ishmael built the Kaaba, Muhammad developed rituals and established a bastion of monotheism in the Arabian wilderness. The Qur'an says Abraham and Ishmael built "the House" (2:125), and as we shall see in Chapter 2, Muslims believe the Qur'an to be the spoken word of Allah (God).[26]

Signs in the Bible

According to Islamic scholars, the Qur'an as a book was not compiled until the years 646-50. From materials written by Muhammad before his death in 632, scholars, with the help of Muhammad's Companions, pieced together the completed manuscript we recognize today as the Qur'an. On the other hand, the Bible is a compilation of writings that Christians acknowledge as the Old Testament and the New Testament. Thirty-nine books make up the Old Testament, but the first five are of the most interest. Genesis, Exodus, Leviticus, Numbers, and Deuteronomy represent the stories, laws, and struggles of the Jewish people's earliest days. These chapters are sometimes referred to as the Pentateuch, the Jewish Bible's core writing, the Torah. They were composed in the days of Moses and even possibly written by Moses circa 1400-1500 BC.[27] Hebrew tradition indicates that Moses was literate, having grown up in the court of an Egyptian pharaoh. The Bible gives credence that Moses could read (Exodus 24:7) and write (Exodus 17:14). However, most Old Testament scholars put the earliest documentation of these stories starting in Solomon's court, approximately the ninth century BC.

By the time of Moses, writing technology was over two thousand years old, but it was a specialized skill.[28] Even then, literacy was low, ranging from one percent[29] to 15 percent.[30] More than likely, the ability to transcribe records and record events was unavailable to the mass of Jewish tribes wandering in the Sinai wasteland. It is a distinct possibility that the Pentateuch's writings came from verbal stories handed down from one generation to another. The other 30 or so chapters in the Old Testament represent the history of the Jewish effort to invade, capture, and domesticate their Promised Land, the land of Canaan. The Old Testament presents no sunshine history of Israel. Kings ruled, tribes dissolved, outsiders invaded, wars were lost, other gods were worshipped, and covenants broken. Best efforts to estimate the time of documentation are around 1000 BC to 100 BC.[31]

The New Testament is mainly about the Gospels, the stories of Jesus, and the Epistles, the efforts to spread the word of God's coming kingdom of which he was part. Twenty-seven books make up the New Testament, but the Gospels of Matthew, Mark, Luke, and John are of the most interest as the core writings about Jesus' sermons, his followers, his miracles, and his teachings. The other books represent stories about his disciples and their efforts to proselytize to the people. The earliest book of the New Testament written was 20-25 years after Christ died.[32] This date would have put the complete New Testament timeline somewhere between the years AD 48 to 110.[33]

Both the Old Testament and the New Testament were scripted centuries before the Qur'an was. Yet, Islamic scholars can point to scriptures in the Bible that indicate the Prophet Muhammad's coming. Muslim scholars argue that there are prophecies of Muhammad in the Bible that predate his birth and his teachings. Muslims have expanded on these viewpoints and have claimed that they can recognize references about Muhammad in the Jewish Torah and the Christian New Testament. Christians may not think much about it, but to a Muslim, these scriptures validate their religion. So, what are some of those signs located in the scriptures?

Deuteronomy 18:18-20

I will raise up for them a prophet like you from among their brothers; I will put my words in his mouth, and he will tell them everything I command him. If anyone does not listen to my words that the Prophet speaks in my name, I myself will call him to account. But a prophet who presumes to speak in my name anything I have not commanded him to say or a prophet who speaks in the name of other gods must be put to death.[d,34]

Today, many Muslim religious scholars suggest this scripture has four points. First, they claim that the reference to "brothers" in Deuteronomy 18:18-20 might consist of any person who is a descendant of Abraham. Since Muhammad was an assumed descendant of Ishmael, Abraham's first son, Muhammad qualifies as a "brother" to the Israelites. There is also a passage in Genesis 16:12 written about Ishmael referring to his "brothers" on Isaac's side of the family.

Second, in those verses, God told Moses that the Prophet would be "like you." Muslims list the similarities between Moses and Muhammad and the dissimilarities between Moses and Jesus as proof that Muhammad is the foretold Prophet. The argument poses that Muhammad is like Moses because of his ability to wage war, make and enforce laws, lead and govern tribes of men, be born with natural parents, and marry and have children. None of these things did Jesus do.[35]

The third point is that the 18th verse says, "I will put my words in his mouth." The Muslims argue that the four gospels do not consist of words that God put in Jesus' mouth. The story of Jesus that comes from the gospels only tells us the story as interpreted by outside observers. All the gospels' narrative is from an external third party who, in many cases, we cannot identify. Muhammad (unlike Jesus[e]) was illiterate, and the words for the Qur'an were put "into his mouth" as exactly foretold in the prophecy.

The fourth point is that the verses indicate the coming of a prophet. A prophet was considered a mortal man, not a deity or the Son of God. Muhammad was considered a true prophet because of his mortality. If this passage were about Jesus, this would lend credence to the Muslim belief that Jesus was mortal and not the Son of God.[36]

Psalms 84:6

As they pass through the Valley of Baca,
they make it a place of springs;
the autumn rains also cover it with pools.[37]

The word "Baca" appears in this verse as well as in the Qur'an (3:96). Baca, as it occurs in Psalms, and Bakka, as spelled in the Qur'an, is a slang word for Mecca, depending on the dialect of the tribe. Mecca is the location of the Kaaba, the house of worship that Abraham and Ishmael built. A well-known spring called Zamzam is close to the Kaaba, still flowing after all this time.[38]

Isaiah 29:11-12

For you, this whole vision is nothing but words sealed in a scroll. And if you give the scroll to someone who can read, and say to him, "Read this, please," he will answer, "I can't; it is sealed." Or if you give the scroll to someone who cannot read and say, "Read this, please," he will answer, "I don't know how to read."[39]

This scripture is important to Muslims as it relates to Muhammad's first encounter with the angel Gabriel. One of Muhammad's biographers, Ibn Ishaq (d. 767), tells this story:

When it was the night on which God honored him and his mission and showed mercy on his servants; thereby, Gabriel brought him the command of God. "He came to me," said the Apostle of God, "while I was asleep, with a coverlet of brocade whereon was some writing, and said, 'Read!' I said, 'What shall I read?' He pressed me with it so tightly that I thought it was death; then he let me go and said, 'Read!' I said, 'What shall I read?' He pressed me with it again so that I thought it was death; then he let me go and said 'Read!' I said, 'What shall I read?' He pressed me with it the third time so that I thought it was death and said, 'Read!' I said, 'What then shall I read?' – and this I said only to deliver myself from him, lest he should do the same to me again. He said: 'Read in the name of the Lord who created, who created man of blood coagulated. Read! Thy Lord is the most beneficent who taught by the pen – taught that which they knew not unto men' (96:1-5). So, I read it, and he departed from me. And I awoke from my sleep, and it was as though these words were written on my heart."[40]

In his young adult years, Muhammad was a businessman and a trader, managing his first wife's caravans. Evidence shows he was illiterate but knowledgeable in the ways of the world. Muhammad could negotiate contracts and was knowledgeable about trade routes and markets. He understood what goods people wanted, but he required others to read and write out the details.

Matthew 3:11

I baptize you in water for repentance. But after me will come
one who is more powerful than I, whose sandals I am not fit
to carry.[41]

This prediction by John the Baptist is said to refer to Muhammad.
Islamic scholars think that the very proposition "after" clearly
excludes Jesus from being the foretold Prophet since both John
the Baptist and Jesus "were both contemporaries and born in
the same year."[42] Another reason given is that if John the Baptist
knew that Jesus was the Messiah, why did he not pick up and
follow him like an apostle or a disciple?

John 14:16

[Jesus said,] "And I will ask the Father, and he will give you
another Counselor to be with you forever."[43]

John 15:26

When the Counselor comes, whom I will send to you from
the father, the spirit of truth who goes out from the father, he
will testify about me.[44]

John 16:7-8

But I tell you the truth: It is for your good that I am going
away. Unless I go away, the Counselor will not come to you;
but if I go, I will send him to you. When he comes, he will
convict the world of guilt in regard to sin and righteousness
and judgment.[45]

John 16:12-13

I have much more to say to you, more than you can now
bear. But when he, the Spirit of Truth, comes, he will guide
you into all truth. He will not speak on his own, he will speak
only what he hears, and he will tell you what is yet to come.[46]

In the four scriptures above, Christians assume Jesus is referring to the Holy Spirit as the Counselor. Given the fact that Muslims do not believe in the Trinity of the Godhead and given that the term Counselor has a legalistic twist (a twist that puts a spotlight on Muhammad as he is considered a lawgiver), Muslims would have reason to interpret this as a reference to the coming of Muhammad. Notice in the last verse the concern about speaking "only what he hears." Muslims see that as a reference to Muhammad receiving the Qur'an from the Angel Gabriel.

There are additional scriptures and sources that Muslims insist refer to Muhammad, but their inclusion would not strengthen or weaken the point. The fact is that Muslims can make a case to their community that Muhammad's arrival was preordained. Christian scholars make the opposite case that the scriptures are out of context. In either case, it does not matter, for the bias of the interpreter determines the outcome.

Chapter Summary

The Old Testament contains the remnant of the Torah with all the Jewish laws, genealogies, and history of the Jewish nation. The story of Islam starts with Abraham's journey in the Old Testament and his ties to monotheism. Throughout the Old Testament and the New Testament, Muslims believe some verses mention the coming of their Prophet, Muhammad. Most Christian scholars vehemently deny the affiliation. For the most part, Muslims believe that the Biblical scriptures lend credence to their religion, but more than that, they lend credence to their *connection to Abraham*.

End-of-Chapter Notes

b.   The Hebrew word is Yam Suph, sometimes identified as the Red Sea and sometimes identified as the Reed Sea, two different landmarks.

c.   These legends come from hadith, which are a collection of sayings of the prophet Muhammad. This hadith comes from al-Bukhari, Volume 4, Book 55, Number 584.

d.   While this passage shows the connections to Muhammad, let it be noted that Samaritan eschatology in the first century also justified one of their prophets through this same verse. Unfortunately, Pontius Pilate also killed him. Helen K. Bond, *Pontius Pilate in History and Interpretation*, Cambridge University Press, 1998, 90.

e.   In Luke 4:16, Jesus went to the synagogue in Nazareth and read aloud from the scroll of Isaiah.

Chapter 2

The Qur'an

This chapter explains the building blocks of Islam. Once you understand what role the Qur'an plays and other supporting pieces like hadith and sunna, the religion starts to make sense to the uninitiated. For example, as Jesus is God incarnate to Christians, the Qur'an is Allah's unfiltered word to Muslims. Christians can turn to the Bible for inspiration. Muslims study hadith (stories about Muhammad). Muslims and Christians have their theological categories, and each camp must understand the similarities and differences of the other camp to make any sense of the opposing religion.

The word "qur'an" in Arabic means "recitation," referring to the origin of Muhammad's quotations that came from the angel Gabriel. The Qur'an says that Allah, through the Angel Gabriel, told Muhammad what to say and memorize. Thus, Allah's message given to Muhammad reaches our ears spoken in the Arabic language. The exact transliteration of the Arabic character for "recitation" when translated into English is "qur'an," but in Europe, theologians didn't accept this spelling until recently. In the seventeenth century, many Arabic words became staples in the English language. Vocabulary such as algebra and alchemy originated from Arabic to mean the study of math or chemistry. The "al" was the Arabic equivalent of "the." The French spelled the word "qur'an" in a phonetic manner using the name "coran." In Europe, Muhammad's holy book was initially referred to as *The Alcoran*, which wrongly fused the Arabic definite article al, with the French spelling coran. Technically, when Europeans alluded to the book as *The Alcoran*, they were actually saying "the the Coran."[1] "Koran" was a common spelling that evolved in the eighteenth century. George Sale, a British Orientalist scholar, used this title in 1734 when he authored the translation sold to Thomas Jefferson in 1765 and now located in the Library of Congress.[2]

Let us review a short biography to bring the reader up to date on Muhammad. He was born in the year 570 in Mecca. His parents were both dead before he was three, and his uncle raised him to be a trader.[3] His extended family was the powerful Quraysh tribe, who controlled the caravan trade in Mecca. He married an older but wealthy widow, and he engaged in business for himself. He was often away on trading ventures going north into the Byzantine territory in Syria and Palestine. While not proven, he likely met many traders from Christian and Jewish locales and learned their religions and cultures.

Often, Muhammad visited a cave at Mount Hira's base a few miles north of Mecca to meditate and contemplate issues, ideas, and his purpose in life. In his fortieth year (610), the angel Gabriel visited Muhammad during a retreat to his cave. Gabriel confirmed to him there is only one God and gave him many messages from God to memorize. Since Muhammad was illiterate, he must have someone else write the words down. Over the next 23 years, Muhammad received messages from Gabriel in dreams, visions, and trances and narrated what the angel tells him to scribes, family, and friends.

Eventually, after Muhammad died in 632, the writings are assembled as the Qur'an. The finished text is a collection of 114 chapters (suras) shorter than the New Testament. In the suras, Allah tells believers how they shall live, worship, conduct business, treat one another, and other "People of the Book" and how they shall treat unbelievers. Two-thirds of the Qur'an is about dealing with the "kafir," the unbeliever or infidel.[4] Muhammad sees himself as the final Prophet of Allah and the recitations as God's final revelation.[5]

The Hegira

Once the angel, Gabriel, relays to Muhammad the information about Allah's plans, Muhammad starts preaching to his tribe, the Quraysh. Muhammad advocates the worship of one God, Allah, while the Quraysh worshipped many gods.

Consequently, tensions rise between Muhammad and his extended family. In 622, Muhammad fears for his life and flees to Medina, an oasis city 200 miles to the north, with his followers. The departure from Mecca is called the "Hegira," and Islam dates its calendar from this year. It is worth noting that all suras in the Qur'an written in Mecca are of peace and conciliation. That will not be the case for the rest of the suras written in Medina.

By 630, Muhammad has won over the Quraysh, partly through persuasion and partly through military victory. Before his death in 632, Muhammad has joined all the Arab tribes of the Peninsula into a new unity, a unity based on faith in Allah, the One God, and allegiance to Muhammad, his Prophet. One of the last revelations from the angel Gabriel is, "The believers are naught else than brothers. Therefore, make peace between your brethren and observe your duty to Allah that haply ye may obtain mercy (49:10)."[6]

This scripture is known as the "Verse of Brotherhood." Fundamental Islamic belief is that believers are nothing else than brethren and should treat each other as brothers. On a brief trip I took through Jordan in 2019, I experienced a short example of this. Our guide, a retired veteran from the Jordanian Air Force, spoke to me about the brotherhood as it relates to "People of the Book." To paraphrase his comment, he said, "We are all brothers of a different mother, but the same father." The *sura* above from the Qur'an is also the source of the name of the "Muslim Brotherhood." Founded in Egypt, the Muslim Brotherhood is one of the most significant political organizations in the Islamic world. The collective brotherhood referred to in verse is called the *Umma*. Membership in the Umma or the "Muslim community" brings with it both duty and privilege.

The Five Pillars

Muhammad gave his followers a new and strict code for living. He set aside five requirements that Muslims must do, or try to do, called the "five pillars."

- First, to become a Muslim, one must say in Arabic, "I bear witness that there is no God but Allah, and that Muhammad is his messenger." This is the same phrase on the top of the ISIS black banner and the Saudi Arabian flag.[7] This phrase was often encrypted on the bills and coins of several Islamic dominant countries, much like we have "In God We Trust" on our money. Sometimes this is referred to as the *Shahada* from the way the phrase sounds when pronounced in Arabic.

Side Note: One of the early Islamic dinars minted in Egypt in 798 by the Abbasid Caliph Harun Al-Rashid. This side has the inscription "There is no God but Allah, Muhammad is the Apostle of God."

Source: The author's private coin collection.

- Second, one must pray five times daily, facing towards the Kaaba in Mecca.
- Third, one must give alms or *zakat* – one-fortieth of one's income and savings to the poor and needy.[8] There is more about this in Chapter 8, "Sharia Finance."
- Fourth, one must take no food or drink from sunup to sundown during the period of Ramadan.
- Fifth, a pilgrimage to Mecca, which is called the *Hajj*, is required of the faithful. This last requirement only happens once in a lifetime and only if the believer is physically able to do so.

Side Note: Judaism, which dates to the time of Moses (circa 1500 BC), had three pilgrimage festivals that predated the Islamic pilgrimage by 2,000 years. Exodus 23:14-17 states:

> Three times a year you are to celebrate a festival to me. Celebrate the Feast of the Unleavened Bread (Passover). Celebrate the Feast of Harvest. Celebrate the Feast of Ingathering. Three times a year, all the men are to appear before the Sovereign Lord.[9]

To appear before the Lord meant a trip to the Temple in Jerusalem; thus, it became a pilgrimage. Psalms 120-134, referred to as the Songs of Ascent or the Pilgrim's songs, are associated with the pilgrim's journey to Jerusalem.[10] After the destruction of the Second Temple and until the Third Temple construction, the actual pilgrimages are no longer obligatory upon Jews and no longer take place on a national scale.

While Muslims have five daily prayers to which they are obligated, the Jews have three daily prayers. "Evening, morning and noon I cry out in distress, and he hears my voice" (Psalms 55:17). Exactly when these three times of prayer first began to be observed is unclear, but it is mentioned first in Psalms and next in the Book of Daniel (6:10) when we read that Daniel was thrown into the lion's den because he observed his three daily prayers. Psalms 55 dates to the sixth century BCE, and Daniel dates to 164 BCE.[11]

The Miracle of the Qur'an

The Qur'an, for Muslims, is the pure word of God with no admixture of human thought or content. Because of this, Muslims routinely kiss the book, place it to their forehead, and store it on the highest shelf in their house.[12] Many Muslims have such intense jealousy for the Qur'an that they keenly resent a non-Muslim possessing it. Muslims affirm that the Qur'an was given to Muhammad in the Arabic language, piece by piece, over 23 years until his death.[13]

Most Christians are familiar with the numerous miracles that Jesus performed, such as raising the dead, healing the sick, and feeding the multitudes. The Qur'an testifies that Muhammad worked no marvels except one, the revelation of the Qur'an itself.[14] Muslims do not believe the Qur'an is a miracle solely because of its eloquence and beauty but because Muhammad was illiterate. In verse 7:157, Muhammad is called "the Prophet who can neither read nor write."

As mentioned earlier, the Qur'an is the Arabic language word for recitation. Muslims believe the language of the Qur'an possesses divine power. The angel Gabriel dictated to Muhammad what Allah had told him to. Gabriel literally gave Muhammad the word of God. After Gabriel's visit, Muhammad would then recite the verses to other believers or scribes as available. For the majority of Muhammad's lifetime, a cadre of companions memorized the content of the Qur'an, who then could recite the entire dialogue as needed. The Qur'an's intent was to be heard, not read. This situation was the case up until

AD 632, when Muhammad died. Later that same year, during the Battle of Yamamah, where Muhammad's successor Caliph Abu Bakr defeated a challenger, more than 70 Muslims who had memorized the Qur'an were martyred. It became evident to the newly appointed Caliph that the content needed to be collected and placed in one manuscript, which it was.[15]

A few of the most critical revelations – those dealing with legal or economic matters – were preserved on scraps of leather or bits of parchment. It was not until about 50 years after Muhammad's death that Muslim scholars collected the bulk of the Qur'an's suras.[16] Only then was the revelation split into specific verses. This form of a collection made it incredibly hard to place the Qur'an's verses into historical context, much less chronological order. This work was deliberate on their part. Muslims perceive the Qur'an as God's dramatic monologue, recorded without a human filter. Scholars felt that changing content, adding commentary, or reorganizing verses would interfere with God's direct revelation. Eventually, the placement of chapters was by their length of material, the longer sections first and the shorter ones last.

Even today, there is no higher goal in Muslim life than to become a human repository of the Holy Book; there is no more common sound in the Muslim world than the sound of Qur'anic recitation. "The language of the Koran has the ring of poetry. The sentences are short and full of half-restrained energy, yet with a musical cadence."[17]

Reciting the Qur'an is the backbone of Muslim education. Traditionally, madrassas are institutions of higher studies, where students learn sharia law, Islamic studies, and philosophy.[18] With the Qur'an being the leading textbook, madrassas are created as needed to provide poor and needy students a means to improve their worth. Their education is to study, learn, and recite the Qur'an. There may be additional studies such as agriculture or basic sanitation and medicine, but this is education on the cheap, financed primarily throughout the world by rich oil-producing nations.[19] A Pakistani journalist in Afghanistan aptly describes the situation:

> the younger Taliban barely knew their own country or history, but from their madrassas, they learnt about the ideal Islamic society created by the Prophet Muhammad 1,400 years ago, and that is what they wanted to emulate.[20]

Madrassas populate the entire Muslim world. The best and brightest from these madrassas can wind up in tournaments that can attract audiences in the hundreds of thousands – the Super Bowl, if you will, of the Muslim world. The winners' CDs and other audio and video recordings become instant bestsellers. It goes even further – it is also possible to get university degrees from your ability to recite the Qur'an.[21] In the meantime, most students learn Islamic principles that reinforce its powerful belief system.

The angel Gabriel dictated the words of Allah to Muhammad in Arabic. Arabic has, of course, many different dialects, and Arab literature is full of poetry. During Muhammad's days, poetry competitions were frequent, as one poet would challenge another, usually from different tribes or clans. Pageants were held in the major markets of Arabia to determine whose command of the language was best. The Qur'an was known to have rhythm and prose that vastly surpassed the best poets of the day.

Recitation of the Qur'an in Arabic or even reading it in Arabic will work for the believer if they know and understand Arabic. As Islam spread, how would the holy book be disseminated? After all, the content was to be heard, not read. During the seventh, eighth, and ninth centuries, few people could read or understand Arabic in the countries that fell to Islam during Islam's expansion phase. At the same time, Muslims were very possessive of the Qur'an and its knowledge. Three solutions to the issue of literacy evolved in the Muslim world. First, the madrassas, wherever they are, teach the Qur'an in Arabic. The student may not understand how to speak conversationally in Arabic, but they know how to recite the Qur'an in Arabic and what each chapter and verse means. Second, Islamic clerics, all of them men – as women were and are still not allowed to enter the clergy (except in extraordinary circumstances) – are ordained to define the meaning and the message of the Qur'an. In medieval times, the Catholic clergy were the only people capable of reading the Bible because it was written and spoken in Latin. Imams, usually ordained clerics trained to lead the prayers in mosques, and the ulama, trained religious scholars, know the law that stems from the Qur'an and the sunna.

Third, translations of the book gradually leaked out to the masses. To the orthodox faithful, this was a problem. The inherent sacredness of the Qur'an has historically created an unusual situation for the Muslim faithful. Based on its recitation in Arabic, the Qur'an has a significant impact on its followers; however, translation into any other language causes the material to lose its message. Muslims believe that translating the Qur'an into any different language will violate the divine nature of the text.

First, some words and phrases may turn into meaning things that are different, so the way one chooses to render a specific term from Arabic to English has a great deal to do with one's prejudice and biases. Here is verse 4:34, which interprets as allowing husbands to beat their wives: "As for those from whom ye fear rebellion, admonish them and banish them to beds apart, and scourge them" (adribuhunna).[22] The problem is that adribuhunna can also mean "turn away from them" or even "have sexual intercourse with them."[23] It depends on the context in which the word is used.

Second, the interpreter can purposely turn the content into an incorrect message. For example, George Sale, an English citizen, was one of the first translators of the Qur'an, publishing his work in 1734. Over the next few decades, people like Voltaire, Thomas Jefferson, and John Quincy Adams bought his translation of the Qur'an. However, his early English translations willfully distorted critical aspects of the Qur'an, with the political aim of representing Islam as a heresy and the Prophet as an imposter. Sale's immediate goal was to remind his Christian readers that Islam was a false religion, and he intended his work to help convert Muslims to Protestant Christianity.[24] That is why translations can present a problem.

Because translating the Qur'an caused the content to lose its divinity, the third solution that emerged was to consider a translation as commentary. It is as if one had written a hymn for a Christian service. The chorale might pertain to the holiness of God, but most people would not consider it sacred or holy like the Bible. It would be an opinion piece of the "real" thing.

Side Note: The Bible, in contrast to the Qur'an, has the unique quality of being easily translatable and understandable. Consider that the complete Bible translates into 683 languages and the New Testament into 1,534 native tongues. If you add in selected parables and verses, the total rises to 3,350 dialects with some Biblical references. This list includes every language and even every important dialect spoken in the Muslim world.[25] In contrast, the complete book of the Qur'an has been translated into only 47 idioms and selected verses into 114 languages.[26] The strength of the Qur'an is in recitation in the original Arabic. By reading it in another language, you get the gist of the message without the emphasis on rhythm.

Sale's translation of the "Alcoran" was purely in English. Muslims regard any transcription of the Qur'an out of the Arabic language into another language as just plain commentary. It is not an actual holy book, per se, whereas a Qur'an in Arabic is the word of Allah, literally.[27] A Qur'an in English would be regarded as sacred and divine if it had Arabic scriptures as well. One of the earliest translations of Arabic scriptures provided the way to handle a holy Qur'an. In AD 1320, the Arabic Qur'an with Turkish commentary was made available for officials in the emerging Ottoman Empire.[28] A Qur'an only in English, or for that matter in any language (except Arabic), is just plain commentary.

Side Note: Quite a few translations of the Qur'an are now available. *The Sublime Quran* (2007) is the first by an American woman, Laleh Bakhtiar. *The Quran: A Reformist Translation* (2007) by Edip Yuksel claims to be non-sexist. *The Message – A Translation of the Glorious Qur'an* (2008) claims to be from a group of progressive Muslims called The Monotheist Group. Without the Arabic scriptures included, they are plain commentary, just an opinion of the true scriptures.

Despite the Qur'an being the primary source of Islamic law, it is not a legal text. On close analysis, less than 10 percent of the Quranic text relates to a body of law and judicial issues.[29] The legal jargon separates into passages on the acts of worship and readings related to social contact. The rituals of religion are definitive and are not subject to deviation. However, the passages that deal with social contact lack specific details because social dealings are subject to change depending on environmental and social influences. Principles for buying and selling, marriage and divorce, inheritance, and other social issues are also in the Qur'an, but the specific details are absent. That brings us to the purpose of the sunna. The sunna provides the details.

Sunna

The Sunna (or sunnah) that accompanies the Qur'an represents the traditions of the Prophet, his Companions,[f] and the first four Caliphs.[30] From a historical view, sunna is a pre-Islamic Arabic term used chiefly in poems, meaning how someone or a community lived.[31] Sunna is mentioned sixteen times in the Qur'an, mostly when describing the customs and lifestyles of various peoples mentioned. Frequently, sunna comes from documented accounts of Muhammad's (and sometimes his Companions') words and commandments. Sunna is the body of conventional, social, and legal practices of the Islamic community.

Islamic law (sharia) is shaped from different sources of community expectations. Some sources have more importance than others. For example, the Qur'an represents the first source of social expectations as it was given to man by Allah. If the law were shaped like a pyramid, the Qur'an would be at the top, with lesser essential sources of the law coming underneath the Qur'an. It was not until the second Islamic century (eighth century AD) that the term "sunna" became a legal term occupying the second source of Islamic law. The sharia pyramid of constitutional jurisprudence would put the sunna as the next most crucial body of knowledge under the Qur'an. Sunna offers examples of ethics and living based on the events of the life of Muhammad. In Islamic law, sunna means an action a Muslim is advised to follow because that is what Muhammad did or would have done in a similar situation. There are a few verses in the Qur'an that support the use of sunna as a source of legal jurisprudence. Probably the most pertinent is this one: "Verily in the messenger of Allah ye have a good example for him who looketh unto Allah and the Last Day, and remembereth Allah much."(33:20)[32] This verse suggests that Muhammad's manner of governing, decisions, customs, and way of life would provide an excellent standard by which people should live their lives.

Hadith

The Arabic word *hadith* means communication, story, and conversation, whether religious or secular, historical or recent.[33] The inexperienced practitioner often uses hadith interchangeably with sunna.[34] Each hadith is a narration of the life of the Prophet and what he said during specific situations. Sunna is the action or direction a person should take based on what the Prophet would do, based on reliable documentation revealing what the Prophet did or said (the hadith).

While the Qur'an represents the apex of Islamic law, there is much detail it does not cover. Consequently, the reports of Muhammad's sayings and actions were tirelessly collected by scholars from subsequent generations to supplement the Qur'an. The corpus of hadith is enormous; individual collections contain thousands of these records. As they provided the primary source of information for the Prophet's life, the grouping, assimilation, analysis, and verification of these oral documentaries evolved into a science. The science of hadith focused on classifying them, evaluating their reliability, and using them to determine the law. There were attempts to compile those hadiths that were perceived to have guaranteed or likely authenticity. Of course, scholars were aware that many hadiths were forged, fabricated, or otherwise faulty, and those reports relevant for law or jurisprudence needed to be subject to rigorous examination. Those not required for legal purposes (dealing with good manners or cleanliness) were not subject to such scrutiny.

The two most important hadith collections are Muhammad ibn Ismail al-Bukhari (d. 870) and Muslim ibn al-Hajjaj (d. 875), commonly referred to as al-Bukhari and Muslim. Religious scholars widely accept their collections as the most authentic and reliable. These two Islamic scholars were both Sunnis, and while other Sunni and Shi'ite scholars have extensive collections, al-Bukhari and Muslim represent the gold standard in the hadith.[8]

Most Muslim scholars realize the compilation of the Prophet's sayings by al-Bukhari to be the most genuine collection of Muhammad's words and deeds. Al-Bukhari rigorously checked these hadiths for their compatibility with the Qur'an. The integrity of the people who reported them was also painstakingly established. Bear in mind that it was 50 years after Muhammad died in 632 that the Qur'an was assembled. By the time al-Bukhari was interviewing people, it was two centuries after the Prophet's death. Al-Bukhari tried to establish accuracy by mainly examining family members of the Companions. Al-Bukhari spent 16 years compiling his research, and he selected only 7,300 out of 600,000 narrations for fear that the others may have been fabricated or forged.[35]

The compilation by Muslim ibn al-Hajjaj was a much broader collection. Muslim, a student of al-Bukhari, evaluated 300,000 hadiths and, using less stringent criteria, accepted 12,000 into his group.[36] Other religious scholars have put forth collections of hadiths but none as substantial as al-Bukhari and Muslim.

Some aspects of the sunna are obligatory, and some are recommendations. Reading hadiths can go a long way toward helping Christians understand the lifestyle of a Muslim. Two examples would be:

Do the opposite of what the pagans do, cut the mustache short and leave the beard (as it is) (al-Bukhari, Volume 7, #781).[37] [Author's note: more on beards in Chapter 12.]

A companion asked Allah's Apostle (Muhammad) about liquor. He forbade (its use), and he expressed hatred that it should be prepared. He (the Companion) said: I prepare it as a medicine, whereupon he (the Holy Prophet) said: It is no medicine, but an ailment (Muslim, Book 23, #4892).[38]

Practically every action Muslims take, from how they get

dressed, to what they wear, to their hygienic standards, has a precedent in the hadiths.

Side Note: Throughout the New Testament, there are references that Jesus said this and Jesus did that. However, one Gospel specifically focused on what Jesus said, much like the hadith collected on Muhammad. The Gnostic Gospel of Thomas, found in 1945 in Nag Hammadi, Egypt, is composed of 114 sayings attributed to Jesus. Almost half of these sayings are familiar and like those found in the Canonical Gospels, while the rest represent a Gnostic line of thought.[39] Various scholars place the composition of the Gnostic Gospel of Thomas between AD 50 and AD 250.

Note the level of urgency of what Jesus says and does, and what Muhammad says and does. What Jesus says and does is essential in a theological setting or a religious environment. Muhammad's actions and sayings are also salient in theology, but even more than that, Muhammad's sunna, after the Qur'an, is the basis of Islamic law. The Holy Qur'an does not speak to all events that an individual or a government may need for guidance. Thus, some passages order Muslims to follow the Prophet in all his deeds and sayings. Scriptural authority to follow the Prophet's traditions and commandments comes from the Qur'an in multiple verses (24:54 and 33:21, for example).

While hadith and sunna are considered the second most important source of Islamic laws, there is discord among Muslims regarding many of the hadiths' authenticity. Scholars, such as Muslim and al-Bukhari, were strict on those hadiths that served as a base for Islamic law. While some hadiths they encountered were superstitious and unbelievable, religious scholars granted a liberal license to the "afterlife genre." Descriptions of the reward or punishment that awaited certain deeds in the afterlife were accepted, whether they could be proven or not. Scholars accept it now that many hadiths were doctored or fabricated in later times to serve political or sectarian agendas.[40] As a result, Muslim scholars are sometimes unsure and often confused about what they should practice as their religious duty.

This finding strikes a dagger to the heart of Islamic religious tradition. Authenticity is critical to Muslim scholars. The Qur'an (29:46) rebukes earlier Jewish and Christian communities for adulterating their holy books, an inequity from which Allah avows to shield the Muslims.[41]

Because of hadith forgeries and fraud, there is a high demand for Islamic scholars or ulama. The law's ambiguity causes each legal, educational, and economic organization to employ one, if not many, Islamic clerics and scholars to interpret the law in their favor. Ordained ulama can issue legal rulings or *fatwas* that can make one's actions legitimate. We see this a lot in the ongoing battles between terrorist groups, especially ISIS and Al-Qaeda. One area I discuss later is the excommunication of a person or a group from Islam or *takfir*. Whereas ISIS is quite strict about who can remain a Muslim, Al-Qaeda is much more tolerant. It all depends on how the law reads and how credible your ulama or your religious scholar is.[h]

The Satanic Verses

In 1988, a British citizen, Salman Rushdie, wrote a book entitled *The Satanic Verses*. In 1989, Iran's Ayatollah Khomeini condemned Rushdie and his publishers to death for writing and publishing the book. Rushdie and his cohorts went into protective hiding, but over the years, Iranian hardliners have pushed the bounty on Rushdie's head up to $4 million (as of 2016).[42] Rushdie's crime was writing a book that mocks the Prophet Muhammad for an incident where he mistook "satanic suggestion" for divine revelation. While this episode in the Qur'an has numerous variations and many reasons to dispute its historical accuracy and relevance, the primary elements of the account are the same.

When the incident occurs, Muhammad lives in Mecca but has been receiving verses from the real God through the angel Gabriel. Mecca is polytheistic, meaning there are many gods to worship; some sources say there are over 360 idols representing gods and goddesses in the Kaaba.[43] Meccans worship Allah as the High God, but they also worshipped subordinate deities. At first, Muhammad rejected these other deities, insisting that Allah alone is worthy of worship. The people of Mecca became upset. To gain favor with the Meccans, Muhammad endorsed the worship of three local gods, Allat, Manat, and Al-Uzza, whom the Meccans have worshipped as daughters of Allah.

If true, these implications have potent repercussions for Islam. They indicate that Muhammad was bending to local polytheist pressure and that perhaps not all of Muhammad's revelations were divine. Muslims are insistent that Allah has no offspring, not Allat, Manat, and Al-Uzza, and certainly not Jesus, who they consider a mortal Prophet. Perhaps Muhammad was trying to curry favor with the tribal elders who controlled Mecca and the shrine of the Kaaba at the time.

Later, Muhammad admitted he had fallen prey to the whispering of Satan. The verses in question are still in the Qur'an (53:19-22), but the angel Gabriel gave Muhammad new words such that the passage could be revised to reflect Allah's words. As to Satan's influence, Muhammad claimed that Satan tests all prophets, just as he tested Jesus in the wilderness (Matthew 4:1-11). Why would Muhammad even mention the goddesses' names in such a holy book if the story were not true? Still, skeptics wonder if there are more Satan-inspired passages in the Qur'an.

The Doctrine of Abrogation

"Abrogation is the act of canceling, nullifying, or repealing something, almost always in a legal context."[44] A new law can repeal an old rule. Muslims believe the Qur'an abrogates all the holy books which precede it. Also, Muslim theologians use abrogation as a way of explaining the inconsistencies of the Qur'an. If verses seem to contradict each other, the scripture's chronology determines their significance and proper interpretation. Later verses abrogate earlier contradictory verses.[45] Abrogation has evolved to become a legal principle, and Islamic legal scholars are required to master the science of understanding which verses cancel earlier scripture before they can be appointed a judge (qadi).[46]

Since the Qur'an was revealed to Muhammad over 23 years, Islamic scholars claim Allah needed to change some of the scriptures as the people became adept at following them. Because of this "progressive revelation," some laws were replaced with others.[47] As the Qur'an itself puts it: "Such of our revelation as We abrogate or cause to be forgotten, but we bring (in place) one better" (2:106).

The Qur'an has 114 chapters (suras), of which 86 originated in Mecca, followed by 28 in Medina. Almost all the serenity and tolerance verses of the Qur'an come from the earlier period of Muhammad's life in Mecca. At that time, the Prophet still hoped to convince the Christian and Jewish tribes in Arabia that his religion had compatibility with their beliefs. When Muhammad's efforts to persuade the Jews and Christians that he was the final and authoritative Prophet of God failed, the verses of the sword, fire and destruction, and oppressive slavery for those who do not convert to Islam became unleashed. These verses, which emphasized force and violence, originated during his time in Medina. The location of the "Sword" verse is sura (chapter) 9, verse 5:

Then, when the sacred months have passed, slay the idolaters wherever ye find them, and take them (captive), and besiege them, and prepare for them each ambush.[48]

This verse comes from a chapter that is considered the most militant, violent, anti-Jewish, and anti-Christian chapter in the Qur'an. Although scholars disagree on the exact number of verses that became abrogated, estimates range from 124[49] to 140[50] verses that initially encouraged tolerance. The Prophet reveals this chapter when he is in Medina, and it is one of the last revelations from the angel Gabriel. Thus, it has a final word status in the Qur'an and would abrogate any earlier chapters. One classical jurist from the fourteenth century, Ibn Rajab (d. 1393), maintained that abrogation did not cancel previous scripture. Instead, later verses clarified, explained, and sometimes provided exceptions to general rules laid down in preceding verses.[51] As to the "sword verse," he maintained that war and defense were exceptions to the general direction of peace only after persecution became intolerable.

Abrogated verses are helpful to show how their faith evolved from tolerant and peaceful to aggressive and assertive. They are used in early training and education to soften the religion to neophytes. Also, the abrogated verses are usually applied disingenuously by Muslim propagandists and naively by their Western devotees to present a far more appropriate and much less threatening image of Islam to the West (see the explanation of *taqiyya* in Chapter 9).

This misdirection generates a massive issue for those in the West who insist that Islam is a religion of tolerance and peace. Moderate Muslims characterize the body of the Qur'an as being equally weighted towards forbearance as well as militarism. However, abrogation is a doctrinal instrument that Islamic jihadis use to justify their case of extremism.

Side Note: Is abrogation in the Bible? Many Biblical scholars believe that the Old Covenant Laws, sometimes known as the Mosaic Laws, have been set aside by the laws of Christ. The Bible nowhere explicitly defines what precisely is the law of Christ. However, most Bible teachers understand it to be what Christ stated were the greatest commandments in Mark 12:29-31:

> (Jesus says) The most important one is this "Love the Lord your God with all your heart and with all your soul and with all your mind and with all your strength. The second is this: Love your neighbor as yourself. There is no commandment greater than these."[52]

Most of the Old Covenant Laws were related to Judaism, while the Law of Christ is inclusive to all – Jews and Gentiles alike. However, this scripture from Matthew 5:17-18 would suggest abrogation is not intended:

> (Jesus says) Do not think I have come to abolish the law of the Prophets; I have not come to abolish them but to fulfill them. I tell you the truth. Until heaven and earth disappear, not the smallest letter, nor the least stroke of a pen, will by any means disappear from the Law until everything is accomplished.[53]

Thomas Jefferson's Qur'an

Jefferson's Qur'an was placed in the national spotlight in January 2007 when Keith Ellison, the United States' first Muslim congressman, chose to swear his private oath of office on it instead of the customary Bible.[i,54] Again, in January 2019, Rashida Tlaib, a new Muslim congresswoman, used Jefferson's Qur'an to repeat what Ellison had initiated.[55] To date, there have been four Muslims elected to Congress, but only two have used Jefferson's Qu'ran as their swearing-in book. While Jefferson is a patriot to emulate, it is questionable they knew of Jefferson's real feelings about Islam.

Newly elected members of Congress must take an oath of loyalty to the U.S. Constitution. Newly elected members of Congress do not place their hands on any book during the official swearing-in ceremonies when they raise their right hand to take the oath of office in January. They stand in front of the Speaker's podium altogether, raise their right hands, and pledge a commitment in which they swear to uphold the Constitution. Members, individually, may choose to carry a sacred text. After the official swearing-in, Ellison, and later Tlaib, used Jefferson's two-volume Qur'an borrowed from the Library of Congress for a photo-op.

McClatchy, a news organization, posted an article about Tlaib's swearing-in. Their report notes that George Sale translated Jefferson's Qur'an in a manner "that sheds a less-than-favorable light on Islam."[56] Early English translations willfully distorted vital aspects of the Qur'an, with the political aim of representing Islam as a heresy and the Prophet as an imposter. Sale's immediate goal was to remind his Christian readers that Islam was a false religion, and he intended his work to help convert Muslims to Protestantism.[57]

Finally, Jefferson himself subscribed to the anti-Islamic views that were common in the colonies at that time.[58] His exposure to Islamic piracy in the Mediterranean Sea during his Presidency and the Islamic pursuit of bribes, tribute, and slaves caused him to question their legitimacy as a religion. During the last few years of his life, his feelings about the Qur'an and the Prophet did not wane, and he wrote about them in disparaging terms.[59]

The congressmen who hastily grab the Jefferson books seek legitimacy in a government system using an English language book unknowingly anathema towards their religion. Jefferson's fame as one of our nation's founders dazzles these Muslims as they want to show that their faith is credible and now part of the mix but little do they realize that Jefferson, a statesman who sought equal rights for all, was not their best friend.

Chapter Summary

Muhammad had numerous spiritual encounters with the angel Gabriel, resulting in a holy book that gives direction on living a pure, monotheistic life. The Prophet Muhammad becomes a leader, a warrior, a preacher, a counselor, and an imam guiding his adherents on how to live a good and holy life. The Qur'an and sunna serve as points of light to those believers who need structure and direction. One weakness in Islam's religious writings is the validity of some hadiths. In the early years after Muhammad's death, many Companions (and later, their family members) forged hadiths to make the religion what they thought it should be, not what Muhammad said or did.

End-of-Chapter Notes

f. Whereas Jesus had his disciples, Muhammad's followers are referred to as his "Companions."

g. In the Sunni sect, there were six collectors of sacred hadith that reached canonical levels. They were al-Bukhari (d. 870), Muslim (d. 875), Abu Dawud (d. 888), al-Tirmidhi (d. 892), ibn Maja (d. 886), and al-Nasa'I (d. 916).

h. This is covered in more detail in Chapter 12. Because they are religious scholars and "know" the Qur'an, the sunna, and all consensus rulings, the ulama are authorized to make religious rulings on any topic.

i. In this same election, voters in Georgia and Hawaii elected the first two Buddhists – Democrats Hank Johnson and Mazie Hirono – to the U.S. Congress. Johnson, citing tradition, elected to use the Bible. Hirono did not use any religious book, but in the past, when she was sworn in as lieutenant governor, she used a Bible.

Chapter 3

Islamic Beliefs

This chapter is an attempt to explain the fundamental doctrines of orthodox Islam. Islam is a religion that has many common elements with Judaism and Christianity, as we have seen; however, the Christian community would be surprised to know that many Muslims look down on Christianity as a tainted and corrupt religion. Much as with any other religion, the Islamic faith requires that anyone who has accepted Islam can have no legitimate reason to convert to another faith. According to the hadith, a person who has experienced the superior light of Islam cannot go back to the time of ignorance.[1] In other words, a person who has accepted the Islamic religion cannot easily "backslide" and become a Christian. In some Islamic countries like Pakistan, the person can be sentenced to death.

Islamic concepts are different from Christian ideas, of course, but they are understandable. We do not have to believe in them or even like them, but it is to one's advantage to know them. The Islamic religion has some harsh rules that, in some cases, call for the enslavement of classes of people, the death of people who commit specific actions, and the treatment of people who are non-Muslims. Consider this chapter as the abbreviated guidebook for understanding Islamic rules.

The Nature of Islam

It is incumbent upon Christians to examine the nature of the Muslim god. "Allah" is the Islamic name for God. One Muslim author, Maurice Bucaille (d. 1998), described its origin, "Al Lah means 'the Divinity' in Arabic."[2]

Most Muslims see the strength of their religion as uncompromising monotheism. There is only one God to worship. Period. There is no worship of God's prophets, God's son, or the son's mother, nor the priests or the clergy, the holy spirit, angels, saints, or apostles. There will be no worship for statues or paintings made in the deity's image. There will be no devotion to earthly possessions, houses or shrines, pictures, or valuables that would interfere with such commitment. Allah is one deity unto himself; there are no partners and no lesser gods. This Oneness is referred to as the Unity of Allah and is the most distinguishing characteristic of Islam. In a sense, the Bible reiterates this same theme. Consider the story of the Pharisee who asked Jesus, "Which is the greatest commandment in the Law?" "Jesus replied, 'Love the Lord your God with all your heart and with all your soul and with all your mind. This is the first and greatest commandment...'"(Matthew 22:36-38).[3]

Both religions put a premium on worshipping the one supreme God, but some differences motivate recognizing and honoring him. Christians want to know God and meditate on His essence. Muslims focus on obeying God and submit to His will.

The Nature of Allah

The Qur'an is a religious text with rules about how to interact with Allah. Except for a few verses scattered throughout the book, not much describes Allah's nature. Another way to view Allah is to identify the different names given to him in both the Qur'an and the hadith. Islamic tradition relates that Muhammad said, "Verily, there are ninety-nine names of God, and whoever recites them shall enter Paradise."[4]

Some scholars looking for these names have identified many more than the alleged ninety-nine. The following verses (59:22-24) provide a good sampling of titles:

He is Allah, than Whom there is no other God, the Knower of the Invisible and the Visible. He is the Beneficent, Merciful.

He is Allah, than Whom there is no other God, the Sovereign Lord, the Holy One, Peace, the Keeper of Faith, the Guardian, the Majestic, the Compeller, the Superb. Glorified be Allah from all that they ascribe as partner (unto Him). He is Allah, the Creator, the Shaper out of naught, the Fashioner. His are the most beautiful names. All that is in the heavens and the earth glorifieth Him, and He is the Mighty, the Wise.[5]

These verses suggest that Allah has wisdom, is all-powerful, sovereign, deterministic, eternal, and gives mercy. There is no doubt that Allah is omnipotent, but there is no mention that Allah can grant personal and intimate attention to everyone. Allah, it would seem, is all mighty, but not all caring. The relationship is that basically between Master and slave. God is the sovereign master, and man becomes an obedient slave.[6]

Most Christians would note the difference between the Muslim God and the Christian God is how it relates to them personally. The Christian God is more intimate and personally involved with the individual.

The Corruption of the Bible

To Muslims, Islam's purpose is to finish the job of bringing God's word to the masses in its true meaning. Muslims believe that prior versions of God's word, the Torah, and the Bible, have been misquoted, misspoken, and corrupted. Even the Old Testament acknowledges corruption of the scriptures: "How can you say, 'We are wise for we have the law of the Lord' when actually the lying pen of the scribes has handled it falsely?" (Jeremiah 8:8)[7]

Accusations fall into two categories; first, most Muslims insist Biblical scripture has been changed and forged. Second, most Muslims believe that doctrinal mistakes are evident in the teachings that indicate God's will. Let's look at the first category: how Muslims perceive that Bible scriptures have been changed. An example would be God calling on Abraham to sacrifice his son Isaac (Genesis 22). Every Muslim knows the real story was about Abraham sacrificing Ishmael. The story continues that Abraham was so happy that the Lord allowed a ram to be sacrificed instead of his son that Abraham built the Kaaba as a permanent house to worship Allah. Most Christian and Muslim scholars recognize that the Torah has stories going back 4,000 years, with documentation only in the last 3,000 years. To question the Torah's accuracy is not unexpected, but Muslims also believe the reliability of the New Testament is doubtful. Regarding the New Testament, Muslims feel that Paul, who authored thirteen of the 27 books, wrote of the divinity of Jesus, causing the multitudes to see Jesus as a God.[8]

Let us look at these allegations in more detail. We must recognize that all the folktales, the stories, the legends, and the assertions before the ninth century BC are spoken history, passed on from one generation to the next through oral storytelling techniques. First, the Patriarchs' stories (Adam, Abraham, Noah, Isaac, and Jacob) are 2-4,000 years old, with little or no archaeological evidence to support them. Bible scholars maintain the patriarchs were likely historical figures, but the stories conveyed over time are in the traditional or saga-based form.[9] Sagas are usually long stories encompassing one central character who experiences drama and makes ethical decisions that reflect high personal costs or heroic outcomes. Stories about Abraham, Noah, or King David would be saga-type tales. Next, the documentation of the five books of the Pentateuch comes from different sources at different periods, each written with seemingly ulterior motives for their version of the stories. While Christians may find this as heresy, some of the Old Testament and some of the New Testament may not be factual.

In a series of 24 lectures prepared for a commercial endeavor called "The Great Courses," Bart Ehrman, PhD, the Bowman, and Gordon Gray Professor of Religious Studies from the

University of North Carolina at Chapel Hill, addresses the historical context of the New Testament, and by extension, the Old Testament. In the 24th lecture entitled "Do We Have the Original New Testament?" his straightforward answer is, "No!"

> We do not have the originals of any of the books that were later canonized into the New Testament. What we have are copies, better yet, copies of the copies of the copies of the originals – copies made for the most part hundreds of years after the originals themselves. Unfortunately, all of these surviving copies contain mistakes.[10]

While Dr. Ehrman is not considered a Christian[11] but is a Christian scholar, his research shows that scribes made some errors unintentionally and some changes with purpose. The lack of paragraph and sentence structure limited by no punctuation or even small case letters or even spaces to separate the words caused unintentional errors.[12] Imagine the tedious hours of copying rows of letters with no spaces and no punctuation. Also, intentional changes were made to Biblical scriptures when scribes came upon errors in their copying. Even more consequential are items that copyists took to be theological errors that they then corrected. Here is one of his stories to illustrate the point: The oldest and best manuscripts of the Gospel of John do not contain the story of the woman taken in adultery (where Jesus utters his famous line: "Let the one without sin among you be the first to cast a stone at her"). This line was not added until the twelfth century.[13] In other words, some copied manuscripts left out information that was in other copied documents; that content, when later verified as authentic, was added to the English translation.

Muslims maintain that while the Qur'an came exclusively from Muhammad, both Moses and Jesus produced books to share with their people. Supposedly, Moses guided the composition of the "Pentateuch," a word that means "the five scrolls," but we recognize them as the Torah or the Old Testament's first five books. Jesus supposedly wrote the "*Injil*," the Gospel of Jesus. Islamic tradition maintains that the Jews partially destroyed the original Pentateuch and the initial *Injil* and rewrote parts of them to meet the needs of those in power at the time.

In the Gospel of Matthew, there is an example of creative editing. The chapter starts with a genealogy of Jesus. The writer organized Jesus' line of descent into a "who begat whom" – three sets of 14 generations: 14 from the father of Israel, Abraham, to the King of Israel, David; 14 from David to the destruction of Israel by the Babylonians; and 14 more to the Messiah of Israel – Jesus. To make this sequence of 14 work out to occur during some significant events in Israel's history, Matthew's author had to change some genealogy around. A comparison with other genealogies in the New Testament and the Old Testament shows that the Gospel of Matthew's composer dropped some names to make it fit.[14] Why would he do this? So, he could show that Jesus appeared at the right moment in history. This example illustrates that stories in the Bible may not be factually correct.

Other books in the New Testament have traces of the writings of Plato. One of Plato's most famous discourses is about allusions. An allusion is an indirect reference to something the author wants you to notice without telling you to see it. The book of Hebrews, verses 8:5 and 10:1, has obvious similarities to the writings of Plato. It is not difficult to believe the connection. One of Plato's students, Aristotle, was the tutor of Alexander the Great. Once Alexander the Great conquered the known world, all the Greek classics written by Socrates, Plato, and Aristotle were available to all the literate scribes. The New Testament's connection is that different scholars wrote all 27 books in Greek (not Hebrew or Aramaic, as many think).[15] In that day and age, for someone to have the ability to write in Greek, they would also be literate in the Greek classics.

The author of Hebrews is unknown, but the book seems to be a sermon to a congregation of Gentiles. The preacher is trying to convince the churchgoers why Christianity is better than Judaism. Two verses seem to mirror what Plato wrote in his "Allegory of the Cave."

They serve at a sanctuary that is a copy and **shadow** of what is in heaven (Hebrews 8:5).[16]

The law is only a **shadow** of the good things that are coming – not the realities themselves (Hebrews 10:1).[17]

Colossians 2:17 also reiterates this same theme.

The writer is suggesting that the Old Testament sanctuary and law are both mere "shadows" of the existence of Christ. The imagery of "shadow" versus "reality" reflects philosophical metaphors back to Plato nearly 500 years earlier. Plato insisted that things that appear to be real were only shadows of a higher reality.

An allegory is a story that reveals a hidden meaning, typically a moral or political one.[18] If not trained otherwise, Plato's allegory suggests that people will perceive illusions as reality. While this is not the place to review Plato's work, the description of "shadows" does illustrate that Greek classics influenced the Books of Hebrews and Colossians in the Bible.[19]

As discussed earlier, there is conclusive evidence that parts of the existing manuscripts were changed either accidentally or purposefully, depending on conditions. There is also evidence that outside philosophies by Plato may have influenced the epistles. Scholars surmise that other documents exist but have not found them yet. For example, the New Testament Gospels of Matthew and Luke have several stories commonly found in Mark. Since the Gospel of Mark (AD 65) predated Matthew (AD 85) and Luke (AD 85) for several years, their authors probably used Mark as a reference to write the stories that fit their view of Jesus. Matthew and Luke also have several familiar stories not found in Mark, i.e., the Lord's prayer. Scholars now generally believe that those stories came from a Gospel document that no longer survives, which they called "Q" (from the German word *Quelle*, meaning "source"). The Q source is a hypothetical document that contained the material found in Matthew and Luke but not in Mark.[20] The evidence seems to point to missing manuscripts. Essential information and stories about Jesus and his salvation seem to be missing from the Bible. There is no telling what has been left out and there is no way to know how it would affect the Christian eschatology.

Dr. Ehrman also suggests that Paul's writings make Jesus into something he is not – a deity. More than one scholar makes the point that the messages of Jesus and Paul were fundamentally different. Jesus focused on the Mosaic Law; the first two commandments in particular – Love God and Love one's neighbor as oneself – were central to his message. On the other hand, Paul focused on Jesus' death and faith in the resurrection as the way to salvation.[21] According to this view, Paul transformed the religion of Jesus into a religion *about* Jesus. But is the Islamic idea that Jesus is not a deity, and that Paul wrote his epistles so that people would worship Jesus as God possible? It is probably not, as there is still the virgin birth, Jesus' miracles, and the resurrection that say otherwise. Islam does not contest the virginal conception or the miracles. Yet, they do challenge Jesus' return to life after death on the cross.

Muslim scholars have reason to believe that Paul's epistles were not in sync with Jesus, but they do not question that Jesus had miraculous powers and a message about eternal life. In closing, Dr. Ehrman gives us both thumbs up and thumbs down on the New Testament's historical accuracy. Some passages are historically accurate, but he maintains considerable doubt of the authenticity of some selections.[22] Jews and Christians are implicated since this corruption occurs in both the Old Testament and the New Testament.

While Dr. Ehrman presents a compelling case of corruption, other scholars of comparable authority see different interpretations and rationale for these incongruencies. In other words, some Christian scholars see a different view than do Muslim scholars. What may seem an intentional effort to corrupt both New and Old Testaments' content is simply a matter of opinion.

The second type of corruption I mentioned previously was that doctrinal mistakes have crept into the teachings that portray God's will. The three leading doctrines that Muslims complain about would be the incarnation of Christ, the trinity of the Godhead, and the dogma of original sin.[23] These topics we will cover in this chapter.

The Prophets

One of the integral beliefs of Islam is the prophets. God sends prophets to bear his divine message. People have a way of deviating from God's righteous path. History has shown that man is negligent, greedy, and brutal. Man has good nature, but his needs and desires can cause actions not in God's plan. Being imperfect, man needs constant guidance. The prophets are God's way to bring them back in line. Through the prophets, God has repeatedly reminded humankind of the law of God.

Islam emphasizes that a prophet must be a human being. Another essential characteristic is high ethical standards. Prophets must be known for their honesty, truthfulness, intelligence, and integrity. Their reputations for good character must be impeccable. It is also noteworthy that some prophets were capable of sinning, but they always worshipped a single God and sought forgiveness. As to the purpose of the prophets, the Qur'an says this (16:36): "And verily We have raised in every nation a messenger, (proclaiming): Serve Allah and shun false gods."[24]

There are two points to make here. First, someone preaching or evangelizing the word of God is selected for each tribe. Second, each prophet has proclaimed the same underlying message; that people must acknowledge that God is a unique single deity they must worship because of the hereafter. Islamic tradition has put the number of prophets at 124,000.[25] Most of the prophets mentioned in the Qur'an are names we recognize from the Bible. Adam was the first prophet as he was the first man created. Other declared prophets are Noah, Abraham, Lot, Isaac, Jonah, Moses, David, and Jesus. As Christians, our familiarization with these prophets is that some, if not all, have committed sins. For example, Moses was a murderer, and David committed adultery. To the Muslim believer, these prophets recognized only one God and asked for forgiveness. Allah, being a compassionate God, has accepted their repentance.[26] In the Qur'an, there are some 25 prophets mentioned by name, most we know because of their Biblical references.[27] According to the Qur'an (33:48), God sealed the line of prophets with Muhammad as the last.[28]

The Crucifixion of Jesus

At the heart of Christianity is the death and resurrection of Christ. Muslims refute that Jesus died on the cross and rose again from the dead three days later. Let us review what Muslim scholars think. First, Jesus is mentioned in 93 verses in 15 suras in the Qur'an, so he is considered a unique Prophet within the Islamic faith. However, the Qur'an says this about him:

The Messiah, son of Mary, was no other than a messenger, messengers (the like of whom) had passed away before him. And his mother was a saintly woman. And they both used to eat (earthly) food. See how We make the revelations clear for them (5:75).[29]

Muslim scholars do not deny the virgin birth, and they do not deny the multitude of miracles that Jesus performed. They do not deny that he ascended to heaven, much like Enoch (Genesis 5:23) and Elijah (Second Kings 2:11). But they do deny that he is a deity on the level with God. They also deny that Jesus died and came back to life three days later. There is much evidence as to the crucifixion and the following of rituals of the dead. However, there is also much speculation regarding the last hours of Jesus' life on earth. The Qur'an presents its version of what happened:

> And because of their saying: We slew the Messiah, Jesus son of Mary, Allah's messenger – they slew him not nor crucified him, but it appeared so unto them (4:157).[30]

Muslim scholars have speculated about the different ways that the crucifixion could have occurred without Jesus' participation and the various people who might have taken Jesus' place on the cross, either voluntarily or not. Candidates for substitution have ranged from Judas to Pilate to Simon of Cyrene[31] or even one of Jesus' close disciples.

Side Note: Several different Christian sects also believed in Jesus as a mortal person. The Ebionites and the Deists are two of the most well-known groups to espouse this belief.

The Ebionites, an early offshoot of Christianity, believed Jesus was fully human and that worshippers must follow Jewish law.[32]

Deism is a construct that envisions a supreme being as a sort of watchmaker who has created the world but no longer intervenes directly in daily life. Deists take the position that Jesus was probably a real person but NOT the Son of God. Many of the founding fathers – Washington,

Jefferson, Franklin, Madison, and Monroe – practiced this faith called Deism.[33] *The Jefferson Bible,* written by Jefferson in 1820 when he was 77 years old, clarifies and distills Jesus' teachings without references to his miracles or his Father, the Lord God Almighty.

In the sixteenth century, a Spanish manuscript entitled the *Gospel of Barnabas* emerged, depicting the life of Jesus and Judas' death on the cross in Jesus' place. According to Acts 4:36, Barnabas was a Cypriot Jew and not one of the original 12 disciples; instead, he emerged after the crucifixion. Named as an apostle in Acts 14:14, he and Paul the Apostle undertook missionary journeys together.

George Sale published his translation of the *Alcoran* in 1734, and in the Preface, he refers to the *Gospel of Barnabas*. According to Sale, the *Gospel of Barnabas* relates to Jesus' life very differently from the four Gospels of the New Testament. Sale maintains that this "fifth" Gospel agrees with the Qur'an and the hadith in the following ways:

Jesus denies he is the Son of God (*Gospel of Barnabas,* chapter 70)
Judas is crucified instead of Jesus (*Gospel of Barnabas,* chapter 216)
Jesus announces the arrival of Muhammad (*Gospel of Barnabas,* chapter 112)

The English version of the *Gospel of Barnabas* was translated and published in 1907 by Londale and Laura Ragg. It was distributed for the first time in the Muslim world in 1973. In Pakistan alone, it sold over 100,000 copies. It was well-received among Muslims as they believed they had finally found a document – of supposedly Christian origin – which proved that Muhammad is the foretold prophet of Allah.[34]

Jewish and Christian scholars believe that the *Gospel of*

Barnabas does not hold muster as an authentic source. There seem to be many linguistic, historical, and geographical errors found in the book. On the other hand, Muslims have purchased thousands of copies of this book, which fits a niche in their beliefs. It confirms to them that Jesus was a person and not a God.

Islam Versus the Trinity

The Trinity is a complicated relationship that says God is composed of the Father, the Son (Jesus Christ), and the Holy Spirit. According to scripture in the Old and New Testament, the Godhead's three persons are coequal and coeternal. (Theologians sometimes use that term, "Godhead," when they want to relate to the Father, the Son, and the Holy Spirit as three divine Persons in a single God.) What is confusing is that there is only one God, one Supreme Being, but there are three distinct persons. As mentioned, and described in the Bible, **the Father, Son, and Holy Spirit have different characteristics and do different things, all in God's name.** Described in Philippians 1:2 is the Father as God; listed in Titus 2:13 is Jesus as God; and Acts 5:3-4 records the Holy Spirit as God. If there is one passage that most brings all of this together, it is Matthew 28:19: "Therefore, go and make disciples of all the nations, baptizing them in the name of the Father and of the Son and the Holy Spirit."[35]

Most Christians agree that God is of one essence but has three distinct areas of consciousness. Still, they find it hard to explain, and it appears somewhat contradictory based on the number of different explanations put forth.[36]

The Bible does not use the word "Trinity," but there are several scriptures where you will find acknowledgment of the Father, the Son, and the Holy Spirit; here are two:

Jesus' baptism – "As soon as *Jesus* was baptized, he went up out of the water. At that moment, heaven was opened, and he saw the *Spirit* of God descending like a dove and lighting on him. And a *voice from heaven* said, 'This is my son, whom I love; with him, I am well pleased.'" (Matthew 3:16-17) [Italics added]

Prayer – "I pray that out of his glorious riches he may strengthen you with power through his *Spirit* in your inner being so that *Christ* may dwell in your hearts through faith... and to know this love that surpasses knowledge – that you may be filled to the measure of all the fullness of *God*." (Ephesians 3:16-17, 19) [Italics added]

Muslims cannot attribute divinity to Jesus and the Holy Spirit because they believe in one unique God. The idea of God in three persons – Father, Son, and Holy Spirit – is anathema to them. Jews, of course, do not accept Jesus as a divinity, either. To the Muslims, two components of the Trinity are invalid; thus, the Trinity is baseless. Muslims believe for different reasons that the Son of God (Jesus) and the Holy Spirit are not divine or subject to be worshipped as God is. First, let us examine the reasoning that debunks the Holy Spirit from being in the Trinity. In Psalms 104:4 and Hebrews 1:7, the scriptures refer to the angels being spirits. Muslims believe that the Holy Spirit is the angel Gabriel,[37] and according to their beliefs, men do not worship angels. Even in the Bible, angels are not celebrated or idolized (Colossians 2:18; Revelations 22:9). Allah, the supreme God, is the only one worthy of a person's worship. (It is somewhat questionable if Muhammad understood the Trinity concept as one verse, 5:116 in the Quran, implies that Jesus and his mother, Mary, were partnered with God.)

While Muslims agree that Jesus was a prophet, born of the virgin, and performed miracles, they do not believe he was the Son of God and therefore a deity to recognize. Muslims recoil at the thought of worshipping a mortal human being. The Qur'an declares:

> The Messiah, Jesus son of Mary, was only a messenger of Allah, and His word which He conveyed unto Mary, and a spirit from Him. So believe in Allah and His messengers, and say not "Three" – Cease! (it is) better for you! – Allah is only One God. Far is it removed from His transcendent majesty that He should have a son. (4:171)[38]

The teaching of the Trinity is considered a manufactured doctrine from the Apostles. The Qur'an explicitly denies Trinitarian teaching. Muhammad argued that three equal gods are logically impossible:

> Allah hath not chosen any son, nor is there any God along with Him; else would each God have assuredly championed that which he created, and some of them would assuredly have overcome others. (23:91)[39]

Historical records show that the first Church Father to be recorded using the word "Trinity" was Theophilus of Antioch, writing in the late second century. However, in AD 381 at the First Council of Constantinople, the Trinity doctrine evolved into its current form.[40] Other organized religions such as Unitarians and Jehovah's Witnesses consider the Trinity a human-made concept, and many in the Christian faith do not believe in it. Deists such as Thomas Jefferson and the scientist Joseph Priestley were also skeptical of the Trinity concept.[41]

No original sin

The words "original sin" describe Adam and Eve's first sin that caused them to be expelled from the Garden of Eden. Christian doctrine indicates that humanity inherits a tainted nature to sin. The penalty for sinning is death. In Christian parlance, accepting Jesus as our Lord and Savior will give us the grace of eternal life. In Romans 5:12-19, Paul writes that sin entered the world through Adam, but Christ has provided grace and eternal life. The term "original sin" here describes the problem directly into which humanity is born, a condition in which guilt, as well as shame, is involved.

Islamic tradition indicates that Adam and Eve repented after falling for Satan's temptation. They sought forgiveness from Allah, and he gave them the necessary guidance to confront the evil that beset them. Muslims believe Adam and Eve were kept in the Garden as a trial before being sent to the earth. The only way to reenter the Garden of Eden was to oppose Satan relentlessly by obeying the Law of God.

All people are born innocent, pure, and free. Any concept of original sin is contrary to the teachings of Islam. Sin is not hereditary. Humankind is given free will from Allah, and man is personally responsible for his actions. Humans can misuse their freedom and fall into corruption, but at the same time, they are capable of reform and forgiveness.

Consequently, a person's position with Allah is dependent upon what they do with their resources. A person who worships Allah will achieve a better place in the afterlife if they give their blessings to the poor and needy. People do not come out of the womb a sinner, and the doctrine of sinfulness, therefore, has no basis in Islam.[42]

Angels and Jinn

Islamic dogma lists humans as the third spiritual creature created by Allah after angels and jinn. Most Christians are familiar with angels. For example, angels guard the entrance to the Garden of Eden (Genesis 3:24); angels worship the Lord by singing his praises (Isaiah 6:3); angels such as Michael (Revelation 12:7-8) and Gabriel (Luke 1:19) carry messages from God. Islamic tradition indicates that angels do not have free will. Their purpose was to serve God's will, be it guarding critical passageways or communicating specific messages to Abraham, Mary, or even Muhammad. The Bible also appears to indicate an angel hierarchy. In Jude 9, the angel Michael is called an "archangel" – a title that confers authority over other angels. Muslims also believe in angels. In addition to the numberless multitudes of angelic beings, Muslims believe in four archangels: Gabriel, the angel who dictated the Qur'an word by word to Muhammad; Michael, the guardian of the Jews; Israfil, the summoner to resurrection; and Izra'il, the angel of death.[43]

Jinn (jinni singular) are spiritual beings that Muslims place somewhere below angels but above humans. Christians, while not recognizing the category, are probably familiar with the name. Jinn are sometimes known as genies, a title that comes from Western folklore and popular culture. The Western concept of the genie is based on the tale of Aladdin in the book *Arabian Nights*, or formally known as *One Thousand and One Nights*, the story of a magical genie whose abode was an oil lamp. The genie granted wishes to whoever freed him from the container by polishing it. TV shows such as *The Twilight Zone, The X-Files*, and *I Dream of Jeannie* have used variations of this concept.[44]

Islamic tradition suggests the jinn, unlike angels, are beings created with free will. Just like humans, they, too, are required to worship Allah. On the Day of Judgment, jinn will also face their creator and be taken to Hell or Paradise depending on their deeds. Their purpose in life is precisely the same as ours, as indicated in the Qur'an: "I created the jinn and humankind only that they might worship Me" (51:56).[45]

Jinn reside on earth in a world parallel to humankind. They are sturdy, intelligent creatures that are physically invisible to humans. The main difference that the jinn have from humans are seemingly occult abilities. Jinn are associated with deceiving humans by using their supernatural abilities to be ghosts, magicians, or inanimate objects. Jinn use their powers to possess and take over the minds and bodies of other creatures.[46] However, having free will, some jinn do good deeds, but most references reflect evil intentions.

Another example you may be aware of are contemporary cartoons which show a devil and an angel on each shoulder. This image stems from Islamic traditions, where the Prophet informs the faithful that everyone has two entities – a jinn and an angel, one on each shoulder – to direct us towards good or bad deeds.[47]

The jinn are spiritual beings, and there are several inferences to them in the Bible. For example, in Leviticus 19:31 and 20:6, and 1 Samuel 28:3 and 28:9, there is a condemnation of people who use mediums and "spiritists."[j] In Chronicles 10:13, God castigates Saul for using a medium for guidance instead of the Lord. While the Bible does not recognize the word jinn or any equivalent, it does acknowledge that there is trouble with rogue spirits. Muslim theology takes this a step further and identifies these spirits' source as coming from the jinn.

Satan

The Qur'an says (16:50) that angels cannot disobey God, yet Satan did. The rational explanation is that Satan is not an angel, but one of the jinn and the Qur'an (18:50) confirms this as well. According to Christian tradition, Satan is a fallen angel, but Muslims do not accept that theory because they think angels do not have free will.[48]

Chapter Summary

In summary, if one is blind, how does one understand a color? That would be the same logic here. How do you describe the relationship between God and a Muslim? In the Bible, adherents describe the relationship between God and his people as one of love. In Islam, the association is one of submission. "God is fully aware of all things" and "He hears and sees everything" are phrases used frequently in the Qur'an. Islam is a comprehensive religion with its own rules, dogma, and expectations, which are quite different from that of Judaism or Christianity. Muhammad structured the Islamic faith to encompass all hours of the day. Islam is literally a 24-hour per-day obligation.

Parts of Islam maintain that specific components of Christian doctrine are incorrect. God is monotheistic, thus believing the concept of the Trinity is wrong. Believing Christ died on the cross is false. Believing in original sin is wrong. Muslims believe the Jews corrupted the Bible and the Torah. Muslims believe their religion is the logical evolution of all religions. That's why they frown on Muslims who leave Islam to join Christianity, as we will see in Chapter 5.

End-of-Chapter Notes

j.   A spiritist is someone who believes they can communicate with the dead.

Chapter 4

Islamic Fundamentals

This chapter explores the governing rules and principles of Islam. Every religion has them, but they are often unwritten or not well understood by members of other faiths. The greatest strength of Islam is its strong belief in ONE God. If any adherent violates this rule, fellow Muslims must take corrective action. Two-thirds of the Qur'an is about dealing with the *kafir* – the unbeliever or infidel.[1] Some specific activities and words can cause an individual to be excommunicated. Banishment can mean death, so one must be careful what they say, do, or indicate in their actions. Even in today's world, there are still 13 Islamic countries that allow capital punishment against apostasy, i.e., the renunciation of Islam.[2] The verse from the Qur'an that supports this action reads as follows: "Whoso denieth the faith, his work is vain and he will be among the losers in the Hereafter" (5:5).[3]

If a Muslim believes in the one-god concept but doesn't believe in the specifics of Islam, then, according to the Qur'an, they will suffer in the fires of hell. If other Muslims recognize the shortcomings of the one with deficient beliefs and they do nothing, then they are as guilty as the first. What is it others should do if they recognize someone with deviant thoughts? They should brand them as an apostate. Most Islamic countries have religious courts that provide due process. Excommunication from the religion is the result of a guilty verdict of apostasy. This process, called *takfir*, is like excommunication in the Catholic Church. In many Islamic countries and terror groups like ISIS and Al-Qaeda, to be tried and found guilty of apostasy results in the death penalty. Death is usually by hanging, but sometimes by stoning.

Kufr

The Arabic word *kufr* occurs 525 times in the Qur'an in 14 derived forms. It means to hide something or to conceal something.[4] In the Qur'an, the term refers to individuals who are acquainted with the truth, but they cover it up, hide it, or decline to make it known. The individual who is a disbeliever is called a kafir. Kufr becomes a crime when an individual who had previously affirmed Islam by speaking the shahada (i.e., the first pillar of Islam: There is no God but Allah and Muhammad is his Prophet) later denies belief in Allah and his Prophet.

The determination of whether someone is a kafir is reasonably straightforward. The question is whether God is recognized as the sovereign creator of the world, whether God alone is the only God worshipped, whether Muhammad is given his due as God's Prophet, and whether his message is accepted. Ironically, Muslims who question Allah's sovereignty and righteousness are given plenty of slack, whereas questioning Muhammad's legitimacy is considered grounds for excommunication.[5] Muslims agree that Muhammad is human, but their tradition, society, and civilization revolve around his legacies and revere him as flawless. Because Muslims strive to attain his values and match his reverence, they see an attack on Muhammad as an attack on their values. That is why Muslims cannot dispassionately discuss Muhammad.

While most Christians and Jews would accept God as the world's sovereign creator, most Christians would not accept God without Jesus. I think it is questionable whether most Christians and Jews would accept Muhammad as God's Prophet. To most Christians, the Prophet Muhammad is not a household word. His philosophy is not something we are familiar with. Christian acceptance of Muhammad's message would be doubtful. This litmus test would cast most Christians and Jews as kafirs in the parlance of Muslims.

There are secondary repercussions of *kufr*. If a person

knows of someone who denies or doubts Allah or cast dispersions on Muhammad or his message, and they do or say nothing to "out" the culprit, then they too are subject to being labeled with *kufr*.

Shirk

Because of the strong emphasis on Allah's absolute oneness in Islam, the greatest of all sins is called *shirk* or assigning partners to God. To Muslims, God and God alone is worthy of worship. There are no other divinities to be worshipped. Jesus, his mother Mary, angels, other prophets; there are no associates. God alone possesses the attributes of deity. To associate any being or any icon with God is a sinful act. The sin of practicing idolatry or polytheism is *shirk*. *Shirk* is considered the only unforgivable sin in Islam: "Lo! Allah pardoneth not that partners should be ascribed unto Him... Whoso ascribeth partners unto Allah hath wandered far astray." (4:116)[6]

Idolatry

"Concerning the historic city, we will preserve it, and it will not be harmed, God willing. What we will do is break the idols that the infidels used to worship."[7] This comment came from Abu Laith al-Saoudy, the nom de guerre of the Islamic State military commander in Palmyra, Syria. If you remember, in Afghanistan, Taliban jihadists dynamited a pair of sixth-century statues known as the Buddhas of Bamiyan in 2001. The Islamic State, during its short reign as a so-called caliphate, destroyed at least 28 religious buildings in Iraq, including Shiite mosques, tombs, shrines, and churches. Also, IS jihadis razed numerous ancient and medieval sites in Nimrud and Nineveh in present-day Iraq.

In man's early history, the worship of "idols" was common practice. In Abraham's time, circa 2000 BC, the worship of other gods such as the Sun God and many others was typical. Even

Abraham's father, Terah, "worshiped other gods" (Joshua 24:2).[8] However, as the chapter of Genesis reveals, Abraham became the first to worship a singular god. This choice was the birth of monotheism, but polytheism still flourished. Moses, circa 1500 BC, had problems dealing with the golden calf during the Jewish exodus from Egypt. In 700 BC, King Hezekiah purged idols from Solomon's temple in Jerusalem.[9] The history of iconoclasm is multidenominational, as well. History shows that Muhammad dealt with rampant idolatry during his years as the Prophet of Islam in the seventh century.

So, what exactly is idolatry? Strictly speaking, idolatry denotes a deity's worship in a tangible form, such as a picture, a statue, or even an altar to make sacrifices. These images are just symbols that represent a god in which a person believes. Their prophets have instructed Christians, Jews, and Muslims to worship the one true God. Throughout history, pagans have found ways in which to worship their gods. Examples would be:

- Nature worship, in which a sacred life force or animistic spirit is venerated in animals and plants, in topographic features like hills and rivers, and celestial bodies such as the sun, moon, stars, fire, and wind.
- The idolization of great leaders and the exaltation of deceased ancestors.
- Greek Gods such as Zeus, Poseidon, Apollo, and Aphrodite.
- Roman Gods such as Jupiter, Neptune, Venus, and Mars.
- Satan.

Advocates of Islam would expand the list:

- Dead prophets and saints as expressed in statues and pictures (paintings and stained glass) and shrines.

- Mary, mother of Jesus, as expressed in scripture, statues, and pictures.

- Jesus as expressed in scripture, statues, pictures, and crucifixion symbols.

- Muhammad, as expressed in scriptures, statues, and pictures.

There are three other forms of shirk in the Islamic tradition that are worth mentioning. One type of shirk includes the worship of wealth, other material objects, and one's ego. This type of glorification is like the tenth commandment in the Bible, which warns against coveting things that belong to others and the Biblical warnings about excess pride.

Another form of shirk is to treat eminent religious scholars, monks, priests, or rabbis as Lord(s) in practice by obeying their doctrines and their rulings on what is lawful when it is at variance with the principles prescribed in the Qur'an (41:38) or sunna.[10]

The final form of shirk represents a design change for houses of worship. The tendency for most mosques is to display colorful designs and patterns, and verses from the Qur'an. There are no pictures or statues in the mosques. They are a temptation to the faithful who come to worship Allah. The Prophet himself was aware that people would soon start praising him if people saw his face portrayed in an image.[11] He made it known that he did not wish his image depicted in paintings or statues. The Qur'an does not explicitly prohibit pictures of Muhammad, but there are a few hadith that do (al-Bukhari, 7.834, 7.838, 7.840, and 7.846).

An interesting story illustrates how Muslims abide by the Prophet's wish to remain obscure, unseen. It begins with Voltaire, who wrote the play *Mahomet, The Impostor*, in 1742. During the Revolutionary War, the play was performed for the British in 1780 and the Americans in 1782.[12] Voltaire's knowledge of Islam was weak, and of course, much of what he wrote was untrue or incorrect, but he was known for insulting all the religions in his philosophical essays. The critical part of the play was a character who played Muhammad in the flesh. It was a radical insult to the prophet, but no Muslims were around to notice at the time. Fast forward to December 9, 2005, when the play was revived and scheduled for a public reading in a small French theatre near the Franco-Swiss border. Representatives from mosques of both countries formally protested but to no avail. The issue of free speech was considered paramount. Consequently, a small riot broke out the day of the scheduled presentation causing the theatre to close temporarily.[13] Fortuitously, Muhammad's image remained in shadow.

There is one public place in America where there is a detailed visual depiction of Muhammad. Constructed in 1935, The U.S. Supreme Court Building in Washington DC has a frieze decorated with a bas-relief sculpture of 18 influential lawgivers. Located on the north wall, between Justinian and Charlemagne, is Muhammad's image. In 1997, the Council on American-Islamic Relations petitioned the Supreme Court to remove the sculpture. Chief Justice Rehnquist refused to remove the Prophet's image, adding that to have the figure was a sign of honor, and the sword, a universal symbol of justice.[14]

On the North Wall Frieze, Muhammad is the fourth character from the right.

Photograph by Franz Jantzen, Collection of the
Supreme Court of the United States.

Here is a close-up of Muhammad from the picture above.

A description provided by the Office of the Curator, Supreme Court of the United States reads as follows:

> Muhammad (c. 570-632) The Prophet of Islam. He is depicted holding the Qur'an. The Qur'an provides the primary source of Islamic Law. Prophet Muhammad's teachings explain and implement Qur'anic principles. The figure above is a well-intentioned attempt by the sculptor, Adolph Weinman, to honor Muhammad, and it bears no resemblance to Muhammad. Muslims generally have a strong aversion to sculptured or pictured representations of their Prophet.[15]

Side Note: According to the New World Encyclopedia, "Iconoclasm is the deliberate destruction of icons or monuments, usually for religious or political motives."[16] While we understand that some Islamic fundamentalists still practice this activity, it was also engaged in by the ancient Egyptians, the Jews in the Old Testament, the Byzantines, Protestant Reformers, and communist nations like China.

In approximately 1458 BC, Hatshepsut, the bearded female king of Egypt and step-aunt of Thutmose III, died, leaving her nephew as pharaoh. It is not known why, but her nephew had all statues, inscriptions, and monuments with her reference destroyed, trying to erase her footprint from history.[17]

After their long trek through the Sinai, the Jews were preparing to invade the land of the Canaanites. Moses instructed them, "Destroy completely all the places on the high mountains and on the hills and under every spreading tree where the nations you are dispossessing worship their gods. Break down their altars, smash their sacred stones and burn their Asherah poles in the fire; cut down the idols of their gods and wipe out their names from those places." (Deut. 12:2-3)[18]

The Byzantine emperor, Justinian II (AD 705-711), had his image cast on the reverse side of gold coins minted with Jesus Christ on the obverse side. In the picture below, a Byzantine coin shows Jesus with the crucifix behind his image.

Source: The author's private coin collection.

Soon after Justinian died, Christian bishops of the Eastern Roman empire adopted the Islamic belief that icons were offensive to God. Icons fell into the category of graven images as described in the Ten Commandments. In AD 726, a massive underwater volcanic eruption in the Aegean Sea caused tsunamis and much loss of life. Emperor Leo III interpreted this as a judgment on the Empire by God and decided that the use of images had been the offense.[19] Leo later passed an edict in AD 730 that forbade the worship of religious icons. During that period, the Emperor confiscated all the gold relics decorated with religious figures.[20]

In the 1500s, Protestant reformers, invoking the Ten Commandments' prohibition of idolatry and the manufacture of graven images, encouraged the removal of holy images.[21]

Iconoclasm was also a hallmark of the communist revolutions in Russia and China. Communist authorities consider religious imagery a necessary means of perpetuating "bourgeois ideology," countering propaganda designed to promote the state's socialist values. Consequently, they encouraged the widespread destruction of all religious paraphernalia.[22]

Blasphemy

Most Christians are familiar with the term blasphemy. It comes to light in the Old Testament book of Exodus that set the law in writing: "Do not blaspheme God or curse the ruler of your people" (Exodus 22:28).[23]

To question the integrity and holiness of God was to revile God directly or those appointed on his behalf. The concept of blasphemy is to say anything or behave in any manner that would insult God or offend others' religious sensibilities. Later on in Leviticus 24:10-16, we learn that the penalty for blasphemy is death as it is in Islam.[24] Furthermore, in the New

Testament, Jesus teaches that blasphemy against the Holy Spirit is an unpardonable sin; all other blasphemies, particularly those against "the Son of Man," may be forgiven. So, what are the different kinds of blasphemy?

- Idolatry is blasphemy. Idolatry wrongly attributes worship and glorification to an object that is not truly God. When we find comfort in praying to things other than God, we are guilty of blasphemy.
- Arrogance is blasphemy. When writing to the churches in Galatia, the apostle Paul tells us: "If anyone thinks he is something when he is nothing, he deceives himself" (Galatians 6:1).[25] When we reside as though we do not need God within our lives or live without proper regard to our need for God, we deceive ourselves.
- False teaching in God's name is blasphemy. Inaccurate depictions of God obscure the real character of God. The Bible warns Christians always to beware of false prophets and their messages.
- Criticism of Muhammad, the Qur'an, and Islamic teachings is no longer protected free speech in Europe and Canada and is considered as hate speech.[26]
- Two other forms of blasphemy include apostasy and heresy. Apostasy is to abandon or renounce a religious belief. In Christian theology, "Forsaking Yahweh" was the original and oft-recurring sin of the "chosen people," especially during the early years (Exodus 20:3).[27] In Islam, apostasy comes into play when Christian missionaries attempt to convert Muslims. In the Middle East or North Africa, a Christian conversion can lead to a death penalty for both the evangelist and the Muslim.[28] Even today, proselytizing for Christianity can get you executed or imprisoned in Somalia, Afghanistan, Sudan, Pakistan, or any one of a dozen or more Islamic countries.[29] Heresy

refers to a self-chosen path or doctrine not emanating from God,[30] very similar to false teaching (2 Peter 2:1).

The Qur'an and the sunna also have rules and teachings as regard blasphemy. First, blasphemy in Islam is like the way it is in Christianity. Impious language and behavior against Allah, the Prophet Muhammad, the angels, or the other prophets are unacceptable. Worldly punishment is not specified in the Qur'an, suggesting that the blasphemer will have to face God themselves on Judgment Day. The hadiths, another source of sharia (Islamic law), suggest various punishments, which may even include death.

Laws prohibiting apostasy and blasphemy are most common in the Middle East and North Africa. Most nations in that region criminalize blasphemy and apostasy. Apostasy laws are rare worldwide, but blasphemy laws are prevailing throughout Europe and the Middle East. Of the 30 Islamic countries that impose blasphemy laws, 13 impose the death penalty for the offense.[31] For example, anyone critiquing Muhammad's relationship with a nine-year-old girl (he was 53 years old), later to become his fourth wife, could find themselves on the end of a hangman's noose.

While Western governments are reluctant to enforce or enact blasphemy laws, radical Islamic groups embedded in Western societies are not. Mob violence and assassinations have occurred. Recent examples have included the 2015 *Charlie Hebdo* magazine murders and the riots outside numerous Danish embassies for a Danish newspaper that published cartoons mocking the Prophet Muhammad.

One critique against the concept of blasphemy is that, when enforced, it curtails freedom of expression. The freedom to speak freely is a fundamental human right. Every country with a liberal democracy needs to guarantee this right to its citizens. While freedom of speech is imperative for society's progress and development, this freedom, like all other freedoms, is not limitless. The truth is that religious sensitivities and freedom of speech are essential. Both need to be protected. There is no clash if both operate within their limits and do not trespass into each other's domain. However, there will be times when sensitivity and freedom will conflict.

The Doctrine of Takfir

Excommunication or *takfir* results from being judged guilty of kufr or shirk, which are both considered heresy. Religious scholars maintain that only the doctrinally pure merit the name Muslim. Excommunication is a crucial issue since, in Islam, heresy is punishable by death. Hence, takfir constitutes a religious license to target and kill an individual.

Muslims maintain that followers must have a high degree of belief in Muhammad's faith. For those who commit shirk, excommunication is customarily considered the outcome. Some states and groups take it one step further. The founder of Wahhabism, the state religion of Saudi Arabia, describes it as "Whoever does not excommunicate the polytheists or is doubtful about their unbelief, or affirms the validity of their doctrine – he is an unbeliever by consensus."[32] In other words, a Muslim, himself, or herself, is subject to excommunication if they fail to alert the authorities of supposed polytheists. It's a tattletale religion. Christians understand the term "polytheists" to mean the worship of more than one God. To extremists, Muslims that participate in polytheistic acts such as voting in a democratic system or even supporting rulers or public officials who fail to rule by sharia are subject to takfir. It is possible to be guilty by association, such as having family or friends who are not believers and participating in events supporting Western ideals and values. Excommunication of a person, tribe, or group makes them subject to death.

The inquiries about who is Muslim and who is not, and under

what conditions and circumstances, are critical questions for Islamic fundamentalists. They are fundamental questions for jihadis since takfir is pivotal to identify the enemies who must be fought and killed. The issue of takfir was one of the significant contention points in the conflict between Al-Qaeda and the Islamic State. Al-Qaeda holds the more moderate position, according to which takfir applies to selected individuals. In contrast, IS leaders use it more freely and do not hesitate to brand as heretical entire movements, communities, or sects, such as the Shi'ites.[33]

The Islamic Hand Gesture

Muslims contend that there is only one God to worship. Under Islam, the so-called Trinity is blasphemous as it suggests that the Son of God, Jesus (a mortal man), and the Holy Spirit (an angel) are to be worshipped in addition to God. This unitary nature of God known in Arabic is *tawhid*.

Religious fighters for Islam, sometimes referred to as jihadis, signify God's unitary feature by making a hand gesture with the index finger pointing up. Simultaneously, the thumb wraps underneath and presses against the digital phalange of the center finger. The remaining digits are squeezed against the palm to spotlight the long forefinger. The single finger pointing up is a reminder to others that there is only one God. All believers understand the hand gesture to be a symbolic form of the shahada, the Muslim affirmation of faith, and one of the pillars of Islam. Quite often, in propaganda videos put out by the Islamic State, jihadi fighters will show the hand gesture with the finger as if it is pointing to heaven when, in fact, it stands for the number one – as in a unitary God.[34] For a while, during their 2014 to 2018 reign of terror, you could recognize an ISIS jihadi in the media by watching for the hand gesture. You can still find those pictures on the Internet. Do an Internet search for "ISIS Islamic hand gesture images." Make sure you click on the "images" selector. You will see all kinds of hand gestures, but if you look closely, quite a few show the single index finger pointing to heaven. Even one picture shows President Obama making the hand gesture, but the actual video where it occurs catches him out of context. While the hand gesture is known and understood by all Muslims, it is ISIS that has branded it for their identification.

Innovation

Innovation originates from the Latin *innovates*, meaning "introducing something new" or "to bring in new things, or to alter established practices."[35] When technical developments or brand-new inventions surface within the realm of science, we describe them as innovation. In Islam, innovation refers to an alteration in religious rituals. Muslim theology interprets innovational change as a novelty, heretical doctrine, or heresy. Several verses in the Qur'an suggest the recitations are pure and truthful, and any hadith that would indicate change under the guise of being better or more fulfilling would be heresy (10:32; 5:3; 4:59).

The concept of innovation predates Islamic theology. The allegation that something was new and different meant that it violated the tribal code. In Arabia, the pre-Islamic governing structure was tribes. Tribal elders were the non-elected governors. An action or idea that lacked precedent and challenged established custom was considered a creative act. Tribal customs worked, or they would not have been around long enough to be a custom. In these circumstances, change indicated something negative, and sunna meant something positive. In pre-Islamic Arabia, sunna represented the reservoir of tribal codes and traditions. Sunna was indicative of life; it embodied the norms of acceptable thought and practice in tribal behavior.

While there were situations where innovation was considered positive and sunna as unfavorable, they were few and far between. References to change are frequent in hadith. One hadith spoken by the Prophet comes from Muslim's hadith collection: "He who innovates things in our affairs for which there is no valid (reason) (commits sin) and these are to be rejected."[36]

The dominant opinion of Islamic scholars is that the Prophet's warning was *not* a categorical prohibition of innovative ideas or practices but a sign to stay within sound legal parameters to accept or reject them. New ideas and procedures were not intrinsically wrong but had to be consistent with established precedents and recognized principles of the law.

So how does this concept of innovation affect Muslims and non-Muslim scholars who study Islamic theology? In a nutshell, it means Islam will not mutate or undergo a reformation like the Christian theology did in the Middle Ages. Islamic theology will stay as originally intended; there cannot be a middle ground where beliefs and rituals will change as society changes. Islamic innovation forbids changes in the place of worship, the time or number of prayers, the ceremony's manner, the type of devotion, and the cause or reason for the celebration. If these ritualistic changes are prohibited, it would be challenging for the underlying beliefs and doctrines to change. If innovation is brought about by good intentions to achieve closeness to God, it does not have support from the Qur'an or any authentic hadith.

This idea about innovation is not to say that some reform will never happen, but it is unlikely. The Prophet anticipated there would be attempts at metamorphosis, but this concept of innovation nips that in the bud. Even now, the Sunnis blame the Shi'a for change in Islamic theology, causing one group to cite the other for heresy. Heresy is grounds for excommunication, which, of course, allows Sunni fundamentalist groups like the Islamic State to justifiably kill Shi'a Muslims.

Islam, a Religion of Peace?

It is common for Muslims, when conversing with non-Muslims, to refer to their religion as one of peace. In Western countries, Muslims are generally taught that Islam is a religion of peace, and it is as they have experienced no religious wars in this country because of the rule of law. However, Muslims in the Middle East are not as docile as they are taught that Islam is superior to all other religions.[37] In those countries, like Somalia, Libya and Syria, Islam can be violent. It all depends on where you live and what you are taught.

Most recently, in 2017, King Salman of Saudi Arabia presented those same qualifications of being a peaceful religion to President Trump at the end of Trump's visit:

to promote a genuine partnership with the friendly United States of America in a way that serves our common interests and contributes to achieving security, peace, and development for all mankind, which is confirmed by our Islamic religion. Our way to achieve purposes of our religion and win the paradise is to spread the tolerant values of Islam based on peace.[38]

The first reference that Islam was called a religion of peace went back to the 1930s in a book entitled *The Religion of Peace*, written by Ishtiaq Hussain Qureshi (d. 1981), a Pakistani historian, which was published to promote Islam to Western audiences.[39] The term was slow to take off, but by the 1970s, it appeared more and more frequently. For the first 1,300 years of Islamic history, this description was unknown; it occurs nowhere in Islam's texts or traditions right up until the last century.

The phrase "religion of peace" has been steadily publicized by Western leaders in response to terrorism: George W. Bush and Jacques Chirac after 9/11, David Cameron, after Muslim terrorists killed British tourists in Tunisia in 2015, and François Hollande after the *Charlie Hebdo* shootings.[40] In 2015, President Obama used the term to counter a perceived anti-Muslim bias following the San Bernardino attack.[41]

Adherents of Islam want non-Muslims to think that Islam provides a philosophical high of its seemingly peaceful nature. In other words, if you practice Islam, you are not violent unless you are provoked into it. However, Islam does not have a monopoly on peacefulness. John Locke, the most famous British theorist about limited, liberal government and Thomas Jefferson's mentor, wrote that Christianity is "the most modest and peaceable religion that ever was."[42] Christian theologians tell us that the *visio beatifica* – the beatific vision of God – is the highest pleasure known to man (1 John 3:2).[k] Both Islam[43] and Christianity share this reward with their followers. In any case, true religion will bring its followers to a point where they want to share with non-followers, thus being the case with Islam and Christianity.

Chapter Summary

Islam contains a very high-strung belief system that utilizes punishment to keep people in line. Islam's mechanics involve specific labels that promote discipline: kufr, shirk, idolatry, heresy, blasphemy, and apostasy can all get a member excommunicated from the religion. Being excommunicated or takfir, for a Muslim, can result in the death penalty. On the other hand, the doctrine of tawhid or God's unity is a critical ripple of the belief that permeates Islam.

Muslims today try hard to convince others that Islam is a religion of peace. Western leaders espouse those thoughts, especially after nauseous terror attacks. That line of thinking did not evolve until the mid-1900s, but it has grown and permeated Western thought. Interestingly, minority religions, such as Islam and Judaism, have found ways to gain credibility and recognition. In another chapter, I mention how the "Judeo-Christian" concept originated in the late 1900s.

End-of-Chapter Notes

k.   The Bible teaches that God "who alone is immortal and who lives in unapproachable light, whom no one has seen or can see" (1 Timothy 6:16), but when God reveals himself to us in heaven "then we shall see face to face" (1 Corinthians 13:12).

Chapter 5

Where Islamic Fundamentalists Stand on Select Issues

There are several concepts in the Islamic faith that challenge cultural values in secular Western democracies. These pertain not only to religion but to all facets of life. So, let us look at some of the topics:

Can Muslims Convert to Other Faiths?

A 2013 Pew Research Study found that Muslims worldwide agree that Islam is the one true faith that leads to salvation and eternal life. In 34 of the 38 countries surveyed, more than half of the Muslims also say it is their religious duty to convert others to Islam and prevent people from leaving the religion.[1] Sharia law forbids Muslims to convert to other religions. Converts are considered apostates and subject to takfir. This apostasy is equated to treason by Muslim clerics in fundamentalist countries like Pakistan and Somalia, making it a criminal offense punishable by stoning. There are several verses in the Qur'an and in the hadith that set the tone. Here is but one of several: "Lo! those who disbelieve after their (profession of) belief, and afterward grow violent in disbelief: their repentance will not be accepted. Theirs will be a painful doom and they will have no helpers." (3:90-91)[2]

Many Muslim countries no longer prescribe death for apostates but hand out some lesser form of punishment such as imprisonment or fines. Some countries, including Iran, Saudi Arabia, and Pakistan, still hand out death sentences. One case came to light in the Afghan media in 2006 involving a legal motion by a plaintiff named Abdul Rahman. He petitioned the court to let him convert to Christianity. The Afghan court struck down the petition, and his penalty was to be death for apostasy. The court later reversed the decision following international pressure. The court released Rahman, who then fled and sought asylum in Italy.[3] Recent cases in Egypt, Jordan, and Kuwait have been handled similarly, with the converts serving jail time.

In some cases, the publicity turns the case into a political free-for-all with diplomats from foreign countries and even famous personalities getting involved. In cases like that, the governing authority usually finds some technicality to release the accused, who then flees the country. Sometimes, Islamic vigilante groups take the law into their own hands and administer their punishment. One example in 2006 occurred in Bangladesh: "... the president of CFI (Christian Freedom International) indicated that Muslim women who convert to Christianity may be subject to beatings, abduction, rape, forced marriage, and forced reconversion to Islam."[4]

Side Note: In the fourth century, Christianity adopted similar conversion laws. For example, during that time, it was illegal for a Christian to convert to Judaism.[5] Christianity started as a Jewish sect that followed Jewish eschatological expectations. The inclusion of Gentiles led to a growing split between Jews and Christians that caused much criticism and persecution from the Jewish leaders. After Christianity became a state church in the Roman Empire, the criticism and abuse reversed, and the Jews were sanctioned, much like the Muslim *dhimmi*, as we will discuss later in this chapter.

Can Muslim Women Have Abortions?

In general, Muslim scholars consider abortion as an act of interfering in Allah's role, the only author of life and death. The Qur'an does not offer much guidance on this matter but provides direction on related issues listed below. The high priority that Islam gives to the sanctity of life is the crucial viewpoint. The Qur'an states: "We decreed for the Children of Israel that whosoever killeth a human being for other than manslaughter or corruption in the earth, it shall be as if he had killed all mankind, and whoso saveth the life of one, it shall be as if he had saved the life of all mankind." (5:32)[6]

Muslim tradition asserts that a fetus in the womb is recognized and protected by Islam as human life. Islam rarely permits abortion after 120 days because that is when the soul enters the fetus. However, there are several different legal schools of thought, and they have their reservations on when abortions can happen. Here are some circumstances:

When the baby is born into poverty

The Qur'an makes it clear to families that a fetus is not aborted just because of fears that they will not be able to provide for the forthcoming child – they should trust Allah to look after things: "Slay not your children, fearing a fall to poverty, We shall provide for them and for you. Lo! the slaying of them is great sin."[7] (17:31)

The same texts also forbid abortion on social or financial grounds, such as that the pregnancy was accidental or that the baby will hinder the mother's life, training, or profession.

When the baby has a defect

An irreparable defect found in the fetus early in the pregnancy is an acceptable reason for abortion. Under these circumstances, many scholars would point out that it is permissible to abort, provided that the pregnancy is less than 120 days old. There is an almost unanimous opinion that after 120 days, abortion is not allowed unless the mother's life is somehow in danger from the defect in the embryo.

When the mother's life is at risk

There is a religious principle called "the lesser of two evils"[1] in which an abortion can save the mother's life. Abortion is considered a lesser evil in this case because:

- the mother is the "originator" of the fetus, the mother's life is well-established
- the mother has duties and responsibilities
- the mother is part of a family
- allowing the mother to die would also kill the fetus in most cases.[8]

When the soul enters the baby

After the fetus receives the soul, Islam prohibits the termination of a pregnancy. There's disagreement within Islam as to when this happens. The three prominent opinions are:

- at 120 days
- at 40 days[m]
- when the fetus moves on its own, sometimes as late as 20 weeks.[9]

A pertinent hadith indicates that the point of ensoulment occurs in 120 days:

Allah's Apostle, the true and truly inspired, said, "(as regards your creation), every one of you is collected in the womb of his mother for the first forty days, and then he becomes a clot for another forty days, and then a piece of flesh for another forty days. Then Allah sends an angel to write four words: He writes his deeds, time of his death, means of his livelihood, and whether he will be wretched or blessed (in religion). Then the soul is breathed into his body..." (al-Bukhari, Volume 4, Book 55, Number 549)[10]

Side Note: In the U.S., the right to have an abortion has

evolved into a political schism. The pro-choice movement wants to ensure that women have the right to choose an abortion, whereas the pro-life movement wants to restrict abortions against the unjust taking of human life.

The Bible provides two viewpoints on abortion. First, in Exodus 21:22-25, a life for a life applies to the unborn child's death. Second, this opinion found in Deuteronomy 30:19-20: "I have set before you life and death, blessings and curses. Now choose life so that you and your children may live and that you may love the Lord your God."[11]

Honor Killings

The majority of honor killings worldwide happen within Muslim communities.[12] However, such killings are also frequent in Hindu (and Sikh) communities.[13] Even though the outcome is the same, the causes of this type of femicide are different, arising from different cultures and other values.

The premeditated murder of a relative (usually a young woman, although the number of young men is on the increase) who has been accused of impugning her family's honor is known as an honor killing. It tends to predominate inside communities where patriarchal authority structures, tribal opinions, and intolerant religions control specific rights. Subject to such conditions, control over marital life and reproduction is critical to the socioeconomic status of kinship groups, and the regulation of female behavior is essential to perceptions of honor.

When it comes to such an environment, a woman who will not enter a prearranged marriage, seeks divorce or even fails to avoid just the conjecture of immoral conduct is seen by her relatives as having dishonored them. Other families will shun male relatives in such an environment, and the siblings of the accused will have problems finding suitable candidates to marry. Killing the accused is supposedly the only way the family can restore its honor, regardless of whether she is, or can be proven, guilty of the alleged offense.

Hindu society has a caste system, membership of which is hereditary and virtually permanent and unchangeable. According to Hindu religious law and tradition, marrying or having sexual relations with a member of a different caste is strictly forbidden.[14] Honor killings act as an enforcer of this.

Some honor killings involve allegations of adultery or apostasy within Islam, which are punishable by death under sharia, as we have seen. Going a step further, the Qur'an (18:66-81) contains a story that ostensibly supports honor killings in Islam if the accused has disgraced their parents. In the story, Moses follows a man around to learn wisdom from his actions.

Moses said unto him: "May I follow thee, to the end that thou mayst teach me right conduct of that which thou hast been taught? He said: Well, if thou go with me, ask me not concerning aught till I myself mention of it unto thee. So, they twain journeyed on till, when they met a lad, he slew him. (Moses) said: What! Hast thou slain an innocent soul who hath slain no man? Verily thou hast done a horrid thing. He said: As for the lad, his parents were believers and we feared lest he should oppress them by rebellion and disbelief. And we intended that their Lord should change him for them for one better in purity and nearer to mercy."[15]

In her 2010 study on honor killings, researcher Phyllis Chesler showed that the average age for an "honor killing" victim in the Muslim World is 23. Usually, multiple people conscripted by the family of the victim are involved in the killing. The victim is frequently tortured before death, such as gang-rape, beating, stoning, or burning. The top two reasons for these murders are "too Western" and "sexual impropriety."[16]

On more than one occasion, after an honor killing has taken place, people from the Muslim community will flood the newspapers and social media with statements that Islam had nothing to do with the murder. They claim that sensationalizing domestic violence is not only racist but a form of Islamophobia. In a sense, honor killings are a type of domestic terrorism meant to ensure the subjugation of Muslim women through wearing the veil, procreating, marrying, and socializing only within the faith.

Side Note: Christians should be aware that the Old Testament in the Bible also endorsed honor killings. There are several scriptures of which Deuteronomy 21:18-21, Exodus 21:17, Leviticus 20:9, and Leviticus 21:9 are the most notable references. That last reference from Leviticus reads as such: "If a priest's daughter defiles herself by becoming a prostitute, she disgraces her father; she must be burned in the fire."[17]

Child Marriage

As mentioned in Chapter 3, Muhammad, the Prophet of Islam, is often labeled as a pedophile because of the age of his bride, Aisha. Critics allege that when Aisha was just six years old, she was promised to Muhammad as a bride, who was in his 50s. Later, when she was only nine, the marriage was consummated according to hadiths found in al-Bukhari (Volume 5, book 58, number 234) and Muslim ibn al-Hajjaj (book 8, number 3309).

In seventh-century Arabia, adulthood was considered to begin at the onset of puberty. Puberty in girls usually starts between the ages of 8 and 13 and ends by around 14. In the United States, the average age for girls to get their first period is around age 12.[18] It seems that Muhammad waited from the time Aisha was six (when the marriage ceremony took place) until she turned nine to consummate the marriage because he was waiting for her to begin menstrual cycles – thus becoming a woman.

95

Side Note: Child marriages were common throughout history. Europe was a hotbed of child marriages as royal families, quite often with the Pope's help, tried to forge alliances with different kingdoms. Some examples:

- 33-year-old King John of England married 12-year-old Isabella of Angoulême (1200).[19]
- Agnes of France was 12 when she was married to Andronicus Comnenus, Byzantine Emperor (1182).[20]
- Isabella de Valois (France) was seven years old when she was married to Richard II of England (1396).[21]
- Mary, the mother of Jesus, was probably between 12 and 14 years old when she gave birth to Jesus. Jewish maidens were considered marriageable at the age of 12 years and six months.[n,22]

Today, child marriage is still widespread, particularly in developing countries. Arguably, the worst area in the world to be a young girl is in South Asia's rural regions.[23] The eight countries in that region of the world include Sri Lanka (predominantly Buddhist), Pakistan (Muslim), Afghanistan (Muslim), Bangladesh (Muslim), Nepal (Hindu), India (mainly Hindu), Bhutan (Buddhist), and the Maldives (Muslim).[24] Notice that the larger countries are either Muslim or Hindu.

In developing countries worldwide, one out of nine girls will be married before their fifteenth birthday.[25] Most of these girls live in poverty, are illiterate or poorly educated, and live in rural areas. Some parents genuinely believe that marriage will secure their daughters' future, while others see their daughters as a burden or commodity. Both Muslim and Hindu families believe blessings will come upon them if they marry off their girls before their first menstruation; thus, the perpetuation of child marriages has more of a cultural than religious impetus. In 52 countries, young girls under the age of 15 can marry with parental consent compared with only 23 nations where boys can do the same.[26] This particular absence of gender equality in the law reinforces social norms that dictate it is somehow acceptable for girls to marry earlier than boys.

Married young women are often under pressure to become pregnant immediately or soon after marriage, although they are still children themselves. Nearly 16 million girls aged 15-19 in developing countries give birth every year.[27] In Chapter 10, we explore the reasons for Islam's steady growth rate. Two of the causes are the young age of the family and Muslim families having many children. Starting families early with child brides gives Islam an explosive growth demographic, but it only works when socioeconomic trends are low. In our day and time, it is evident to Westerners that child marriage is not conducive to either the child's mental or physical health or society's well-being. So why does it happen?

Most of the families concerned apply social or emotional pressure or encourage marriage mainly for economic reasons. Either they receive money for the child who is being married off, a dowry, or are not able to afford her upkeep. For example, in food-insecure Kenya, these girls are called "famine brides."[28] In Sri Lanka, Indonesia, and India, young girls were married to "tsunami widowers" to obtain state subsidies to marry and start families.[29] During the conflicts in Liberia, Uganda, and Sudan, girls were abducted and given as "bush wives" to warlords or even in exchange for protection for their families.[30] It would appear that the root cause of child marriage is social dysfunction, not any religious obsession with pedophilia. The person receiving the child bride may indeed be a pedophile. Still, the recognition of pedophilia as the driving cause of child marriages will remain in the shadows if the transactions continue to have such strong economic incentives.

Aisha, Muhammad's favorite wife, is credited with creating over 2,400 hadiths[31] herself and has become a strong female voice in an otherwise patriarchal society. None of her stories or tales have indicated that she was mistreated or had a miserable existence. However, she felt jealous of Muhammad's other wives and concubines and those who tried to occupy Muhammad's time. A mark of her unique position is that the Prophet died and was buried in her house, which today lies within The Prophet's Mosque in Medina.

Homosexuality

Homosexuality is anathema to Islam. It meets with hostility throughout the Muslim world, where state punishments range from hefty fines to the death penalty. It is common in the Middle East and South Asia for extremist groups to persecute gay and bisexual men. In 2016, there were many reports of gay men having been thrown off tall buildings by ISIS.[32] However, numerous scholars and commentators maintain that the Qur'an and hadith rule unambiguously against same-sex relations.[o] So, what has caused homosexuality to become such a hated crime?

Fundamentalists justify the blanket condemnation for homosexuality through references to the parable of Lot as written in the Qur'an (26:161). This version of Lot's story is the same as in the Bible in Genesis, chapters 11-14 and 19. To recap the story, Lot was a nephew of Abraham and made the journey (described in Chapter 1) from Ur to Canaan. Lot then traveled with Abraham through Canaan to Egypt and back to Canaan. Friction within the tribe urged Lot to move on, which he did (Genesis 13:11).[33] Eventually, he settled in Sodom, one of a few villages thought to exist south of the Dead Sea in Moab, in present-day Jordan.

The parable describes two visitors who visited the city of Sodom, disguised angels, sent to destroy the desert cities where "sins of the flesh" were rampant. Lot was the first to encounter the travelers as they entered the city gates. He took them to his house and provided food and board, as was the custom. The parable ending is similar in both the Bible and the Qur'an. The official line is that Sodom and Gomorrah were wicked cities with homosexuality and bestiality running rampant. Because of this wickedness, God allowed Lot and his immediate family to leave but destroyed four towns in the region with fire and brimstone from the heavens (Deuteronomy 29:23).[34] We know that approximately 500 years later, Moses incorporated these values into law so that in ancient Israel, homosexuality was punishable by death (Leviticus 18:22; 20:13).[35] There is much emphasis in the Bible that believers remember this behavior and the consequences, for there are 27 references outside Genesis, where the Bible mentions Sodom.[36] The Qur'an also documents it (27:55). In summation, it may seem that modern Christianity has become progressive and liberal, while fundamentalist Islam has remained rooted in its purest values.

The story of Lot provides the foundation for why homosexuality is deemed wicked in Islam. A survey by the Pew Research Center in 2013 found that most people in the Middle East reject homosexuality: 97 percent in Jordan, 95 percent in Egypt, and 80 percent in Lebanon. Islamic countries in Central Asia and Africa feel the same way: 87 percent in Pakistan, 98 percent in Nigeria.[37]

It did not use to be that way. While homosexuality was never accepted, society was more open to its visibility. When Alexander the Great conquered the world, his armies swept through the Mediterranean Sea's lower lip to Egypt. His soldiers and generals brought Greek culture with them, which the Islamic world inherited and enhanced. The most prevalent and socially significant form of same-sex sexual relations in ancient Greece was between adult men and pubescent or adolescent boys. As the ancient Athenians did, classical Muslim scholars marveled over the beauty of young boys. As heirs to ancient Greek culture, Muslim scholars discovered that men would be drawn to young boys or effeminate males since they manifested the same feminine beauty as women. Sharia has no penalty against looking and lusting, only against actual acts of sexual contact.

In the 1980s, the rise of Islamic fundamentalism coincided with the gay rights movement in America and Europe. In the eyes of many in the Islamic world, the movement caused homosexuality to become synonymous with the West, and Islamic politicians convinced their constituents of the West's moral decay. In some Islamic countries, same-sex marriages are legal, e.g., Turkey; the problem lies with discrimination, harassment, and violence prevalent in many Islamic countries. In those countries, it is a problem beyond control. On a local level, Muslims abide by sharia, and if sharia does not endorse homosexuality, the local citizens will not either.

In countries that prohibit homosexuality, legal punishment ranges from mild to lethal. Muhammad, himself, recognized that what may suit one culture may not be entirely suitable for another. For this reason, he encouraged each community to introduce its customs into its laws, provided that these customs did not contradict basic Islamic principles. As a result, the Islamic rulings of Muslim countries differ significantly on various matters. By reserving space for tradition, the Law Giver (Allah) emphasized the importance of cultural diversity and each society's ability to make its own choices.

Sharia or Islamic law approaches legitimate sexual contact as being a *quid pro quo* arrangement. Understanding sharia is vital to understanding the outcome of the law in Islamic societies. Sharia is concerned primarily with actions as opposed to emotions, desires, and lust. For example, marriage in sharia is not a sacrament; it is a contract. Of course, some ceremonies and rituals express love and companionship, but after the crowds have gone home, all that remains is a binding, lawful contract between a man and a woman. The man supplies the woman with financial support in return for exclusive sexual access. It is a contract that has sex and procreation legal in the eyes of God and legitimate in the eyes of society. The basis for marriage in sharia is vaginal intercourse and financial obligations between a man and a woman. Same-sex couples would have difficulties bridging that gap. They could construct an arrangement for inheritance and shared property that mimicked marriage, but it would not be marriage.[38] The Qur'an would have to be changed for the same-sex union to be considered marriage, and that won't happen.

Let us continue with our exploration of sharia as it pertains to the position of sexual acts. All sexual contact between unmarried men and women is forbidden. Sexual contact other than vaginal intercourse is also prohibited with punishment at the judge's discretion. Based on the Qur'an (24:2), vaginal sex between an unmarried couple is punishable with 100 lashes.[39] In some countries and territories such as Afghanistan or Somalia, family and community jointly execute a person who is married and commits adultery or sodomy by stoning. Stoning adulterers to death is not mentioned in the Qur'an but was a custom in the Mosaic law of Jewish communities living in Medina at that time.[40] Sodomy, its name derived from the city of Sodom in Lot's parable, is understood to be anal sex. The Qur'an does not mention any punishment for sodomy, but several hadiths state that Muhammad favored execution. As described in Chapter 2, the problem is that some hadiths are from unreliable sources or have unauthentic content. Over time, the consensus of Muslim scholars has set the punishment for anal sex between men ranging from a relatively light one at the judge's discretion to the same as illicit fornication (100 lashes) or execution (based on Muhammad's hadith of disputed authenticity).[41] Indonesia and Malaysia impose 100 lashes while Egypt, Libya, UAE, and Oman penalize homosexuality with prison sentences. Saudi Arabia, Iraq, Iran, and Yemen maintain the death penalty.[42] Altogether, there are more than 70 countries that criminalize homosexual acts.[43]

Not to leave out women, since there is no penetration to speak of, sexual contact in this manner did not receive the attention that did sodomy. As with gay men, Islam prohibits lesbian relationships under the general rule against sexual contact outside marriage, with any penalties at the judge's discretion.

The issue of LBGT rights in America is a tough one for Muslims. On the one hand, it is doubtful that one could construct an argument by which sexual contact between men, let alone anal sex, is considered permissible in God's eyes. On the other hand, attempts to ignore sharia law threaten Muslims' ability to have their marriage contracts. Muslims are not, of course, opposed to reason, logic, scientific and historical evidence. There is much ignorance about homosexuality on the Muslim side and much ignorance about sharia law from the Western view.

Issue: Dhimmitude

In most countries that are predominately Islamic, there are communities of non-Muslims. This mixing of religions has been the case since Islam began spreading its message in the last half of the seventh century. A thousand years later, in the late seventeenth century, the Ottoman Empire was more significant than the Roman Empire ever was, ranging from Austria in Europe, North Africa, the Middle East, Central and South Asia, and beyond. Islamic armies rolled through these areas seizing land and people. When they came, the people were either killed, became slaves, became regular citizens by converting to Islam, or became second-class citizens who refused to change religions. Not all the population of these countries accepted Islam, but their rulers allowed them to stay and continue with their lives if they assumed the rules of Dhimmitude.

The concept of Dhimma started in AD 627 when Muhammad and his army overtook Jewish refugees at the oasis of Khaybar, north of the city of Medina. Since the Jews were monotheists, Muhammad offered them an alternative to death. If they would submit without resistance and pay tribute to the Muslim community, they could continue to live as Jews.[44] After Muhammad's demise, the Dhimmi principle expanded as more and more cities and territories capitulated to Islam. It became embedded in Islamic law when the second caliph, Umar, offered the inhabitants of Jerusalem a pact upon capturing that city in 638. Under sharia, captured civilians and their offspring are considered prisoners of war. They can be designated as Dhimmi only if they conform to the terms and conditions of Dhimmitude. If they breach the agreement, they revert to prisoner status. Dhimmis were free to worship in their manner but could not proselytize, build new houses of worship, make a public display of their religion, rule over Muslims, or own Muslim slaves. They could not ride horses or camels but could ride mules; the local government prohibited them from owning guns, and they had to wear distinctive clothing so Muslim citizens could recognize them and not mix with them.[45] An eleventh-century chronicler wrote that "the Caliph of Baghdad... imposed that each male Jew should wear a yellow badge on his headgear."[46] Nazi Germany eerily reintroduced Star of David badges for Jews in 1939 as the Third Reich spread across Europe.[47]

The word "Dhimmi" literally means "protected person."[48] Islam gave Dhimmis security of life and property, defense against enemies, communal self-government, and freedom of religious practice. All the Dhimmi had to do was obey the Dhimmi laws, pledge loyalty to the state, and pay the *jizya* tribute, comparable to Muslims' *zakat* tax. Of course, the jizya tribute would be in addition to the tithe they gave to their religion. Dhimmis were exempt from specific duties explicitly assigned to Muslims (e.g., military service, government service) and didn't enjoy privileges and freedoms reserved for Muslims.[49] For the most part, Dhimmitude as a policy to keep captured populations in check worked. However, there was one period that it did not.

In the Caucasus region of Eurasia, Armenia was the first

Roman province to adopt Christianity as a state religion in 301,[50] even before Constantine did in 313. At the time, Armenia was just a territory in the Roman empire. For the next 1,200 years, Armenia bounced around from one realm to another several times during its history, until 1555, when the Persians lost a war to the Ottomans. The ensuing peace treaty ceded western Armenia to the Turks. For the first time in their history, the Armenians found themselves subservient to a Muslim caliphate. The Ottoman Empire's central government allowed the Armenian community to rule itself under its governance system with relatively little interference as Dhimmis. However, on a local level, their Turkish and Kurdish neighbors would regularly overtax them, subject them to kidnapping, force them to convert to Islam, and otherwise exploit them.[51]

In the late nineteenth century, both Armenian and Bulgarian Christians rebelled, but the Ottomans engaged the Kurds to put them down. Kurds killed up to 250,000 Christians during this stage.[52] Two decades later, in 1912, the Balkan Wars had the consequence of pushing 850,000 Muslim refugees from the Balkans into Armenian territory. While the Armenians were one step above poverty, it was better than what the refugees had, and it acted as fuel for the coming fire.[53]

The Ottoman Empire sided with the Axis Powers during World War I. In 1915, Kaiser Wilhelm II in Berlin pushed Ottoman Caliph Mehmed V to incite Islamic uprisings in British and French colonial holdings to get them to divert their resources from the European theatre. The Caliph's initial proclamation was brief and dealt with the proposed Holy War in a general way.[54] It was difficult to explain that a Muslim should kill Christians in a British colony but not kill Christians in a German colony. For the Germans, the "Berlin Fatwa," as it came to be known since it came from Berlin, was a failure.[P]

Shortly after this Berlin Fatwa, a second proclamation was secretly distributed, giving specific instructions to the faithful.

Henry Morgenthau, the U.S. Ambassador to the Ottoman Empire, wrote:

> This paper was not read in the mosques; it was distributed stealthily in all Muhammedan countries – India, Egypt, Morocco, Syria, and many others; and it was significantly printed in Arabic, the language of the Koran. It was a lengthy document – the English translation contains 10,000 words – full of quotations from the Koran, and its style was frenzied in its appeal to racial and religious hatred. It described a detailed plan of operations for the assassination and extermination of all Christians – except those of German nationality.[55]

Morgenthau believed this second secret proclamation instigated the obligation and justification for jihad causing "the great massacres and persecutions of the Armenian race."[56] This second attempt to incentivize the masses was so inflammatory and the effects so inhuman that the State Department took the unusual step of keeping it classified until 1961.[57]

The Armenians were assigned to work battalions to support the war effort. Putting Armenians into unarmed logistic work details was an essential precursor to the subsequent genocide. They could be sent to locations far from home with no local support and no weapons for defense. Again, Ambassador Morgenthau wrote:

> Let me relate a single episode which is contained in one of the reports of our consuls and which now forms part of the records of the American State Department. Early in July, 2,000 Armenian "amélés" – such is the Turkish word for soldiers who have been reduced to workmen – were sent from Harpoot to build roads. The Armenians in that town understood what this meant and pleaded with the

Governor for mercy. But this official insisted that the men were not to be harmed, and he even called upon the German missionary, Mr. Ehemann, to quiet the panic, giving that gentleman his word of honour that the ex-soldiers would be protected. Mr. Ehemann believed the Governor and assuaged the popular fear. Yet practically every man of these 2,000 was massacred, and their bodies thrown into a cave. A few escaped, and it was from these that news of the massacre reached the world. A few days afterward, another 2,000 soldiers were sent to Diarbekir. The only purpose of sending these men out in the open country was that they might be massacred. In order that they might have no strength to resist or to escape by flight, these poor creatures were systematically starved. Government agents went ahead on the road, notifying the Kurds that the caravan was approaching and ordering them to do their congenial duty. Not only did the Kurdish tribesmen pour down from the mountains upon this starved and weakened regiment, but the Kurdish women came with butcher's knives in order that they might gain that merit in Allah's eyes that comes from killing a Christian. These massacres were not isolated happenings; I could detail many more episodes just as horrible as the one related above.[58]

While there is absolutely no consensus regarding the number of Armenians who lost their lives between 1914 and 1918, estimates vary between 600,000 and 1 million.[59] While most governments worldwide recognize the atrocities that occurred, the Turkish government passed in 2005 Article 305, making it a criminal offense to discuss the Armenian Genocide.[60] To the Turks, the Armenians were Dhimmi who violated their covenant and thus reverted to the prisoner of war status. Under those terms, the bloodshed that followed was legal and warranted.

Chapter Summary

There are numerous issues in the West that Muslims (and other religions) approach differently than Christians. For example, Muslims treat people converting from Islam to Christianity as apostates, which in some countries warrant the death penalty. In Western countries, conversion is frowned upon but is allowed. Abortions, honor killings, child marriage, and homosexuality are social problems that are handled differently in Christian societies than in Islamic societies. Depending on the issue, the criminal laws are also different in Western cultures, and in some cases, Muslims will follow their religious dictates even when it violates domestic laws.

The issue of Dhimmitude was discussed and presented for those readers who had never heard of it. Primarily, in Muslim-dominated countries, residents with different faiths are treated as second-class citizens. There are rules on both sides to keep the Muslim faithful separated from non-Muslims, and non-Muslim citizens are not generally afforded equal rights.

End-of-Chapter Notes

l.   This principle only pertains to matters of life and death. If by necessity you break God's law, then God understands. The Qur'an, 5:3, 6:119, 6:145, 16:115. Later in Chapter 9, you will see how Muslims have expanded this rule to include political involvement.

m.   More stringent scholars rely on another tradition that states that after the first 40 days, an angel endows the fetus with hearing, sight, skin, flesh, and bones. This clearly indicates the formation of a human being, and to abort after this period is deemed as forbidden.

n.   According to the proto gospel of James of early Christian apocrypha, at 12, Mary was given in marriage to Joseph, an elderly widower with grown children.

o.   There are no references to homosexuality in the hadith

collections of al-Bukhari or Muslim, regarded by Muslims as the two most authentic collections in existence.

p.   When issued by the proper authority, fatwas are "formal legal opinions that have the force of law." This fatwa was issued by the caliph at the insistence of the German Kaiser.

Chapter 6

Sharia Law

Sharia Law, or just sharia, really means Islamic law. The Islamic religion is the backbone of its legal system. Some form of sharia governs some 1.8 billion Muslims globally, and this chapter explores that connection.

In October 1765, the *Virginia Gazette*, the local newspaper in Williamsburg, Virginia – which also served as the only bookseller in what was a British colony at the time – sold to Thomas Jefferson a two-volume set of the Qur'an. Back then, it was titled *The Alcoran of Mohammed*.[1] George Sale had translated it in 1734 from Arabic to English, and law professors of that time considered the Qur'an a book of the law, as well as religion. At the time of purchase, Jefferson was 22 years old and had studied law for three years. He openly acquired other classics as well, but his acquisition of the Qur'an was to gain an insight into Islamic law.[2] To Westerners, the Qur'an represented the law of the Ottoman Empire, a conglomeration of countries and territories governing over 25 million people,[3] thus making it worthy of study. As a matter of course, Jefferson viewed both the Qur'an and the Old Testament as repositories of religious law. Jefferson did study the Qur'an, but it did not contribute much to his private practice of law or his public practice of legislating.[4]

Islamic Law has many inputs that affect its existence, and just learning one source is like the parable about the elephant and the blind men.

A group of blind men heard that a strange animal, called an elephant, had been brought to the town, but none of them were aware of its shape and form. Out of curiosity, they said: "We must inspect and know it by touch, of which we are capable." So, they sought it out, and when they found it, they groped about it. In the case of the first person, whose hand landed on the trunk, said: "This being is like a thick snake." For another one whose hand reached its ear, it seemed like a kind of fan. As for another person, whose hand was upon its leg, said, the elephant is a pillar, like a tree-trunk. The blind man who placed his hand upon its side said the elephant, "is a wall." Another who felt its tail described it as a rope. The last felt its tusk, stating the elephant is that which is hard, smooth, and like a spear.

– *The Parable of the Blind Men and the Elephant*[5]

From the parable, we can gather that one's subjective experience can be real. Such knowledge is limited as it fails to account for other truths or a totality of facts. What Jefferson learned about Islamic law from the Qur'an was accurate, but it provided only a tiny window into functioning Islamic jurisprudence.

In the last few years, the word sharia has been absorbed into the English-language lexicon. But what does it mean? The literal Arabic translation of the word sharia is "the road to the watering place."[6] Muslims think of sharia as the road they must follow according to Allah's will. The concept of sharia, however, is not restricted to legal norms but communicates a more holistic picture. Oddly enough, sharia, unlike Canon law, does not just stand for religious rules and regulations. It addresses a broad range of secular laws and ordinances. These contain topics as diverse as international commercial law, criminal law, constitutional and administrative law, humanitarian, and human rights law. Appropriately, this chapter is composed to articulate and look at the secondary and primary sources of Islamic law.

Primary sources of Islamic law mainly consist of the Qur'an and Prophetic Tradition (sunna). Secondary sources include consensus, analogy, public interest, and independent reasoning.

Before we get into the basic parameters of how each secondary source came into being and affected Islamic law, it is essential to understand the law's environment. One must be aware of two rules as we examine the complexities of Islamic law or sharia.

The first rule to know is that Islam is a complete way of life. In most discussions of Islam, one is likely to find a statement to the effect that Islam is not just a religion but a way of life. Often read as a throwaway line to those unfamiliar with the topic, the statement represents a position that is meant to be deliberate and genuine. Consider these two points: first, Islam is not a religion along the norms of Christianity or Judaism to be practiced once a week in a church or synagogue – mostly, as practiced in the West, as part of the broader secular community. Second, "as a way of life," Islam is governed by laws that encompass every aspect of life. "Islam is not just a religion but is a complete way of life" puts readers on notice that Islamic law governs all actions of all believers. Consequently, readers should base their assessment of Islam on its "total way of life" reality. One sura from the Qur'an summarizes that call: "And there may spring from you a nation who invite to goodness and enjoin right conduct and forbid indecency" (3:104).[7]

The second rule to understand is that sovereignty belongs to Allah alone. Islamic law comes exclusively from Allah. The verse of the Qur'an, "Judgment is for God alone" (6:57), is often cited in support of this principle.[8] As the exclusive law-creating authority, Allah is the sole lawmaker and the only sovereign. Because Allah transcends mortality, time, and space, his revealed law applies to all humankind through time and space until the Last Day. This concept is closely associated with the idea of Allah's absolute timeless unity and oneness – the dogmatic doctrine known as tawhid.[9] Islamic law reflects Allah's exclusive sovereign status by further stating that temporal legal authority empowerment comes from a theory of delegated sovereignty. If Allah enjoys individual autonomy, his laws can never be legally overruled by non-sovereign entities, including humankind. If Allah's law is eternal and eternally applicable, one cannot ascribe temporal or time-fixed notions to his rulings. This assumption challenges Western concepts of democracy that argue that man has the right to legislate law on his authority – which is another way of saying that man has the right to assume the sovereignty that allows for the making of his rules. A disconnect between Islamic and Western theories of preeminence exists that may not be reconcilable.

Another level in this concept of sovereignty is its temporal anchor. In other words, sharia does not have a limited application for a specific era. It will suit every age and time. The laws documented in the Qur'an in the seventh century are still valid in the twenty-first century. They will remain legitimate and shall continue to be until the conclusion of this life on earth. Sharia neither becomes obsolete nor does its general principles and fundamental theories need to be changed or renovated.

The Islamic theory of sovereignty undercuts Western notions of democracy at the conceptual level. Not understanding this dynamic undermines the national security objectives of Islamic countries that seek to initiate democratic forms of governance when their constitutions state that "no law shall contradict Islamic law."[1]

Putting these two concepts together creates an environment that allows religious law to be the supreme law of the land. Islamic law defines the way of life that reflects Allah's sovereign law-creating authority. When Islam is a complete way of life, sharia governs both the believer and his community. Islamic law is the sole source of governance for both Muslims and non-Muslims, both Dhimmi and foreigners, and embraces all human activities – both personal and communal. Islamic law is a series of duties and obligations that cannot be severed from Islamic theology and is "totalitarian" in its application.

Primary Sources of Islamic Law

Putting the body of Islamic law beyond the reach of man reflects the sacred nature of its primary sources, the Qur'an, and hadith. Revisiting the earlier discussion from Chapter 2 on the Qur'an and sunna, both bodies of law represent a form of the binding ordinance when used to support issues of Islamic law.

The Qur'an, according to this theory, is the first source of law. Its importance is religious and spiritual, no less than legal because it is the Word of Allah. It is because of this that the verses of the Qur'an are of paramount authority. While there are over 6,000 verses,[5] depending on the source used, there are estimates from 200 to 800 scriptures related to legal codes or actual legal rulings in the Qur'an.[9] One source provided this classification:

- 350 verses on repealing objectionable customs such as banking and gambling
- 140 verses on holy matters and religious law
- 70 verses on family law
- 70 verses on commercial law
- 30 verses on procedural and administrative law
- 25 verses on treaties and international law.[10]

Other supporting verses are too general to have the precision and point of legal rules. For example, the Qur'an prescribes that a Muslim ought to act in good faith, that he must not bribe judges, and that he must refrain from gambling and exploitation. Still, it does not stipulate what legal effects apply if these commandments are disregarded. Jurists and religious scholars are not in agreement as to how much judicial content lies hidden in the Qur'an. Computations of this nature differ according to one's understanding of, and approach to, the meaning of the Qur'an. In short, the purpose of the Qur'an is not to regulate people's relationships with each other but their relationship with their creator.[11]

The second source of law is the sunna, the traditions, and practices of the Prophet. The sunna was used in pre-Islamic times to describe an activity that came from ancient and traditional usage that the community was well acquainted with; later, scholars applied the term to the practice of the Prophet. In a sense, this concept is reminiscent of common law in the U.S., a code originating from community customs and judicial precedent rather than statutes. Sunna must be distinguished from the word hadith. The mixed-use of the two terms sometimes leads to confusion. Hadith is the story of a specific occurrence; sunna is the "practice" of the Prophet, his model behavior. Both the Qur'an and sunna are considered primary sources of sharia.

Side Note: Islamic jurists have always viewed the Qur'an as the primary source of Islamic law. After Muhammad died in 632, the first few caliphs of the empire found that the Qur'an had limited information on what requirements to apply and how to apply them. Emphasis was placed on the caliphs' independent reasoning until an abundance of sunna and hadiths became available. From the ninth century on, Prophetic Traditions were employed on equal footing with the Qur'anic rulings and considered a primary source of Islamic law.[12]

Non-Primary Sources of Islamic Law

The third source of Islamic law, *Ijma*, or the consensus of scholars, indicates the benefits of delegated legislation in the Muslim community. Muslim society requires such a rulemaking power to meet the practical problems for the implementation of sharia. Ijma means the consensus of the jurists over a religious matter. The word "consensus" in this context means an agreement of most authoritative scholars or jurists. It would be like a decision by our Supreme Court, where a majority of judges can decide the fate of legal cases. Because the third source of law constitutes the acceptance of judicial rulings immediately derived from the Qur'an and hadith, any legal judgments are beyond the reach of judicial review.

The fourth most important source of sharia is reasoning by analogy or *qiyas*. Analogy in this context means to compare one case with another. The law used for one can fit the other if the instances are similar enough. To use qiyas for similar issues, the reason for the Islamic rule must be apparent. For example, because the Qur'an clearly explains the idea that alcohol consumption is restricted (since it will make the user lose control over his actions), an analogy can be drawn with drugs that induce the same effect. But simply because the Qur'an does not explicitly point out the explanation as to why pork is prohibited, Muslims cannot rationalize banning another meat product with a similar cholesterol level, for example. When Muhammad's Companions asked him to deal with challenging issues relevant to the new Muslim community, he applied qiyas. After Muhammad's death, the Companions used qiyas to set regulations and codes to govern their society.[13]

Masalih al-Mursala, which means public good or the public interest, was employed in developing sharia laws during the immediate period after Muhammad's death. In cases where there was no direct text in the Qur'an or sunna, seventh-century Muslim society based its rules on what was in the best public interest. Since public affairs change over time, sharia laws developed in this manner have not been kept up.[14]

A sixth source was *ijtihad* or the application of critical personal reasoning in interpreting Islamic law. Before there was much hadith or case law to fall back on during Islam's early days, ijtihad was commonly used. Reportedly, the Prophet himself encouraged the permissibility of deducing secondary rulings through critical thinking. Critical thinking, in other words, presupposes that a Muslim jurist does not invent rules but assists norms and principles that are already there to become evident, albeit in a concealed or gnomic form, in sacred texts.

By the turn of the ninth century, independent reasoning and consensus-based doctrines led to the growth of a sizeable corpus of rulings and precedents. From this point onwards, however, most scholars, generally representing the Sunni tradition, claimed that the leading legal schools of thought had resolved all the critical questions. Hence, the personal interpretation of Islamic law was no longer necessary.[15] This policy finally assumed an official character, and Islamist jurists decided to "close the door" for the exercise of ijtihad. Consequently, many Islamic jurists today claim that the lack of critical thinking in their society has caused Islamic legal, scientific, and political achievements to fall behind Western leadership.[16]

In the developing Islamic Empire, jurists have extended the non-primary sources to include Islamic rulers and caliphs' practices, their official instruction to commanders and politicians, constitutional laws, and internal legislation of Islamic States, both in the historical and modern era.[17] Non-primary sources have thus provided a degree of flexibility over the development of Islamic law. Although Islamic law owes its origins to the primary sources, it has overwhelmingly flourished due to juridical activity, which was particularly intense during the classical period of Islamic civilization, roughly between the ninth and the twelfth centuries.

The "Fixed" and the "Flexible" in Islamic Law

The Qur'an and sunna are the primary sources of Islamic law and are the products of divine revelation and hence cannot be overruled or changed. Consensus is the third source of governance, and since it is based on acceptance of Qur'anic principles and the hadith, it is also beyond judicial review. Consequently, most of the sharia is fixed. The outcomes of legal jurisprudence in "the four Sunni schools of Islamic law: Hanafi,

Maliki, Shafi'i, and Hanbali, are identical in approximately 75 percent of their legal conclusions."[18] In the U.S. legal system, lawyers call these "settled issues of law." The remaining difference falls in the use of reasoning by analogy or qiyas and how each school of law uses this branch of deduction. Some Islamic schools of law use it extensively (The Hanafi School), while others avoid it altogether (The Hanbali School). Islamic law has some variation but not enough to cause widespread differences throughout the different Islamic nations.

Permutations of Sharia

The evolution of legal thought affects all societies; Islam is not excepted. Just as in the West, there are schools of thought that lean towards being more liberal than others. Some traditions are more ingrained in some countries than in others. These events cause personal and tribal values to be different from their neighbors. These differences are noteworthy in the four schools of law that dominate Sunni theology.

The Hanafi School of legal thought is the most liberal and flexible of the four Sunni schools. There is an emphasis upon qiyas, or reasoning by analogy to formulating legal judgments, a practice deployed extensively by Abu Hanifa (d. 767), the founder of this legal school of thought. This endorsement of logic and reasoning allowed the Hanafi School to carry out detailed investigations of legal sources before forming juridical principles. Today, the Hanafi School is predominant in Central and Western Asia (Afghanistan to Turkey), Lower Egypt (Cairo and the Delta), and the Indian Subcontinent.[19] Historically, the Hanafi School has had the most significant institutional impact of all the Islamic law schools due to its close relationship first with the Abbasid caliphs and then with the Ottomans. To the extent that modern jurisdiction still applies to Islamic law, it is often Hanafi law but subject to legislative reforms in particular areas. It is worth noting that the Taliban, the religious authority in Afghanistan, relies on Hanafi jurist rulings for much of their jurisprudence guidance.[20]

The Maliki School was established in Medina in the eighth century by Malik ibn Anas (d. 795). Malik was a religious scholar who became a great collector of the hadith. In this regard, Malik, it seems, was the first to adopt the use of consensus during his time as a jurist in Medina. The Maliki School has supporters in both North Africa, West Africa, and Upper Egypt.[21] The Maliki School was the dominant legal school of thought in Spain when it was part of the Islamic empire.

Muhammad ibn Idris al-Shafi'i (d. 820) was an Arab theologian who established the Shafi'i School in Cairo in the early ninth century. Al- Shafi'i hailed from southwest Palestine (Gaza) and traveled extensively, training under Malik ibn Anas in Medina, teaching and practicing law in Baghdad, and finally taking up residence in Egypt, where he produced several significant works before his death there. Al-Shafi'i's most important contribution was in utilizing hadith for making law instead of ijtihad. Al-Shafi'i also refined the usage of qiyas, and he curtailed its use as envisaged in the Hanafi school. In addition to establishing Muhammad's sunna as the second of the four "roots" of law, al-Shafi'i defined ijma (consensus) in its classical form and invested it with a power that enabled it to remove ijtihad from jurisprudence, except in the most limited sense. That is, ijma came to be the principle and procedure that the jurists of all the Sunni schools increasingly used to determine what was authentically Islamic. Thus, ijma was extended even to the authentication of the hadith. Today's Shafi'i School is predominant in Malaysia and Indonesia, Southern Arabia, East Africa, Lower Egypt, and most of the Indian Ocean littoral.[22]

The fourth school of law, the Hanbali School, was founded in the ninth century by another contemporary of al-Shafi'i, Ahmad Hanbali (d. 855). Hanbali was thoroughly conservative and believed in a rigorous interpretation of Islam. His deep convictions of the Qur'an and hadith led him and his followers to adopt a rigid interpretation of sharia. His independent-mindedness and resistance to theological approaches led him to suffer imprisonment and persecution by Abbasid Caliph al-Ma'mun. While primarily a theologian, Hanbali's teachings were based mainly around religiously ordained hadith and were only rarely articulated in strict legal jargon. More significantly, Hanbali influenced the seventeenth-century Wahhabi reformation in Arabia. The Hanbali School has flourished in the Arabian Peninsula. It remains the dominant legal school of thought in northern and central Arabia (modern Saudi Arabia).[23]

The Hanbali School rose to prominence with the Saudi royal family in the eighteenth century. Initially, this was the least significant of the law schools; however, that changed as the Hanbali School acquired a prominent position in the Arabian Peninsula.[24] While this particular school is the most conservative of the orthodox schools and relies mainly on the hadith or sunna for its interpretation of the law, as stated earlier in Chapter 2, it has a weak foundation because many hadith may be forgeries or unproven.[25] While this school of law might give legitimacy to the Saudi royal family, it is rarely recognized outside the Arabian peninsula because of its use of unreliable hadiths.

Side Note: In the Middle East, sharia is unlikely to be the only law source. Except for Saudi Arabia, all Arab legal systems borrow heavily from non-Muslim sources for most of their requirements. Frequently when dealing with Western countries and companies, Islamic countries use courts based on European civil-law models. Internal domestic businesses might find their judicial reviews tempered by both civil-law courts heavily influenced by sharia, and for the most part, personal and family claims use sharia.[26]

There is little doubt that blind adherence to orthodox doctrines has been responsible for the decline of Muslim thought in almost all intellectual realms such as art, politics, finance, and science. When any community chokes itself off from innovation and critical thinking initiatives, it ceases to grow. This process has caused artificial shackles to be placed on Islam's inherent dynamics that paved the way for Western domination and colonialism. At the close of the eighteenth century, it became unmistakably clear that the Islamic world's key institutions were in steep decline, as judged against Western standards and progress.

Sharia law and the death penalty

There are three categories of penalties in sharia:

1. *Qisas* crimes: (retaliation or retribution).
2. *Hudud* crimes: (crimes against God).
3. *Ta'zir* crimes: (crimes of the state/society).[27]

Qisas crimes include murder or injury caused by intent or accident. Before Islamic law, families and even tribes would engage in long-running feuds to get retribution. After Islamic law, the Qur'an implemented a death penalty that sometimes can be assuaged by financial compensation or "blood money." One of the more infamous cases of murder involved the brutal death and dismemberment of Saudi journalist Jamal Khashoggi in 2018. While not proven explicitly, it is alleged that the Saudi royal family had ordered his killing; thus, the henchmen worked directly or indirectly for either the Saudi king or prince. In 2020, *Al Jazeera* reported that "The son of murdered Saudi journalist Jamal Khashoggi has released a statement via Twitter forgiving his father's killers."[28] A statement of forgiveness like this can lead to a negotiated settlement where the killers are freed, and the family receives a stipend. While the news source made no mention of money, it would be easy to assume that since the Saudi royal family was alleged to have been involved, the sums of money would be enormous.

Hudud crimes are an offense in which the Qur'an or hadith stipulates a specified punishment. These crimes include adultery, theft, slanderous accusation, and highway robbery. Others suggest that this would also consist of wine drinking and apostasy. These are crimes described in the Qur'an or the hadith with predetermined penalties. All that is needed is proof of the crime and enforcement.[29]

Ta'zir crimes are social or state crimes in which penalties vary from state to state. For example, homosexuality in some countries carries the death penalty versus other countries that administer fines and prison sentences.

Islamic Execution by Beheading

In 2002, Daniel Pearl, a journalist with the *Wall Street Journal*, was kidnapped and later beheaded by jihadi terrorists in Pakistan.[30] Jump forward 17 years, and the ABC News online edition headline reads, "Headless bodies found in mass graves in IS Syrian stronghold thought to be those of sex slaves."[31] Most people do not realize that beheading is the standard method of executing the death penalty under classical Islamic law. As a means of execution, beheading had been abandoned in most countries by the end of the twentieth century. While a few countries such as Saudi Arabia and Yemen still use beheadings as legal executions, numerous non-state jihadist groups such as ISIL, Tawhid, and Jihad also continue to use beheading as a technique of killing their captives. Since 2002, many terrorist groups have spread videos of beheadings as a type of propaganda and terror.

Because of the recent flurry of public beheadings carried out by Muslims acting under Islam's flag during the Syrian Civil War, numerous world political and religious figures in the West have recently weighed in on the subject. Most of these people have taken the position of defending Islam, saying these beheadings are not justified in the Islamic faith. In a 2014 address to the U.N. General Assembly, President Obama stated: "Islam teaches peace," thereby repeating sentiments first expressed by President George W. Bush in 2001. In 2014, in support of President Obama, ex-British Prime Minister Theresa May went so far as to declare that the actions of the Islamic State "... have absolutely no basis in anything written in the Qur'an."[32] Perhaps she was not aware of the two verses listed below. The two primary sources of direction within Islam, namely, the Qur'an and the sunna offer answers to this question that we would be foolish to ignore.

So, make those who believe stand firm. I will throw fear into the hearts of those who disbelieve. Then *smite the necks* and smite of them each finger. (8:12) [Italics added][33]

Now when ye meet in battle those who disbelieve, then it is *smiting of the necks* until, when ye have routed them, then making fast of bonds; and afterward either grace or ransom till the war lay down its burdens. (47:4) [Italics added][34]

The significance of verse 8:12 is essential, but verse 47:4 is the verse that respected Islamic scholars repeatedly cite to justify beheading.[35] All four Islamic jurisprudence institutions (Shafi'i, Maliki, Hanafi, and Hanbali) understand and support 47:4 as an explicit justification – within the sharia – of the practice of beheading.[36]

Next, we have the illustration of the founding father of Islam himself, Muhammad. At the massacre of the Jews of the Qurayza tribe in Medina in the year 627, *Muhammad ordered that 600-800 Jewish captives be beheaded.*[37] The bottom line is: religious scholars and jurists all agree that the practice of beheading is a sanctioned type of execution within the rituals of Islam.

There is one last bit of circumstantial evidence that Islamic law justifies beheadings. The former Islamic Caliph and head of the Islamic State himself, Abu Bakr al-Baghdadi (d. 2019), had a Master's Degree and a PhD in Islamic Studies.[38] Al-Baghdadi, who received his PhD from the Islamic University of Baghdad, focused on Islamic culture, history, sharia, and jurisprudence, sanctioned quite a few beheadings.[39] It is sensible to believe that he may have known even more about acceptable Islamic customs than political leaders for whom the subject is merely an occasional political distraction.

Islamic Execution by Stoning

Execution by stoning is mentioned several times in the Bible (Leviticus 20:10; Deuteronomy 22:22; and Acts 5:59), and one would think that it would be included in the Qur'an as well, but it is not. Stoning, in the Bible, is generally associated with adultery. The Qur'an repealed the practice of stoning and replaced it with one hundred lashes for both the adulteress and the adulterer (24:2). A recent punishment administered in Banda Aceh, the capital of the conservative Muslim province of Aceh, Indonesia, gives a good example.

A dozen young people were flogged in the street in front of a cheering crowd for allegedly having sex outside marriage. In Aceh, alcohol is banned, and adultery, sex outside marriage, and homosexual acts are among the crimes outlawed.[40]

The Qur'an, therefore, attempts to establish a very reformist vision to change the social norms of the time by invalidating the Hebrew law of stoning and educating Muslims to respect the private life of individuals. It was important to Muhammad that the Qur'an be more lenient than Jewish law in family social values.

There were several occasions (hadith by Muslim, #4196, #4205, #4209) where followers confessed to Muhammad of their extramarital involvement, and his decisions resulted in their "stoning." Therefore, most schools of Islamic jurisprudence accept this as a prescribed punishment for adultery. The penalty has been rarely applied, however, owing to Islamic law's stringent evidential requirements.

In almost all cases, stoning has taken place in tribal or disputed areas beyond any state control. The Taliban in Afghanistan, ISIS in Iraq, and Boko Haram in Nigeria and Somalia have used stoning to punish adultery and homosexuality.[41] For example, in Afghanistan, a couple was executed in 2010 for fleeing to avoid the woman's arranged marriage to another man; the two were stoned to death by male villagers.[42]

The actual act of stoning is torturous. Individuals are placed in a stoning pit, buried to the neck (women) or chest (men), and community members hurl stones at them until they escape the stoning pit or are disabled or are dead. These rocks are large enough to mortally damage but not too big to kill on impact – in other words, death comes slowly. The person who has been dishonored receives the "favor" of throwing the first stone. Other family members usually take part after being coaxed. Religious authorities tell them to do it for Allah. "For the next 10 to 20 minutes, the rest of the community joins in until there is nothing left but a bloody stump."[43]

Side Note: Jewish law during the time of Jesus sanctioned different capital punishment types for various crimes. For the crimes of sedition and blasphemy that Jesus was accused of, stoning would have been used for his execution had the Jewish high council (the Sanhedrin) been allowed to follow through.[44] Had Herod Antipas ruled against Jesus on the blasphemy charge when he was brought before him, Jesus would have been stoned to death. Since the ruling against Jesus was issued by Pilate, Roman law stipulated crucifixion for slaves and criminals who did not possess Roman citizenship.[45]

Other Forms of Execution

The most common form of execution used by sovereign states in the Muslim world today is hanging. Islamic terrorist groups have executed gay and bisexual men by throwing them off high buildings. In addition to the common crimes punishable by death, such as murder, terrorism, rape, robbery, kidnapping, drug trafficking, and burglary, some Islamic countries also issue the death penalty for apostasy and blasphemy.[46]

Sharia Law in America?

Not likely, but not for the reasons one would expect. According to the Southern Poverty Law Center (SPLC), "Since 2010, 201 anti-sharia law bills have been introduced in 43 states. In 2017 alone, 14 states introduced an anti-sharia law bill, with Texas and Arkansas enacting the legislation."[47] On one side, legislators support these bills because they protect the United States from terrorism and safeguard Judeo-Christian values. Still, proponents have failed to cite any instance in which personal Islamic observances have threatened U.S. laws or society in any way. On the other side, experts, including professors, attorneys, politicians, and the American Bar Association (ABA), have been quick to denounce anti-sharia-law bills. The ABA has released a formal letter of dissent in 2011, stating in part:

The American Bar Association opposes federal or state laws that impose blanket prohibitions on consideration or use by courts or arbitral tribunals of the entire body of law or doctrine of a particular religion. American courts will not apply sharia or other rules (real or perceived) that are contrary to our public policy, including, for instance, rules that are incompatible with our notions of gender equality.[48]

Far-right activist groups like ACT for America (an SPLC-designated hate group) and the American Freedom Law Center (AFLC) have pushed the initiative to block any influence that Islam might exert in U.S. courts. Another reason that the activists are pushing this legislation is to paint Islam in a bad light. David Yerushalmi, the co-founder of the AFLC, is quoted as saying: "If this thing passed in every state without any friction, it would not have served its purpose. The purpose was heuristic – to get people asking this question, 'What is Shariah?'"[49]

Side Note: When the United States ratified the Constitution in 1788, the Protestants were the majority, and Catholics, Jews, and Muslims were minorities. To refute the national ideal of Protestant supremacy, groups of Protestants, Jews, and Catholics came together in the late 1800s to map out plans to normalize relations between the religions. A "branding" campaign promoted Catholics and Jews as equal to Protestants. The phrase "Judeo-Christian" can be dated to 1899 but did not enter usage in the United States until the 1930s, becoming a common expression in the 1950s.[50] In the same vein of thought, Muslims have also tried to brand their religion as "The Religion of Peace," based on a popular book named by the same name penned in 1934 by a Pakistani official (see Chapter 4).

The reason sharia law is not allowable in the United States is the Establishment Clause in our Constitution. The Establishment Clause is in the First Amendment, and, along with this, the Amendment's Free Exercise Clause forms the constitutional right of freedom of religion. The part of the Establishment Clause that we are interested in prohibits Congress from preferring or elevating one religion over another. Thus, if any part of sharia law were allowed, it would be at the disadvantage of Catholic canon law, Jewish halakha, or even Hindu or Buddha dharma. The State laws that are passed restricting sharia are unnecessary, and Muslims perceive them as discriminatory.

There are a couple of ways that all religious adherents can informally utilize religious laws without going through civil courts in the United States. Frequently, litigants can petition a course for arbitration. Muslims, Christians, Jews, and other religious groups, according to the 1925 Federal Arbitration Act, can use ecclesiastical tribunals to arbitrate conflicts, and "state and local courts give the judgments that result in the force of law."[51] The arbitration can and frequently does use religious practices to reach a consensus among the parties.

Frequently, Muslims skip the state and local court systems in favor of sectarian courts. Litigants can use doctrinal courts to handle activities such as inheritance, business, and matrimonial disputes sorted out by Islamic scholars, who base their decisions on theistic principles. Consider that sharia law allows a Muslim man to have four wives. The man may indeed go through the process of arranging marriage contracts with various women. Still, he cannot go through civil laws or officially registering these marriages in the United States as he would be charged with bigamy. However, the women involved in such cases know they are married, and under sharia, are allowed certain rights regarding inheritance and upkeep. Under sharia, even in the United States, the Muslim community protects women just as they would in a Muslim country.

In most Muslim nations, sharia courts handle issues of matrimony, divorce, inheritance, and other personal status matters, where judges tend to be very conservative. Yet, some experts say the interpretation of sharia law in these courts is outdated. Professor M. Cherif Bassiouni, an expert on Islamic Law at DePaul University College of Law, says, "Sharia judges are usually educated in academic institutions which do not favor intellectual independence."[52] They are not usually graduates of notable law schools but come up through the madrassa route, having memorized the Qur'an and the hadiths. Other legal experts declare that sharia judges merely interpret Islamic law favored by most of the world's Muslims.

Our mother country, Great Britain, has, in recent years, conferred legal validity on decisions that affect sharia law under an arbitration law like the one in the U.S. Critics in Britain have questioned the application of sharia law as compromising core democratic values. Research indicates that the top three dispute issues in this arbitration court are divorce, child custody, and inheritance.[53] British jurists argue that the danger of sharia law stems from the fundamental inequalities in the statutes for women, who would not be able to escape abusive relationships, and the welfare of children, who would suffer from living in such an environment. Recognizing that there are some illegitimate sharia courts that Muslims turn to when the secular judicial system does not fit their needs, Britain has attempted to authorize the use of sharia in arbitration. The British legal system has made efforts to train their arbitration judges to use adequate procedures governing fairness, transparency, and consent, expand the arbitration process to appellate review, and provide strong regulatory oversight of the courts' professional quality. The goal is to accommodate the Muslim community's religious needs while asserting state sovereignty over a transnational religion. A secondary goal is to establish a moderate but standard national code of law acceptable to all Islamic sects.

Chapter Summary

Islamic constituencies are affected by two rules that affect their perception of the Islamic religion. First, Muslims believe that Islam is a way of life. They practice the precepts of Islam daily, not just weekly, as many Christians or Jews do. Second, they believe that Allah and his laws are sovereign. In other words, legislation, democracy, and other human-made regulations take a back seat to requirements presented in the Qur'an and sunna.

Sharia is Islamic Law that originates from the Qur'an, the sunna (the traditions of the Prophet and his Companions), a consensus of Islamic scholars, and reasoning by analogy (qiyas). Critical thinking and reasoning were allowed in the early years after Muhammad's death, but Muslim religious scholars felt that this did not closely follow Islamic doctrine. The four Islamic schools of law differ in how much of the Qur'an and sunna they follow, as opposed to consensus and qiyas. The Hanafi School is the most liberal, while the Hanbali School is the most conservative. The Hanbali School is closely associated with the Wahhabi sect and serves as the foundation of Saudi Arabia's kingdom. Since this school of law relates heavily to sunna and the underlying hadith, their foundation can be considered weak, as many Muslims believe particular hadith to be illegitimate.

Could there be sharia law in America? According to existing arbitration rules, legal cases in which civil or criminal statutes are not involved can use sharia where it is considered acceptable to the parties involved. As to actual Islamic laws, the Establishment Clause in the First Amendment in the U.S. Constitution prohibits this. Consider that if there are significant populations of Muslims in several cities in the U.S., they will go to "underground" courts to obtain their style of justice. It may fill a social need to authorize a sharia court where the proceedings would be transparent, fair to women and children, and appealable to higher courts.

End-of-Chapter Notes

q.   The principle of *tawhid* is the dogma of the unity of Allah. It unequivocally holds that God is one entity and single. If there is one thing in which Islam will not temporize or compromise, it is the dogma of the absolute unity of Allah.

See "The Islamic Hand Gesture" in Chapter 4.

r.   Virtually, all Islamic countries have constitutions with this phraseology. For example, Pakistan, Egypt, Jordan, Iraq, and Saudi Arabi are all Islamic Republics and state such in their constitution.

s.   The exact number of verses is disputed due to different methods of counting.

Chapter 7

American Islam

This chapter documents the early exposure of Islam to the North American continent. While there were many Muslims among the slaves brought into America in the seventeenth and eighteenth centuries, Islam did not take hold. Two centuries later, one religious movement did sprout that grasped the Islamic moniker, i.e., the Nation of Islam (NOI). While the name implies an Islamic connection, the religious doctrine behind it does not, which is the beginning of American Islam.

The year 1619 is the year most people point to when discussing the beginnings of slavery in the United States. That is the year that 20 African slaves arrived in Virginia. At that time, Virginia did not allow the ownership of slaves but did allow indentured servants. The 20 African slaves were bartered to the colonists for goods and ship repairs and later allowed to work off their debts before being freed.[1] However, the transatlantic slave trade that had begun in the mid-fifteenth century was more brutal to those who were its victims. Led by Portugal and followed by other European kingdoms, slave traders sailed to Africa. The Portuguese were the first to kidnap people from the west coast of Africa and take them back to Europe. Soon after, the Spanish and the British took the slaves to their colonies in the new world. The Spanish brought their first African captives to the Americas from Europe as early as 1503. By 1518, the first captives arrived in the Caribbean from Africa.[2] In 1619, an English privateer captured the slaves from a Spanish slave trader headed to Mexico and brought them to Jamestown, Virginia.[3]

While 1619 is considered the beginning of the slave trade in the North American British colonies, the British, by that date, already had numerous settlements in the West Indies where their sugar plantations needed lots of labor to harvest the sugar cane. The tobacco plantations in the Chesapeake region initially drove the need for slaves in North America. Later, the demand for slaves was exacerbated by the cotton plantations in the southern colonies. While the Portuguese originated the practice, the Spanish, Dutch, English, and French participated in that illicit trade. Slaves were "sourced" primarily from West Africa, between the Senegal and Niger rivers.[4] We would recognize that geographic area today as Mauritania, Senegal, Gambia, Guinea, Ghana, and Sierra Leone. Later regions would include all west African countries south to Namibia and around the Cape to include states on the continent's east coast. Inland areas adjacent to the coast, such as Mali and the Congo, were also raided.

By the late eighth century, Islam had spread through North Africa and into Spain. But it was also creeping south down the west African coast, initially into Mauritania and Senegal.[5] Over time, many of these regions developed Islamic enclaves, and many inland ethnic groups converted.

Fast forward 700 years, and it becomes conceivable that many of the slaves captured by European traders and sent to the Americas were Muslims. One source estimates that some 90 percent of the Africans came from four areas where Islam was a part of the tribal culture: those areas being west-central Africa (Congo and Angola), the Senegambia Confederation, the Gold Coast (Ghana), and Sierra Leone.[6] Historian Michael Gomez estimates that over half of the 481,000 West Africans "imported into British North America" due to the slave trade "came from areas influenced by Islam."[7]

While these slaves represented the arrival of the first Muslims to the "New World," slave owners kept them under control by repressing their previous culture and forcing new languages and customs into their lives. Restrictions of Islamic rituals and worship removed almost all mention of Islam, with only a few exceptions, from the slaves during that period.

Side Note: Historians still debate the number of Africans
forcibly transported across the Atlantic between 1500 and
1866. An extensive research effort started in the 1960s
places the total at more than 12 million people.[t] Of that
amount, less than 10.7 million made it through the so-called
"middle passage" over the Atlantic because of the inhuman
conditions they encountered while being transported and
the brutal suppression of any onboard resistance.[8]
While there was a vibrant slave trade from Africa's west
coast to the Americas, there was also a lively slave trade
from Africa's east coast to the Islamic Arab states such
as Egypt, Saudi Arabia, and Yemen. The total number
of Africans taken from the continent's east coast and
transported to the Arab community is between 9.4 million
and 14 million. These figures are estimates due to the
absence of documented records.[9]
The forced deportation of up to 25 million people from
the African continent impacted population growth there.
It was in that period from 1500 to 1900 that Africa's
population stayed stagnant or even declined.[10]

Islam Returns

In the late eighteenth and early nineteenth centuries, Muslims
emigrating to the United States were predominantly Sunni,
mainly from the Levant (Palestine, Lebanon, Syria, and Jordan).
War and revolution caused much of this migration to the West.
After World War I and the decline of the Ottoman Empire,
there was an influx from old Ottoman territories; World War II,
both during and immediately after, caused many countries to
change their borders and change their governments. India and
Pakistan separated, many colonies in North Africa shook off
their European masters, and of course, Israel became a sovereign

nation. Masses of refugees sought out new opportunities to move to stable countries. These changes opened the door for Muslims from Central Asia, Pakistan, India, North Africa, and the Middle East. The Iranian Revolution in 1979 created another wave of Islamic refugees. Wherever there is turmoil, Muslims (as do many others) immigrate to the U.S. Sometimes the immigrants are students heading to American universities; many come as refugees. Afghans came to escape the 10-year Russian occupation in 1979; Bosnians came during the Yugoslavian Civil War in 1992. Numerous wars, conflicts, and rebellions such as the Lebanese Civil War in 1975 and again in 2012, the Gulf War of 1991, the Iraq War of 2003 caused significant immigration to the United States.[11] These immigrants were the forerunners of a new and distinct type of Islam. Islam in other countries is different from Islam in the United States because it is subject to the American melting pot and a Muslim melting pot. Muslim immigrants come from a myriad combination of Islamic countries.

Side Note: There is an urban legend amongst Detroit's local Yemeni community that Henry Ford told a Yemeni sailor on one of his cruises about how much he paid his automobile factory workers. It was more than the sailor made, so he went to work in the Detroit factory and brought his whole family. Word spread to friends, and other sailors, which led to significant migration from Yemen and other countries in the Middle East to Detroit.[12] Of course, the story is unsubstantiated, but Ford was more than willing to hire Arabs in the early days than some other immigrants, mainly Africans.[13]

A new Arab community, one that now included many Muslims, sprang up around Ford's first factory in Highland Park, Michigan. Recruitment of workers from Syria, Lebanon, and Yemen to help build the Ford River Rouge Plant in the early 1900s resulted in a high concentration of Arab Americans in Michigan. Initially, the workers who arrived were Christian, but as time went by and the numbers of recruits increased, the percentage of Muslims increased. Hundreds of Syrian refugees were working in Henry Ford auto factories by 1916. Since that time, various groups and populations have emigrated from Arab countries and flourished in Michigan. The highest concentration of Arab Americans in Michigan is in Detroit and Dearborn.

Muslims from different regional and ethnic origins formed customs and enjoyed experiences that were not likely to be allowed in their original home country. Muslims in America have historically incorporated into their traditions secular activities such as voting, working, and education. Their children adopt hybrid customs in American culture. For the most part, they do not assimilate, but they do participate. In the United States, they form organizations, associations, political parties, schools, mosques, halal restaurants and associate with different groups to protect and enhance their political leanings. Consequently, their quality of life is better; their life expectancy is longer, and their choices to enjoy life are more diverse. Islam in America represents all the best variations in Islamic religion experienced around the world.

Islamic scholars have often said that the Islamic rule in the Iberian Peninsula (Spain) from the eighth century to the fifteenth century was one of the most productive periods in history. This period marked the Golden Age of Islam and a period of coexistence and cooperation between Christians, Muslims, and Jews. Tolerance and collaboration between religions resulted in significant progress in medicine, mathematics, philosophy, law, architecture, and commerce. Perhaps, this toleration and coexistence are happening again in the U.S.

A 2018 Pew Research report estimated that there were

3.45 million Muslim residents in the United States.[14] Muslim immigrants originate from at least 77 different countries, with the largest single country of origin being Pakistan.[15] The Sunni and Shi'a branches of Islam are roughly in proportion to worldwide population patterns, with the Ahmadiyya branch coming in third.

Side Note: The Ahmadiyya branch of Islam, formed in India in the late nineteenth century, is the oldest continuous Muslim community in the United States. While both the Sunnis and the Shi'a came to America for good-paying jobs and a better way of life, the Ahmadiyya came as missionaries. In the early 1920s, they focused their attention on African Americans as the civil rights movement failed to offset the deep-seated racial tensions and discrimination rampant at the time.

While the number of Muslims in the U.S. is just an estimate, we can quantify the number of mosques in the U.S. Albanian Muslims established the first mosque building in 1915 in Biddeford, Maine. The first purpose-built mosque was in Highland Park, Michigan, in 1921. By 2010, the number of mosques and Islamic Centers in the U.S. had grown to over 2,000.[16]

An Islamic Wannabe

Although traces of Islam had all but disappeared among African Americans until the Civil War, remnants of the religion were well suited to make a return. Africans and their descendants had been oppressed through slavery and later racial discrimination up through the twentieth century. Islam was a religion associated with Africa and a tradition independent of and distinct from European culture. Islam could also lay claim to the Ottoman Empire, which at its peak was more significant than the Roman Empire. It had a straightforward theology, at least compared with Christianity, a conventional social ethic, a legal justice system based on their holy book, the Qur'an, and an economic system promulgated on social justice and equality of distribution. It also stoked fear among white Christian Americans as they were not prepared for a unified underclass to challenge their beliefs or rules.[17]

When there is a need for a specialized product, one will emerge that will take on the features of an existing product but will be custom fitted for the task at hand. In a sense, this is what began to happen for African Americans still feeling the bitterness of racial discrimination in the early twentieth century. Former black slaves and their families were looking for that tonic to ease their pain. They sought to consolidate their fear, hatred, and disgust towards the individuals and the institutions that allowed slavery to go on for so long. The "product" that began to emerge was an activist-based religion that was intolerant of racial equality. It was a "product" that promoted racial superiority, and it found a ready market in the African American community.

Contemporary Islam would not work in these conditions as it promotes racial equality. While traditional Islam does not promote gender equality, religious equality, or LGBTQ rights, it promotes racial equality. The "American product" was modified to look like Islam but promote a superior racial position over whites. It had to provide a rationale for why blacks did not fit into the white social structure. It had to give a path to circumvent the white community. That product, known today as The Nation of Islam, had a rough beginning dating between 1910-1920.

The Nation of Islam evolved from several different organizations which assumed the peculiarities of their leaders. Timothy Drew developed the first uniquely American form of Islam when he founded the Canaanite Temple in Newark, NJ, in 1913 and later the Moorish Science Temple of America in 1928.[18] He referred to his followers as "Moslem" and used the word "Temple" for his meeting place. He claimed his calling from Allah, and he changed his name to Noble Drew Ali. Drew Ali claimed to be a prophet, and his publication of *The Holy Koran of the Moorish Science Temple of America* focused on Jesus, not Muhammad. He taught that African Americans were Moors and that the Founding Fathers had obscured their real identity and enslaved them in the process. Traditional Islamist groups were infuriated that Drew Ali would claim himself to be a prophet, believing that he was blasphemous because the Qur'an claimed that Muhammad was the last prophet. Drew Ali got the message and quickly moved on to Chicago, where he started the process again.

Drew Ali died in 1929 under suspicious circumstances. His movement peaked with some thirty thousand members in the 1930s. Even today, there are still chapters that teach his theology and view him as a prophet. Many of his precepts, which entail Jesus being a black man, Islam as the epistemologically superior religion, and opposition to racial integration, would all become key concepts in the Nation of Islam.

The Nation of Islam

Wali Fard Muhammad received credit for establishing the Nation of Islam (NOI). Although there are many mysteries and suspect stories regarding his name's origin, his real name, according to FBI records, was Wallace Dodd Ford. There is no definitive birthdate and no definite place of birth. Both Los Angeles police records and prison records list him as Caucasian or white, married, and a father. He was arrested in 1918 by the LA police and again in 1926 for the possession of drugs. Upon his release, he moved to Chicago and then to Detroit. God uses troubled men to achieve his goals – perhaps, in this case, that was Fard Muhammad's rise to notoriety.[19]

Fard (pronounced "Farrad") Muhammad worked as a door-to-door salesman. His gift of gab paid off as he began teaching a version of Islam that emphasized the evils of alcohol and pork. He attacked the Bible and Christianity on racial grounds, and he had a willing audience. In the 1930s, the Civil Rights movement was yet to begin, but racial discrimination was rampant throughout the nation. As before, with Drew Ali's case, Fard Muhammad ran afoul of the law and disappeared. His time with the NOI had not been in vain, however. He amassed several thousand followers, founded a second temple in Chicago, and established a school known as the University of Islam. It's noteworthy that a 1934 NOI publication, *The Final Call*, describes Fard Muhammad as a prophet.[20]

His disappearance initiated a power struggle within the movement, but soon a new leader emerged named Elijah Poole. He had risen rapidly in the organization and had changed his name on Fard Muhammad's instruction to Elijah Muhammad. For the next 20 years, the NOI multiplied, establishing over 50 temples, a weekly paper, the University of Islam, and prosperous businesses, including farms, stores, restaurants, and bakeries.

In the late 1950s, the Black Muslim Movement had gained much notoriety because of a charismatic convert named Malcolm X. Other new members, including heavyweight boxing champion Muhammad Ali (formerly Cassius Clay before joining the NOI), added visibility to the group.[ii] Another new member recruited by Malcolm X during this period was Louis Farrakhan (originally Louis Eugene Wolcott and then Louis X).[21] Before joining the NOI, Farrakhan was a cabaret singer, but he rapidly advanced through the ranks, with Malcolm X's support, as a superb speaker and organizer.[22] The onset of the civil rights movement and the violent reactions it provoked made the NOI's portrayal of the "white devil" pertinent to a much more significant proportion of black America. By 1959, Martin Luther King was cautioning his congregations of "a hate group arising in our midst that would preach the doctrine of black supremacy."[23]

Side Note: Elijah Muhammad, the NOI leader from 1934 to 1975, preached that NOI converts should take a name that reflects Islamic genealogy. Before receiving their Islamic name, the member had to demonstrate, through their lifestyle, that they were a decent, respectable person. While awaiting their formal name, the member carried the surname "X" to symbolize the shedding of the slave master's name, acknowledge that black Americans are a lost tribe, and demonstrate acceptance that having an original Islamic name is an honor.[24]

As people adopted this convention, it caused identification problems. In NOI temples, there would be multiple people with the same first name. To handle this problem, members would be assigned numbers in front of the X to distinguish them. Examples of actual names were Edna Mae 2X, Clifton 3X, Larry 14X, and Samuel 25X. Sometimes, this terminology would leak over into press reports. For example, newspaper recounts of the murder of Malcolm X have listed the two co-conspirators as Norman 3X (Butler) and Thomas 15X (Johnson).[25]

After demonstrating acceptance of the NOI theology's tenets, a member may petition a full Muslim name. Initially, upon its founding in 1930, the NOI allowed people to purchase their original name for 30 dollars. The NOI now awards members this new name based on merit after an extended service period to their community.

While the NOI had a strong uptake of membership within the black American community, it also caught the eyes of American Muslims. Immigrant Muslim communities confronted the NOI with objections to it using the Islam "brand" as Islam does not condone racism. Additionally, orthodox Islam recognizes that the last "real" prophet was Muhammad, who died in 632, not Fard Muhammad, who disappeared in 1934.

Elijah Muhammad encountered two sources of conflict in Islam. First, his two sons had grown up privileged, and while one son had gone to Egypt to learn more about Islam, both sons grew increasingly critical of the NOI's theology. For example, at his son's insistence, the temples where they worshipped were changed to mosques, as they are in Islam. Second, as Malcolm X moved up the NOI organization, he became more aware of the so-called "true" – orthodox – Islam. Many law enforcement professionals speculate that Malcolm X's deviation from NOI theology caused his assassination.

Elijah Muhammad died in 1975, and Louis Farrakhan eventually won the power struggle that ensued. Farrakhan had rapidly risen to prominence following his mentor Malcolm X's departure. Farrakhan made the correct assumption that the essence of the NOI was their racial teachings. While America was slowly addressing civil rights and racial discrimination was illegal, progress was too slow, with many adherents supporting Farrakhan's push for radical change. He reinvigorated the NOI in 1977, with all of Elijah Muhammad's original teachings. Farrakhan was no stranger to controversy. He made anti-Semitic speeches, accusing Jews of promulgating the slave trade; organized a large gathering of African American men in Washington, DC to confront lawmakers about civil rights, which was consequently labeled as the Million Man March in 1995; bashed the LGBTQ community, Catholics, Caucasians, and most recently in 2010, embraced the Church of Scientology's philosophy of Dianetics.[26]

Racial separation is one of NOI's primary goals. Nation of Islam members pool their resources and purchase products from black-owned enterprises to keep money circulating within the community. They desire to establish a separate territory which former slave masters are obligated to support for 20 to 25 years until they become self-sufficient. Until they can have an independent nation, the NOI wants segregated schools, exemption from all taxation, and the prohibition of intermarriage.[27] This concept of segregation fits into the demand for reparations being voiced by several congressmen. An interesting irony is that Farrakhan's separatist effort has allied his views with white supremacist organizations that agree that the races must be separated.

The stature of the NOI vis-à-vis Islam remains problematic. The NOI once enjoyed a near-monopoly on Islam's interpretation for black Americans, using the faith as a vehicle to promote separatism. It now competes with groups ascribing to the more traditional and inclusive Islam, followed by millions of Muslim immigrants and their offspring. For the NOI to survive, it must turn more to mainstream Islam.

The NOI will not specify its membership numbers. Still, the estimate is about 50,000, with an ardent following in prisons, where there is much emphasis on black identity and the struggle against racism.[28] NOI also has members in England and the Caribbean.

The NOI resembles traditional Sunni Islam by following their version of the Five Pillars. Other doctrines of the NOI dealing with Muhammad not being the last prophet, a different Messiah other than Christ, and the teaching of Yakub, a story of human breeding that produced the white race, have not been acceptable to other Islamic sects.

If one asks a Muslim scholar what they think about the Black Muslim Movement, they will say that it is not genuinely Islamic. To the orthodox believer: 1) Islam is universal; it does not tolerate racial discrimination; the vitriolic rhetoric emanating from the Black Muslim Movement suggesting the black race is superior is wrong; 2) it is blasphemy to believe that other prophets came after Muhammad as this conflicts with the Qur'an (33:40); and 3) one can be committed to the black community and have a black-only plan and still be an orthodox Muslim, but you need to follow traditional Muslim thought. For example, before his assassination, Malcolm X left the NOI and changed his position on orthodox Islam. He refuted black nationalism, instead moving to pan-Africanism, which aligns African Americans with their cultural and religious heritage in Africa.[29]

The Nation of Islam's legacy of hate cannot be undone. Still, there is a possibility that the group could turn itself around by censuring its bigotry and focusing its energy on community service projects instead. Farrakhan's reign is ending; he is in his eighth decade, and his successor could choose to make the organization a force for good instead of hate.

Chapter Summary

During the seventeenth to the nineteenth centuries in American history, black slavery played a big part in developing commerce and culture. European slave traders took most of the black slaves from areas of Africa that were Muslim. Not much documentation remains from that early period of slavery. Even when President Lincoln emancipated the slaves in 1863, white Americans treated them in uncivilized ways. This racial discrimination opened the door for an American form of Islam to become an acceptable religion even though that new form preached hatred for white people. American Islam, predominately in the form of the NOI, had its Prophet and its temples, but orthodox Muslims saw it as illegitimate and its members as apostates. Civil rights laws have helped to tamp down racial discrimination, and membership of the NOI has slowly dissipated. While so-called American Islam is still present, it has become secondary in affiliation to true Islam. Orthodox Muslims will tell us their religion does not discriminate against blacks or whites, which is why American Islam fared so well for a limited time. What orthodox Muslims do not tell us is that Islam does discriminate against women, LGBTQ groups, and people who do not believe in Islam.

End-of-Chapter Notes

t.   The www.slavevoyages.org website catalogues 36,000

individual trans-Atlantic voyages made during this period.

u. An interesting story about Cassius Clay is that he reportedly refused to be drafted into the U.S. military for fear of being killed by Elijah Muhammad, who opposed the draft and had avoided it himself. In the 1970s, Ali told reporter Dave Kindred: "I would have gotten out of [the NOI] a long time ago, but you saw what they did to Malcolm X... I can't leave the Muslims. They'd shoot me, too." Joe Carter (September 13, 2017), "9 Things You Should Know About the Nation of Islam."

Chapter 8

Sharia Finance

Before Muhammad became a Prophet at 40 years old, he was a businessman – a trader who worked caravans. The story of Islam is not without an economic underbelly. This chapter looks at how Islam incorporates economics into its beliefs.

Trade routes between the Mediterranean Sea and the Indian Ocean have passed throughout the Arabian Peninsula since antiquity. The city of Mecca, where Islam originated, arose as a South Arabian settlement close to a religious shrine and acquired significance as a trading community and a religious-spiritual pilgrimage center. Large trading caravans were joint undertakings in which whole tribes participated. The Prophet Muhammad was a successful businessman, as were several of his Companions and successors. One of Muhammad's Companions, Umar ibn al-Khattab, the second caliph, is said to have claimed: "Death can come upon me nowhere more pleasantly than where I am engaged in business in the market, buying and selling on behalf of my family."[1]

Trading was in the blood and the DNA of the Arab entrepreneur. The Islamic Empire had one thing going for it – location. First, there was Mecca, the spiritual capital of Islam. Mecca was on the caravan trail through the Arabian Peninsula, where it split to either continue to Persia or Egypt. It was enhanced further by the Zamzam water well, which made Mecca a convenient stop throughout antiquity.[v] Also, Mecca was known for having a sacred area and a house built to worship God, the Kaaba. Mecca became a destination for pilgrimages during the religious months for celebrating the harvest. These locational advantages allowed Muhammad and the caliphs that followed in the seventh and eighth centuries to expand the influence of Islam.

Next was the length and breadth of the geography united through the new faith. From the ninth century through the twelfth century, Islam flourished as Egypt, Persia, and Rome declined as world powers. The Arab armies expanded into the neighboring lands and found new markets that spread from western Turkestan to the Atlantic Ocean. Three-quarters of the Mediterranean coastal regions, including the Islamic Al-Andalus (modern-day Spain), now belonged to Islam. Further, the Arab expansion ended the great Roman-Persian conflict, and the Islamic Empire now forged economic and political links that stretched from the Mediterranean to the Indian subcontinent. During the early Middle Ages, a *Pax Islamica* was the cornerstone of a marketplace economy.

At the core of this marketplace were Islamic rules and guidelines that were put into effect to guide traders and merchants. Because of the long Arab history in trading, the ways and means did not change much, but they were codified into the region's ruling religious doctrines. Islamic business practices still recognize that the market created by trading goods and services is subject to specific economic forces but simultaneously requires its adherents to submit to "divine authority" and follow all subsequent commands to fix problems emanating from the marketplace.[2]

Consistent with this ideological framework, Islamic law, or sharia, governed both private and public affairs. While managing all aspects of an individual's life, these laws also ruled the mechanisms of the Islamic marketplace. One dynamic of sharia not mentioned before is that it focuses on creating a unified society by regulating the economic currents that flow through the social order.

The other side of sharia discourages the consolidation of capital via its wealth-splintering principles; it diminished the investment capabilities necessary for keeping pace with the progressively capital-intensive modes of trade. A stable and prosperous commercial class emerged in New York, London, Paris, and Rome from the transatlantic trade between North America and Europe. Bankers and industrialists were able to turn the political scene in their favor. They limited their kings' and rulers' absolute power and fought for the rise of a constitution and other democratic institutions. In summary, the Islamic economic principles that allowed the Muslim world to escape from constant feuding and flourish in the pre-industrial era also limited their growth potential in industrial markets starting in the eighteenth century. As we will see, the Protestant acceptance of usury led to large-scale shipping trade and capital-based industrialization.[3]

Distributive Justice

The Islamic business model is based on both distributive and commutative justice. Distributive justice is concerned with the norms of resource allocation and the perception of fairness by the recipients. Aristotle equates distributive justice with a proper ratio of contribution to reward. In other words, people should receive returns commensurate with their investment, be it capital or labor.[4] The Islamic version of distributive justice includes the following three elements:

1. Guarantee the fulfillment of the basic needs of all.
2. Equity, but not equality in personal incomes; and
3. The elimination of extreme inequalities in personal income and wealth.[5]

The issue of essential need fulfillment from an Islamic perspective is that Allah has promised such in the Qur'an. The Qur'an recognizes this right of necessities for living in these words (51:19): "And in their wealth the beggar and the outcast had due share."[6] In other words, under Islam, the wealthy are obligated to share their wealth with the impoverished.

In the verse above, the "due share" of the poor and needy comes from the rich. Once basic human needs are taken care of, merit or contribution takes over as the Islamic standard of resource allocation.[7] Although Islam does not prescribe a ratio between minimum and maximum income, it does discourage extreme inequalities. The concept of *zakat* is a redistribution of resources and minimization of disparities. The Qur'an commands Muslims to give to the poor and needy. This charity is called *zakat* and is one of the Five Pillars of Islam. Muslim governments can prosecute a person for not paying the required amount of zakat or refusing to pay it at all. Abu Bakr (d. 634), the first caliph after Muhammad, initiated jihad on those citizens who refused to pay the zakat during the early days of his rule.[8] The zakat is customarily 2.5 percent (or 1/40th) of a Muslim's total savings and wealth above a minimum amount known as the *nisab*. The nisab varies depending upon whether your wealth is in real estate, agriculture commodities like cotton or corn, livestock like sheep, cattle, horses, gold, and silver.[9] In the West, citizens are used to income taxes and sales taxes. The zakat would be classified as a wealth tax.

From the Muslim perspective, Islam stands for social cohesion, mutual love, affection, social harmony, and brotherhood. Therefore, it strives to rid Muslim society of those inequalities, which can cause hatred, malice, and ill-feeling among individuals. The zakat incentivizes the rich to help the needy by promising them a reward in the hereafter. The zakat is for mostly charitable purposes, but there can be other uses as well. The following eight categories of people are considered deserving of zakat:

1. The needy (someone who is in difficulty).
2. The poor (low-income or indigent).
3. Those who are designated by the state to collect *zakat*.
4. Those whose hearts are to be reconciled (new Muslims and friends of the Muslim community).

5. For the emancipation of slaves.
6. For alleviating one from the burden of debt.
7. In the cause of Allah, and
8. Wayfarers (those who are stranded or traveling with few resources).[10]

In the period after the 9/11 terrorist attacks, it was found that many Muslims would contribute to groups designated as terrorist organizations by the U.S. government.[11] They were meeting their obligation to provide zakat to those who labored "in the cause of Allah."

Commutative Justice

According to USLegal, "Commutative Justice refers to that which is owed between individuals, such as in conducting business transactions. Commutative Justice calls for fundamental fairness in all agreements and exchanges between individuals or private social groups."[12] The camel caravans that crossed the great dunes of the Sahara Desert between Yemen, Egypt, and Persia began in antiquity. Still, they reached their golden period from the ninth century CE onwards. This level of trade would not have existed without some degree of contract law. Much of the law was oral. Still, it was an understanding between vendors and merchants that protected the rights of both, not to the exclusion of the other.

Islamic law is concerned with promoting a just distribution of wealth and with ensuring that it is maintained. While there is no general theory of contracts, there are principles surrounding types of arrangements. Much Islamic justice comes from Aristotle. His writings influenced Islamic commutative justice as they did distributive justice. Aristotle claims that commutative justice, which encompasses sales, purchases, loans for consumption, pledging of assets, and depositing of funds, should be based on the principals' intent.[13] The different kinds of contracts are accordingly defined in terms of their purpose, i.e., sales, agency, warehousing, etc. If business parties dispute contract arrangements, the outcome should be fair and equitable between the parties, as judged by sharia.

Sharia finance is a spiritual framework that values human relations above material possessions. It places a balance between individual self-interest and the social good. Maximum profit and maximum efficiency are not the sole objectives. Private property rights are recognized and protected, and reciprocity is encouraged.

Islamic doctrine has several remarkable features, including a dynamic set of redistribution and wealth-fragmenting principles. Indeed, Islam prescribes detailed rules limiting the accumulation of private wealth. Two of the most well-known rules are those governing inheritance and usury. Regarding the inheritance laws, the Qur'an allows for the allocation of two-thirds of one's wealth to various family members, including very distant relatives making it a somewhat equal distribution system.[14] Distributive inheritance laws, coupled with the fact that more wealthy individuals are allowed to have more wives and, consequently, children, were an additional force against wealth concentration.

Business and society leaders are aware of behaviors and actions that result in unjustified and malicious opportunities. For that reason, it is the responsibility of the business community and the social environment to implement policies that remove opportunities for malicious activity. In the Islamic community, usurious interest is recognized as the most well-known irritant to cause friction in the social order.

Usurious Interest

From Commutative Justice, we investigate the most important financial activity looked down upon by sharia finance; their hatred of interest.[w] Other activities are frowned upon, which we will get into, but the best-known characteristic of sharia finance is hatred of usury. Usury is the practice of charging a small fee – interest – over the principal amount of a loan. Because of that, there are no interest payments in an Islamic contract. For much of history, most religious theologies frowned on the act of charging interest. With the rise of European banking conglomerates in the early seventeenth century, the practice of usury evolved to mean the charge of interest above the legal or socially acceptable rate.[15]

Commutative Justice in Islamic parlance deems that interest accrual is not an equitable feature and will not be accepted. There are numerous reasons for this; the first and most important reason is that it was communicated to Muhammad by Allah and written in the Qur'an. The angel Gabriel was specific that Muslims conduct trade without interest.[16] While there are several verses in the Qur'an about interest earnings, the ones below are probably the most relevant (3:130-131):

> O ye who believe! Devour not usury, doubling and quadrupling (the sum lent). Observe your duty to Allah, that ye may be successful. And ward off (from yourselves) the Fire prepared for disbelievers.[17]

Throughout history, until recent times, usury was morally unacceptable. Verses in the Qur'an all but support what was the standard belief system during that time. There is evidence that monetary exploitation had a malicious start almost from the very beginning, some 10,000 years ago. Lending with interest predates writing and the coining of money by thousands of years. The earliest recorded loans date from about 3000 BC, but the practice appears to have been ancient by then. Interest payments on loans probably originated during the beginnings of agriculture, about 8000 BC.[18]

Archaeological research shows that usury as a business had origins in Mesopotamia[19] and India.[20] In India, the earliest records come from the Vedic texts dating back to 2000-1400 BC. In Mesopotamia, the earliest mention dates to the Akkadian Empire, circa 1930 BC, near Ur. This period was when Abraham and his father, Terah, started their journey, as described in Chapter 1.

Side Note: The Code of Eshnunna (ca. 1930 BC) provides the first objective evidence of interest rates. The statutory interest rate for money or silver was 20 percent and 33 1/3 percent for grain. If the debtor borrowed in silver but could only pay back in grain, a formula would convert the value of grain to money or vice versa. The timeframe for lending the money or grain was neither annual (the modern practice) nor monthly (Greco-Roman practice) but was from planting till harvest.[21]

Additional archaeological findings from the Sumerian Empire dating to 2100 BC support these discoveries. Clay tablets with a series of bilingual Sumerian-Akkadian texts dated a few hundred years earlier confirm the interest rates in the Code of Eshnunna.[22] Supplementary findings show anti-debtor laws and even jubilees, when the ruling king would cancel all debt, helped remove problems that the debtors encountered from moneylenders. Even then, moneylenders were part of society.[23]

Two centuries later, ca. 1754 BC, the Code of Hammurabi became the Mesopotamia standard code of law. Based in Babylon, King Hammurabi's system had a much different attitude towards moneylenders. Hammurabi and his administration were very cautious about the formalities of loan contracts and the accurate keeping of records. As an example, one case mentioned deals with *anatocism*, a problem that was becoming persistent throughout the history of interest-taking.[24] This case was the first recorded instance of compound interest in a loan contract. In other words, moneylenders were charging interest on the interest owed. Many of the rules and laws from the

Code of Hammurabi dealt with debt and debtors. Hammurabi recognized that some degree of credit was necessary for wheels to turn and crops to be planted. The problem with borrowing money was the unscrupulous moneylender who had no moral conscience. As with so many civilizations, the leaders tried to legislate morality. The Code of Hammurabi stipulated that contracts show interest rates, oaths, witnesses, and giving and repaying dates.[25] In Babylonia, in 1754 BC, the temples made 80 percent of the loans, and they, for the most part, followed the legal code.[26] The other 20 percent of the credit loans came from wealthy merchants and moneylenders, who mostly skirted the law's edge. With the Code of Hammurabi, banking changed from a religious endeavor to a commercial one.[27]

The story of usury in the Bible is synonymous with exploitation. Explanative verses are in the Pentateuch and other Old Testament chapters (Exodus 22:24-25; Leviticus 25:35-37; Deuteronomy 23:19-21; Proverbs 28:8; Psalms 15:5; Nehemiah 5:7).[28] One colorful story concerns the Hebrew prophet, Ezekiel. He included usury with rape, murder, robbery, and idolatry in a list of "detestable things" that would receive the punishment of God (Ezekiel 18:10-13).[29] These verses also forbade the taking of interest. It is interesting to note that the Exodus and Leviticus verses apply only to lending to the poor and needy. In Deuteronomy, the prohibition applies to all moneylending other than business dealings with foreigners. While there were no exact dates when these rules were handed down, it would appear that in the fifth and sixth centuries BC, charging interest to fellow Israelites was considered a moral transgression, but there is proof that it occurred frequently.[30]

Side Note: This sentence from Deuteronomy 23:20 opened the gate for the Israelites to charge usurious interest: "You may charge a foreigner interest but not a fellow Israelite."[31] Israelites were forbidden to charge interest on loans made to other Israelites. Still, they were permitted to charge interest on transactions with non-Israelites since the latter were often with the Israelites for business in any event. It was this interpretation that interest charged to non-Israelites was acceptable. As the Reformation began to change morality in Europe, the perception of usury began to change also. This verse from Deuteronomy allowed fifteenth-century Jews to justify lending money for profit. As basic banking became acceptable, the Jews could not lend to other Jews but could contract loans to the Christians.

After the early Christian church became the state church for the Roman Empire, money exploitation was prohibited. The Church became wealthy from tithes and offerings, and like the temples back in Babylon, became a source of credit for the faithful. By the eighth century, under Charlemagne, the Church declared exploitation by usury to be a general criminal offense.[32] This anti-usury movement continued during the early Middle Ages and reached its zenith in 1311 when Pope Clement V made the ban on usury absolute. There is a small tidbit worth noting: the previous 300 years had been costly to the church as it financed many of the Crusaders on their forays into the Holy Land. Much of their financing came from the first international bank in existence operated by the Knights Templar. It was a financially astute move on the Church's part to outlaw usury as it saved them from repaying the interest. Eventually, the Church did not have to worry about repaying the principal either as Pope Clement dissolved the Knights Templar in 1312.[33]

The attitudes towards banking and interest began to change in the Middle Ages with the Reformation. Interest was still a moral hazard, but it was tolerable. Sometime in the early 1600s, the church redefined usury as "excessive interest."[34] Interest earnings were acceptable if they remained within socially accepted parameters, whatever they might be. It was apparent at this stage that the Islamic trading guidelines began to differentiate from those in the Western world.

Why was Usurious Interest Considered Taboo?

Unscrupulous people use usury to exploit the poor and needy. This theme is redundant in the Code of Hammurabi, the Vedic texts of ancient India, and the chapters of Exodus and Leviticus in the Bible. Even 1,400 years after King Hammurabi, Plato (d. 347 BC) still thought usury was wrong. Plato's grief was because it showed a lack of generosity toward the poor. Besides, it was contrary to the welfare of the state to set one class against the other.[35] Even in modern times, there are "loan sharks" who make their living off the poor. We think of loan sharks as individuals, but there is a parallel argument related to the role of states and nations in the devastating social impact of the "Third World debt crisis." Pope John Paul II is on file as saying, "Capital needed by the debtor nations to improve their standard of living now has to be used for interest payments on their debts."[36]

Usury is an unearned income. It was considered unnatural that an inanimate object such as money could reproduce like a flock or a field. Plato's student, Aristotle (d. 322 BC), argued that money's natural use was a medium of exchange. Still, usury created an unnatural expectation that "a piece of money cannot beget another."[37] Dante Alighieri, the author of *Divine Comedy*, suggested that to live without labor was unnatural. He consequently put usurers in the circle of hell alongside the inhabitants of Sodom.[38]

Usury creates a love for money. The British economist John Maynard Keynes recognized this and is well known for commenting, "love of money, as an end, not a means, is at the root of the world's economic problems."[39] Keynes marked the distinction between money being merely a mechanism to lubricate the interaction between supply and demand, and money as an end in itself. The Bible also echoes this sentiment (1 Timothy 6:10): "For the love of money is a root of all kinds of evil. Some people eager for money, have wandered from the faith, and pierced themselves with many griefs."[40]

Usury is a mechanism of inequitable wealth redistribution. A familiar axiom of capitalist businessmen is that "the rich get richer and the poor get poorer." It is a saying common to several cultures. To those economies that have put together large pools of money, charging interest is a solid incentive to rent out that capital to the highest bidder. Capital is a precursor to technology, and wealthy countries soon have the technology to make more capital. The capital-technology cycle is a quasi-monopoly that hoards economic surpluses to an elite few. Another way of looking at money is that the provision of currency is a government service to which all individuals should have access.

Consequently, not all individuals have access because the hoarding of cash has become a quasi-monopoly. Each unit of currency has some degree of utility, which increases for the poor but decreases for the rich. Economists say that society has inefficient use of money's utility since the rich have most of the capital.

Usury relates to the practice of discounting future values. As mentioned earlier, the use of compounded interest dates to the Code of Hammurabi some 3,700 years ago. The use of compounded interest rates strikes the balance by which we would rather have the asset in our hand versus lending the investment out for someone else to use. Research shows that the higher the discount rate (the interest rate), the faster we use natural resources.[41] In today's business world, we use a financial technique called Net Present Value. We discount future cash flows from a project to calculate the project's expenditure's net present value. The discount rate is commonly called the "hurdle rate," i.e., the rate at which a project must exceed if it is to be approved. The hurdle rate is usually 400 to 500 basis points (4-5 percent) higher than the prevailing interest rate to offset increased risk and attract investors. A project approved using a hurdle rate significantly higher than the current interest rate is considered a project with an attractive return rate. This type of project incentivizes businesses to operate quickly and effectively. Other studies show that discounting can lead to species extinction if the prevailing rate happens to be higher than the exploited species' reproduction rate.[42] The logical conclusion of using discounted rates guides the decision-maker to maximize their capital even at the expense of future generations.

Usury encourages debt. In a modern business balance sheet, there is a certain amount of debt versus equity. Debt is borrowed money, while equity represents the owner's stake in the business. A high level of borrowed money indicates the degree of leverage. High leverage is risky, but if one is willing to take the risk, they could make lots of money with just a little of their own money. Cultural views on risk are also at work. American companies have higher debt ratios on their balance sheet than do European or Asian businesses. When a person can borrow money with just a tiny regular interest payment, their risk level is low.

So why did the prohibition on usury fade away? First, usury – defined as interest on a loan – changed to usury defined as excessive interest. This evolution of thought occurred in the early 1600s during the Reformation. Second, debt became essential to fighting wars, and the only way to combine large sums of capital was to pay an incentive such as interest. Third, the spread of banking ultimately transformed credit from a personal transaction between neighbors or between a church and its parishioners to a competitive impersonal market.[43]

While Christianity began to accept this modern definition of usury, Islam did not.

Other Prohibitions That Shape Islamic Finance

There are three separate categories under sharia finance that are considered *haram*. Haram means forbidden or proscribed by Islamic law.[44] The element of usurious banking makes up one category. A second category is the issue of speculation. A valid financial contract must not contain ambiguity, uncertainty, or deficiency in the agreement. In other words, anything that was a gamble, high risk, excessive conjecture, speculation, hedging, or high-risk products or transactions are not acceptable. The Islamic aversion to gambling or speculation comes from several Qur'anic scriptures (2:219 and 5:90-91 are examples). Still, the root of gambling is considered to be the desire for something valuable without paying an equivalent compensation for it or working for it. This part of sharia is reminiscent of the verse found in Galatians 6:7: "A man reaps what he sows." This Biblical saying suggests that life is not a lottery; life is an investment.

The Islamic ban on speculative transactions is a poke in the eye of capitalistic finance. Commercial products, such as derivatives, options, and futures contracts, are haram. Sharia prohibits selling things that do not yet exist, such as harvests not yet planted or raw food stores not yet processed. These prohibitions impact selling future commodities or other agricultural or business products that are speculative or require arbitrage.

The third category would represent specific industries that are inappropriate organizations in which to invest. Generally, unsuitable businesses would include gambling and casino establishments, companies that produce or sell alcoholic beverages, pork consumption, pornography and prostitution, weapons manufacturing, and financial institutions that depend on payment of interest.[45]

So how does sharia finance overcome this aversion to

usury and uncertainty? Notwithstanding these requirements, Islamic finance has become a functional, competitive, for-profit industry. Over the centuries, Islamic jurisprudence has developed forms of investment in businesses, such as joint ventures, limited partnerships, insurance arrangements, sale-leaseback transactions, and higher purchase prices on credit sales, which comply with the prohibition of usury.[46]

Sharia finance works to reduce or share the risk and offset the interest with equity financing that focuses more on business performance. When traditional banks lend money, they accept the high risk and set interest rates accordingly. Higher interest rates accommodate high-risk projects. If one has up-front collateral that they are willing to lose if the project goes wrong, the project is accepted. To the entrepreneur, high risk can result in a high reward. Rather than taking a fixed interest rate, Islamic banks have an element of responsibility for operations. They share in the potential returns and losses of the business through shared ownership. At the end of the transaction, the bank transfers the assets back to the company at the fair market value. It is not their business to keep business assets on their books but rather to profit through acceptable means and move on to the next transaction.

To ensure compliance with sharia, all Islamic banks or traditional banks that provide Islamic financial products must establish "Sharia Advisory Councils."[47] These councils have sharia scholars and clerics on their staff who specialize in financial markets to determine whether a particular transaction is structured to comply with Islamic law.[x] For Muslims to perceive a banking service or commercial product as "sharia-compliant," it must receive a fatwa (religious ruling) from a credentialed, established cleric. In conjunction with these clerics and scholars, financial institutions have developed financial products that satisfy Muslim customers and the financial institution's shareholders.

The modern history of Islamic finance began in the nineteenth century in Islamic countries then under colonial rule. It's estimated that some 20 territories were under European control in the early twentieth century.[48] Places like Morocco, a French colony, and Libya, an Italian colony, were places where European banks tried to start franchises and offshore branches. Financial institutions based in Europe and North America were the predominant institutions in the Islamic countries where the occupying government provided a legal foundation for conducting business. Citizens who wanted to employ business transactions used Western methods and abided by Western ethics. The colonial powers offered new systems and symbols of modern success that led to the de-emphasis of traditional Islamic values.

As these countries like Morocco, which gained their independence in 1956, and Libya, which gained their independence in 1951, became self-governing, their Islamic values reemerged. As the twentieth century advanced, the Middle East became more influential in the world. Petroleum exports increased capital flows into the region. As these countries became adept at handling significant capital accumulations, they increasingly reverted to their Islamic roots. While Islamic banking methods have emerged in most Islamic countries, they have not entirely replaced Western banking. In most Islamic countries, one might find Western banks right next to Islamic banks, sometimes even in the same building. It seems that Western banking still fills a need that Islamic banking does not satisfy.

Empirical studies comparing Islamic banks to Western banks show that the two categories fill other businesses' needs in various niches.[49] Western banks have more experience, more customers, and more resources but pursue higher risk in industries that provide products that are not necessarily considered appropriate in Islam. On the other hand, Islamic banks are smaller, have fewer customers, and less experience.

They have an aversion to high risk, promotion of partnership, religious principles, and social responsibility as their guiding lights. There are no investment relationships that make one type of bank better or worse than the other kind.

In summary, Western banking's goal is to maximize profits. They will do this by charging interest commensurate with the risk involved, providing funds for speculative products, and financing industries and products that, in some cases, have questionable social value. They are customer-friendly and meet individual social needs. Western culture works on principles of innovation. Customers expect new and exciting products and services, where the government and industry seek new and cutting-edge approaches to doing things. This innovation exacts a certain level of risk – high risk yields high rewards. Western banks are structured to provide capital for this risk, and, because of this acceptance, Western society has experienced a great deal of success with this acceptance of risk.

Islamic banks attempt to be socially responsible while operating under religious scruples. Islamic law shuns exploitive charges that will disrupt religious harmony. Sharia views interest as exploitive, gambling as speculative, and investments in prohibitive industries as haram. Social justice and responsibility are vital proponents of Islamic Banking.

How Sharia Finance is Different from Socialism

After reading this chapter, the reader might find it interesting to compare socialism and Islamic economic principles. In Islam, the goal of narrowing income inequality was pursued through wealth fragmenting policies and wealth redistribution, all the while encouraging a market economy along with individual property rights. The purpose of socialism is also to narrow income inequality. Socialism is a system that owns the factors of production and operates a command economy with limited property rights for the individual.[50]

Under capitalism, the production factors (capital, labor, land, and the entrepreneur) each share part of the profit from producing a product. Capital gets interest payments, workers are paid wages, landowners are paid rent, and the entrepreneur is paid a profit for his risk. There are no limitations as to the industries and types of speculation that can be undertaken. Under socialism, the capital and the land are provided by the state, there is no entrepreneur, but workers do receive a wage. Under Islam, capital does not receive interest but can receive some profits, landowners receive rent, workers receive wages, and entrepreneurs receive profit. However, there are limitations on the type of product sold and the type of speculation one can invest in. On the surface, capitalism and Islamic economics may be similar, but Islam requires mandatory expenditures called *zakat* that distribute wealth to the poor and needy. There are other wealth fragmenting policies in inheritance laws and marriage allowances. These are mandatory rules resulting in legal action that can be taken against you if you don't comply. In a final analysis, successful capitalism pays profits consummate with the risk that entrepreneurs take. Islamic economics is linked to social outcomes more so than capitalism while incorporating some entrepreneurial incentives. For example, many Islamic governments have bloated bureaucracies just to provide jobs for their constituents. Bloated bureaucracies are highly inefficient and require onerous taxes to support them. While socialism provides equality of society's output, there is little entrepreneurial incentive to produce.

In conclusion, most capitalists are familiar with Adam Smith's "invisible hand" of the marketplace. A similar anecdote is credited to the Prophet Muhammad when asked to raise market prices because some vendors were selling products too competitively. His reply was, "Only Allah governs the market." While Islam is socially conscious, it is not a socialist economy.[51]

Chapter Summary

Islam is a quasi-socialist religion in the nature of its beliefs. In the same breath, you could say that it is a quasi-capitalist system also. Islam encourages community empowerment rather than individual rights. Belonging to a community is always a plus, but being part of a community at the expense of individual rights and freedoms can make Islamic countries illiberal with poor human rights records. Islam endorses a strong work ethic and free markets. However, it does not support innovation, the exchange of ideas, or individual rights. It does not support policies that incentivize capital accumulation as we understand it from a Western perspective. Rules governing inheritance, bigamy, usury, and risk have made it difficult, but not impossible, for Islamic countries to compete in the world market.

End-of-Chapter Notes

v.   Muslims claim that the Zamzam spring is referred to in the Bible – Psalms 84:6.

w.   There are eight verses in the Qur'an which condemn taking interest. In hadith, Muhammad is said to have compared taking interest to committing adultery 36 times as well as to committing incest with one's mother, which demonstrates the intensity and seriousness of the issue in Islamic thought.

x.   See Chapter 12, the section on the ulama.

Chapter 9

Islamic Democracy

An oxymoron is a term that contradicts a connecting word. Some common oxymorons are "act naturally," "Hell's Angels," "jumbo shrimp," and "passive-aggressive." Arguably, another oxymoron is "Islamic democracy." This chapter explains why I consider that to be so. Since American Muslims are encouraged to participate in the democratic process, this chapter looks at the standards they should uphold. In other countries around the world, Muslim participation in democracy is hit or miss. Democracy only works in countries with pluralistic political parties, and in Islamic countries, that is not usually the case. We will look at what works and why in the Islamic world.

In the United States, Muslims did not actively participate in democracy until the beginning of the twenty-first century, but this trend has recently become widespread. This activity is in large part due to the presidency of Donald Trump. The anti-Muslim policies and rhetoric that characterized Trump's presidency have driven American Muslims to act; they contend for elected offices in numbers not seen before. In 2016, more than 80 Muslim-Americans ran for national or statewide offices.[1] One Muslim candidate stated, "Running for public office is about advancing the interests of your constituents... Nothing else."[2] In the 2018 midterm elections, 166 Muslim political candidates cast their hats into the ring, with at least 34 winning their public office election.[3] In the 2020 Presidential elections, the Biden-Harris campaign tried to appeal to one million Muslim voters.[4] In addition to increasing voter turnout, Muslims won 57 races for public office.[5] Each election cycle seems to increase Muslim participation. If Muslim political advocacy is here for real, let's review the interests of the Muslim constituency.

What the Bible Says about Government

Before we can delve into the issue of democracy as it might pertain to Islam, let us first review what Biblical scripture teaches us about government. First, God sets up governments:[6]

> Let everyone be subject to the governing authorities, for there is no authority except that which God has established. (Romans 13:1)[7]

Another similar passage is John 19:11:

> Jesus answered, "You would have no power over me if it were not given to you from above."

Next, the government is supposed to punish the evildoer.[8]

> For the one in authority is God's servant for your good. But if you do wrong, be afraid, for rulers do not bear the sword for no reason. They are God's servants, agents of wrath to bring punishment on the wrongdoer. (Romans 13:4)

Third, we need to ask God to give guidance to those who govern us.

> I urge then, first of all, that petitions, prayers, intercession, and thanksgiving be made for all people – for kings and all those in authority, that we may live peaceful and quiet lives in all godliness and holiness. (1 Timothy 2:1-2)

Fourth, we should honor and submit earthly blessings to those who guide us on earth, but we should also recognize and send spiritual benefits to our spiritual mentor.

Then Jesus said to them, "Give back to Caesar what is Caesar's and to God what is God's." (Mark 12:17)

Last, the government is to provide motivation and acclamation to those who have progressed well.

Do you want to be free from fear of the one in authority? Then do what is right, and you will be commended. (Romans 13:3)

There is no indication in the Bible that the government should provide goods and services, but it firmly emphasizes upholding the rule of law and punishing evil. Government should also praise those who do right and encourage good behavior.

There are numerous occasions of a frail or oppressive government given in the books of Judges, 1 Kings, and 2 Kings. God guarantees to us that kindness, respect, and submission are a part of His plan (1 Thessalonians 5:12-18). Failure to punish evil and praise those who do right results in depravity and anarchy resulting from self-centeredness (2 Timothy 3:1-9).

There are times when governments go past the limits set for them by God. On those occasions, we should choose whether we are to obey God or the government. When Daniel was told not to pray (Daniel 6) or when Peter was advised not to preach (Acts 5), we are reminded of whom we work for.[9] God established human government, and its essential job is to ensure its citizens advance harmony and well-being.

In 1996, the political scientist Samuel Huntington wrote a *New York Times* bestseller, *The Clash of Civilizations and the Remaking of World Order*. One quote from that book summarizes the clash between Islam and Western Democracy:

Some Westerners, including President Bill Clinton, have argued that the West does not have problems with Islam but only with violent Islamist extremists. Fourteen hundred years of history demonstrate otherwise. The relations between Islam and Christianity, both Orthodox and Western, have often been stormy. Each has been the other's Other. The twentieth-century conflict between liberal democracy and Marxist-Leninism is only a fleeting and superficial historical phenomenon compared to the continuing and deeply conflictual relation between Islam and Christianity.[10]

Muslim scholars will point out that democracy did not work well in the Bible. The proof is that when the people joined to make a unanimous or majority decision, they usually got things wrong. Here are some examples where the majority (identified in bold font added by the author) are in disagreement with the decision-makers:

Israel's descendants routinely voiced their desire to return to slavery in Egypt instead of following God into the Promised Land.

In the desert, **the whole community** grumbled against Moses and Aaron. The Israelites said to them, "If only we had died by the LORD's hand in Egypt! There we sat around pots of meat and ate all the food we wanted, but you have brought us out into this desert to starve this entire assembly to death." (Exodus 16:2,3)

Even when the Israelites were on Mount Nebo and could see into the Promised Land, the people cried out against moving into unknown territory.

That night, **all the people of the community** raised their voices and wept aloud. **All the Israelites** grumbled against Moses and Aaron, and the **whole assembly** said to them, "If only we had died in Egypt! Or in this desert! Why is the LORD bringing us to this land only to let us fall by the sword?" And they said to each other, "We should choose a leader and go back to Egypt." (Numbers 14:1-4)

The people wanted a leader to take them back to Egypt because they thought that obeying God would be excessively brutal. People will rarely vote for the severe option, even when it is needed. They will generally vote for the opportunity that produces the most comfort. Democracy can lead to outcomes that may not be practical – in this case, the worship of idols.

When **the people** saw that Moses was so long in coming down from the mountain, they gathered around Aaron and said, "Come, make us gods who will go before us. As for this fellow Moses, who brought us up out of Egypt, we do not know what has happened to him." (Exodus 32:1)

The last example of democracy is the crucifixion of Jesus:

Wanting to satisfy **the crowd**, Pilate released Barabbas to them. He had Jesus flogged and handed him over to be crucified. (Matthew 15:15)

Pilate, the Roman Prefect of Judaea making the decision, wanted to set Jesus free. However, he agreed to put the decision to a vote, and Jesus lost.

Muslim scholars maintain that a system where man establishes the laws can never advance the government of God. Looking at these examples, a reader might understand that democracy is not an equitable form of government. However, what we are witnessing is mob rule. Simple democracy is rule by the majority, which can be swayed and manipulated by a charismatic person, i.e., mob rule. Liberal democracy is a horse of a different color. For my conservative friends, do not let the word "liberal" throw you in this description.

Liberal democracy is a system of government in which individual rights and freedoms are officially recognized and protected and where the rule of law limits political power.[11] Liberal democracy acknowledges that the rule of law is predominant and protected by institutions such as courts and legislatures. The federal government in the United States has a balance of power, with co-equal branches of government being the Executive Branch, the Legislative Branch, and the Judicial Branch. The legislature creates the laws, the President executes the rules, and the courts determine if the codes are valid as based on our Constitution or, if broken, what penalties are relevant. In summation, liberal democracy encourages free and fair elections, due process of law, the separation of governmental powers, and protection of fundamental liberties such as speech, religion, the right to assemble, and the right to own property. Mob rule has no place in a liberal democracy.

Side Note: In the May 2012 issue of *American Political Science Review*, a sociology graduate student, Robert Woodberry, published statistical research that demonstrated that Protestant missionaries heavily influenced the rise and spread of stable democracy worldwide. In the article, "The Missionary Roots of Liberal Democracy," statistical evidence shows that "areas where Protestant missionaries had a significant presence in the past are on average more economically developed today."[12] There is a strong statistical correlation between countries with a solid Christian foundation in their past having strong democracies in their present, more so than any other religion. Research shows that Protestant missionaries were strongly involved in developing and spreading religious liberty as far back as the seventeenth century. These missionaries developed public schools, instituted mass book printing, published newspapers, encouraged voluntary organizations, and petitioned for colonial reforms that created conditions that encouraged stable democracies.

In 1977, Ayatollah Khomeini summarized his understanding of the "ideal" Islamic government, and it is a definition that seems to describe the governments of most Islamic states:

> An Islamic government is neither tyrannical nor absolute but constitutional. It is not constitutional in the current sense of the word, i.e., based on the approval of laws in accordance with the opinion of the majority. It is constitutional in the sense that the rulers are subject to a certain set of conditions that are set forth in the noble Qur'an and the sunnah (traditions of the prophets). Islamic law may, therefore, be defined as the rule of divine law over men.[13]

The third President of the United States was Thomas Jefferson. Before he became President, he penned the Declaration of Independence in 1776, writing: "We hold these truths to be self-evident, that all men are created equal, that they are endowed by their Creator with certain unalienable Rights."[14]

Jefferson noted that a government that grants rights could also take them away, but rights granted by the Creator can never be taken away. The function of government is to protect and secure those God-given rights. It seems ironic that both Islam and the United States government agree on where the power to rule originates. Both institutions believe in the Creator's absolute power but have taken different paths to achieve that means.

When Islamic Movements Won at the Ballot Box

As it turns out, several Islamic countries did adopt democracy, but the outcomes did not always find favor in the West. In 1991, the Algerian parliamentary election resulted in the

Islamic Salvation Front winning a two-thirds majority. The country's military, with the support of the West, intervened to annul the results.[15] In the 2006 elections in Palestine, America's rejection of the Hamas victory seemed to confirm in the eyes of many the idea that the U.S. was unwilling to allow Islamists to govern, even when they won free and fair elections.[16] The 2013 Egyptian coup d'état pitted the Egyptian military against a duly-elected President, Mohamed Morsi, a former Muslim Brotherhood member. While the West was not involved, it showed that an Islamic democracy was not acceptable to that nation's military.

Even when Islamic countries embrace democracy, there are several reasons why Western interests are skeptical of Islam's claim in democratic elections in their own countries. Democracies need political pluralism to work effectively. Representative government is the marketplace of political ideas. However, Islamist parties are inherently opposed to pluralism because they are committed to the spread of sharia. Once in power, a political party in an atmosphere with weak liberal institutions can shut out political opponents.

Another problem is that Islamists distrust liberal democracy because it emphasizes the individual's rights rather than the welfare of the *umma*, the community. Islamists have trouble accepting individuals' unfettered freedom to choose for themselves because they believe that the public has a common interest that overrides individuals. This problem becomes highly apparent when it concerns women's rights and the rights of religious minorities.

Islamist parties do project some positive values that even citizens here in the U.S. would support. Key elements include demands for accountability, constitutional and legal reform where needed, an end to political repression, and an honest government.[17]

The Effects of Faltering Democracy in Muslim-Majority Countries

Freedom of expression has come under sustained criticism through both assaults on the press and encroachments on ordinary citizens' speech rights. Even more abrupt has been the drop in individual expression, as autocratic governments have cracked down on critical discussion among citizens, especially online. In their *World Report 2020*, Human Rights Watch reported that in 2019, Pakistan failed to amend or repeal blasphemy law provisions that provide a pretext for violence against religious minorities.[18] Totalitarianism states across the Middle East and North Africa continued to suppress dissent during 2019. In Saudi Arabia, after the central government drew praise for easing the oppressive ban on female driving, authorities detained several well-known women's rights activists. Most of the women faced charges that were solely related to peaceful human rights work, including promoting women's rights and calling for an end to Saudi Arabia's discriminatory male guardianship system.

The concept of *term limits for executives* has been a popular governmental tool since the eighteenth century to curb the potential for monopoly, where a leader might declare himself a leader for life.[19] This concept spread worldwide after the end of the Cold War but now appears to be weakening. Erdogan, in Turkey, and now al-Sisi, in Egypt, are examples of top leaders changing the laws to secure their tenure. Governments in Saudi Arabia, Syria, and Jordan have a monarchy style of government and do not even contemplate term limits.

An expanding number of governments reach beyond their borders to target *expatriates, exiles, and diasporas* who voice dissent. Some Muslim countries like Turkey, Iran, and Saudi Arabia have recently tried to silence political dissidents abroad using practices such as kidnapping, extradition requests, harassment, and even assassination. The alleged murder of journalist Jamal Khashoggi by the Saudis shines a light on autocratic regimes trying to put a lid on dissent. By its accounting, Turkey has apprehended 104 of its nationals from 21 foreign countries over the last two years in a worldwide crackdown on the state's recognized enemies.[20]

Ethnic cleansing is also increasing. In Syria, hundreds of thousands of Sunni Muslims have been killed or displaced by Alawite Muslims. The Turks are notorious for their dislike of the Kurds.

Election Fraud is increasing. While maintaining a veneer of free and fair elections, autocracies undermine the process by finding ways to control their results. Polls, where the outcome is the result of coercion, fraud, gerrymandering, or other manipulations, are increasingly common. In 2018, in Bangladesh, security forces cracked down on the opposition parties ahead of parliamentary elections, arresting and intimidating prominent party leaders. Widespread irregularities had marred the polls themselves, and interparty violence, which resulted in more than a dozen deaths, was extensive.[21] In 2018, Turkey undertook simultaneous parliamentary and presidential elections despite a two-year state of emergency that included the imprisonment of a critical opposition party's leaders. Political repression worsened in Egypt, where President Abdel Fattah al-Sisi in 2018 was re-elected with 97 percent of the vote after security forces arbitrarily detained potential challengers.[22]

Why Democracy Does Not Fit with Islamic Theology

Khomeini stated earlier; democracy is not divine law; it is a law created by men to rule men. Democracy is secular; it is not subject to or bound by religious rule.

Many Arab-Islamic cultures in the Middle East have a history of undemocratic beliefs and authoritarian power structures. The traditional role of government has not been democratic in most Muslim-majority nations. For 1,300 years, most Muslim countries have been ruled by a caliphate of sorts. There are, in basic terms, two types of responsibilities in a state: theocratic and political. The Prophet Muhammad assumed both. Some later caliphs did both, but some did not. Thus, a sultan took care of political duties. The caliph would be like the Pope, and the sultans would be like kings. In 1919, the last legitimate caliphate, the Ottoman Empire, was disbanded by the Allied Powers of the First World War.

One reason that democracy does not work well in Muslim countries is its colonial legacy. Conventional Islamic theology insists that public life must be guided by spiritual values, whereas colonial domination caused the removal of religious values from the public sphere.[23] While some facets of this theory have some merit, we can look at Tunisia and remember that it was a French colony and still has several functioning parts of actual liberal democracy.

The oil wealth of a few dominant Muslim nations is another reason to deny democracy. The trouble with oil and the wealth it generates is that the rulers of the state or kingdom have the means to stay in power, as they can pay off or repress most potential adversaries. Since there is less need for taxation, there is less pressure to act on behalf of or represent citizens.[24] Furthermore, Western governments call for a stable supply of oil. Therefore, they are more prone to retain the status quo than push for reforms, encouraging citizens to protest their government or revolt.

One last reason is the repression of citizens by secularist Arab rulers like Bashar al-Assad in Syria and Abdel Fattah al-Sisi in Egypt. When you deny citizens the right to participate in their governance, they will fight for social equity. These disenfranchised Muslims do not see democracy as a solution. They believe that implementing an Islamic theocracy will lead to more social justice, as described in Chapter 8, "Sharia Finance."

Circumventing the Problem

Islamic countries consider democracy a secular function, an activity with no religious or spiritual basis. Laws created by men to rule over men are deemed sinful. They get around this because sharia law does not cover many of the problems and issues in the governance of a nation, country, city, or region. Sharia law employs democracy when there are no precedents to follow. Democracy can exist where it performs a function that is coexistent with Islamic values. Many Islamic nations, dependent upon American foreign aid like Jordan and Egypt, will implement some democratic institutions without liberal foundations. In any case, democracy adds window dressing so that Western countries see that the "rule of law" is making headway.

In Western nations, Muslims have circumvented a religious principle to justify their participation in democratic functions. There is a principle called "the lesser of two evils." In religious doctrine, this principle usually relates to matters of life and death. In other words, if necessity causes you to break God's law, then God understands (The Qur'an 5:3; 6:119; 6:145; 15:115). Research demonstrates the emergence of a broad agreement (albeit not a consensus) in Islamic jurisprudence on the permissibility of political participation in the West.[25] This general agreement is based primarily on jurists' evaluation that, in some cases, the partnership brings more benefit than harm. For example, it is acceptable to vote on behalf of a political party trying to establish Islamic law by defeating a secular party. Another example might be to vote for an Islamic candidate in a field of secular candidates. In either case, participation is the "lesser of two evils."

Eight Questions to Ask Your Muslim Candidate

More than any other person, Thomas Jefferson fought for the religious and civil freedoms of every minority in the United States.[26] During his time writing the Declaration of Independence and later the U.S. Constitution in the late eighteenth century, the minorities recognized by the Founding Fathers were Catholics, Jews, Native Americans, and Muslims. Some Catholics were

Founding Fathers and thus part of the First Congress in 1789. In 1960, John F. Kennedy was the first elected Catholic president. The first Jewish member of Congress, Lewis Charles Levin, took office in 1845, and while no Jews have ascended to the Presidency, several have campaigned. The first Muslim member of Congress was Keith Ellison, elected in 2007. A Muslim will probably seek the U.S. Presidency during this century. The Catholic and Jewish religions are similar to the mainstream Christian doctrine and endorse the values of democracy as practiced in Israel and Western Europe. However, some Muslims are known to believe that democracy is blasphemous. In 2012, presidential candidates Michele Bachmann and Newt Gingrich supported the notion that sharia is incompatible with American democracy.[27] So, how can we tell if a Muslim candidate believes in and supports liberal democracy in America? Here are eight questions that would be relevant to ask any candidate running for office. Since this book is about Islam theology, the topics point towards Muslim candidates.

1. *Will you support and uphold the process of democracy, that laws made by men can be used to govern men?*

An orthodox Muslim believes that laws for governing men should come from God's laws already in place. Democracy smacks of secularism and borders on blasphemy.

2. *Will you allow freedom of expression (including the liberty to analyze and criticize sharia)?*

Orthodox Muslims will say they will allow freedom of expression, but they will not accept anyone to criticize their religion. A person can criticize Christianity, Catholicism, and Judaism, but the moment one criticizes Islam, they engage in hate speech. Accusations of racism and bigotry make it tricky to contest. Any concept or idea that cannot stand to be analyzed and criticized becomes brittle and loses its ability to survive over time.

3. *Will you acknowledge that organizations, political groups, and governments that use or condone violence and terror to achieve political goals at the expense of rulemaking and rule-enforcing institutions (legislatures and courts) are organizations that should be boycotted and omitted from economic trade and political discourse?*

Muslims will see this as an attempt to criminalize groups like Hamas or Hezbollah, but it can play to any country that plays outside the rules, including Israel.

4. *Will you take a public stand against cases of abhorrent or criminalized behavior that is condoned or commanded by sharia that has no place in this country? This example includes underage or forced marriage, honor killings, female genital mutilation, polygamy, and domestic abuse, including marital rape.*

Most Muslims will not feel obligatory towards these behaviors, but they will not interfere if others of their faith do it. The real question is, would they take a leadership stand against these behaviors to change the attitude in their community.

5. *Do you see yourself as a Muslim first or an American citizen?*

Sharia-adherent Muslims do not identify with any sovereign nation. They see themselves as Muslims first and part of a future caliphate. Ayatollah Khomeini spoke in 1980 about the country of his birth:

We do not worship Iran; we worship Allah. For patriotism is another name for paganism. I say let this land [Iran] burn. I say let this land go up in smoke, provided Islam emerges triumphant in the rest of the world.[28]

Side Note: According to a Pew Research survey, about half of Muslims think of themselves first as Muslims while only a quarter sees themselves first as American.[29] Approximately one-fifth of Muslims sees themselves as American Muslims. The point here is that public officials who think of themselves first as Muslims will not make public policy decisions beneficial to America if they think the American way of life is immoral and ungodly as Muslims do in dominant Islamic countries. An example of this is the recent tweet Rep. Ilhan Omar made about herself. She wrote, "I am, Hijabi, Muslim, Black, Foreign-born, Refugee, Somali." Many commentators from social media, including an opposition candidate, noted that she left off that she was an American.[30]

---

6. *Will you stand for gender equality and sexual preference equality?*

Islam has a long history of enforcing female gender inequality. For example, in an Islamic court, female testimony does not carry the same weight as a male's testimony. Another example, in Saudi Arabia, "Prominent women's rights activists detained in 2018 remained in detention while on trial for their women's rights advocacy..."[31] Many of the women activists protested the requirement that women, when outside the home or traveling, must have a male guardian to accompany them. While those actions do not meet muster in the United States, the attitudes that allow them to occur are still in place under sharia law.

Islam has a long history of antagonism towards lesbian,

gay, bisexual, and transgender people. LGBTQ lifestyles are forbidden in traditional Muslim countries and are liable to different punishments, including prison sentences and the death penalty. In the United States, attitudes formed from sharia allow and support violence against the LGBTQ community.

A survey by the Washington-based Public Religion Research Institute indicated that 60 percent of U.S. Muslims supported laws that protect LGBTQ people against discrimination in jobs, public accommodations, and housing. Compare this to Jewish (80 percent) and Catholic (71 percent) congregations.[32]

7. *Will you support the toleration of religious diversity and the U.S. Constitution doctrine that supports the church and state separation?*

At the beginning of this chapter, I covered what the Bible says about government. The most familiar Bible verse regarding this, supports separating the physical from the spiritual: in Mark 12:17: "Then Jesus said to them, 'Give to Caesar what is Caesar's and to God what is God's.'"

The bottom line is that the mutual toleration of different religions is accepted and expected. Some religions do not have this tolerance. If my family is Protestant and my sister joins a Catholic church, it is acceptable and tolerated. If my family is Protestant and my sister becomes Muslim, it is fair and tolerated. If my family is Muslim and my sister becomes Christian, her decision could result in her being identified as an apostate, tortured, and killed as an honor killing.

8. *The U.S. Constitution's Article VI Supremacy Clause assures that the Constitution, all Federal Statutes, and U.S. treaties as "the supreme law of the land." The Constitution is the highest form of law in the American legal system. When you take your oath to uphold the Constitution, can*

you put aside all other legal arrangements that might cause
you to compromise your loyalty?

It would be remarkable if we could ask each Muslim candidate how they feel about these topics and if we could get honest answers. Catholics, Jews, Native Americans, and Protestants do not have religious/political affiliations that would interfere with the state's decisions. Orthodox and fundamentalist Muslims would be troubled with some of the topics mentioned. If we want true American patriotism, we need to ask these hard questions.

Taqiyya

In politics, many candidates tend to be less than truthful about the facts, especially if their constituents are not buying what they are selling. In this regard, Muslim candidates are no different than Christians, Jews, or Catholics. However, Muslims have a name for it and justify it as dealing with a non-Muslim. Before engaging a candidate in any political discussion, be aware that Muslim candidates feel justified in deceiving non-Muslims. This justification is called *taqiyya*, as is explained below.

Taqiyya is an idea in Islamic law that translates as "deceit or dissimulation," particularly as it would apply to infidels. It can be taken one of two ways. First, it can mean concealment of one's religious convictions. If people shouldn't know that you are Muslim, then hide it. Second, it can mean lying for the sake of Islam. The closest thing in the Western world that matches it is the Fake News Media, so commonly referenced by former President Trump. Taqiyya comes from one main verse in the Qur'an:

Let not the believers take disbelievers for their friends in preference to believers. Whoso doeth that hath no connection with Allah unless (it be) that ye but guard yourselves against them, taking (as it were) security. Allah biddeth you beware (only) of Himself. (3:28)[33]

A respected modern-day authority on Islamic law, William Gawthrop, has noted, Muslims have used taqiyya since the seventh century to confuse and divide "the enemy." One result is maintaining two messages, one to the faithful while obfuscation and denial are sent – and accepted – to the non-Muslim audience.[34]

A recent example is the dual messaging of the Islamic scholar Yusuf al-Qaradawi. In 2010, he was interviewed in a London-based newspaper, *Asharq Al-awsat*, and extolled the virtues of democracy.[35] Later that same year, al-Qaradawi wrote to a Saudi Arabian newspaper, *The Saudi Gazette*, with an intended Muslim audience that accepting democracy is "downright apostasy."[36] In short, what Muslim audiences need to know about Islam is not the same thing as what non-Muslim Western viewers are allowed to know. Taqiyya provides the legal basis under sharia for this deceptive dual messaging.

An Islamic Achilles' Heel?

Going back to the opening paragraph and reviewing the numbers of Muslims running for office in the U.S., do we need to worry? Probably not. The organizational structure of Sunni Islam impedes collective action by Muslims. Sunni Islam, as an organization, is decentralized.[37] The diversity of national origins found among American Muslims heightens this factor. When Islamic institutions' structural features combine with the obstacle of overcoming entrenched national identities, the possibilities for broad-based collective action on religious grounds are limited.

So, why, here in the U.S., is Islam fractured and fragmented? First, Islam is a decentralized, non-hierarchical religion with multiple and competing schools of law and social requirements.

The exception to this is Shi'a Islam, a relatively small group found mainly in Iran. The Shi'a Muslims have a centralized and hierarchical structure, much like the Catholic Church, but they have the Ayatollah instead of the Pope. In contrast to Catholicism, Sunni Muslim leaders have no enforcement mechanisms to obtain their followers' obedience. There is no established, recognized procedure for the removal of specific imams in a local mosque. Islam's organizational structure cannot easily give exclusive rewards to those who participate in collective action and cannot punish those who free ride. In sum, Islam has no central authority to enforce cooperation, punish noncompliance, or structure an activity. That is why Muslims belong to an overabundance of social and political organizations, associations, and movements. The political consequence is that the lack of a hierarchical organization means comparatively less political power.[38]

In a foreign Islamic country, this lack of political power means that mainstream Muslims cannot confront authoritarian regimes even on a regional basis. However, in the United States, low political power still allows a group to play in local politics, and that is what the Muslims have done.

In the United States, there is no "Muslim vote," just as there is no Jewish vote or Catholic vote. There are a plethora of Muslim voices. In any religion, there are moderates and extremists, separationists, and integrationists. Adherents separate into their political, social, and religious groups. For Islam, there is arguably too much division for there to be strength in numbers. There are two exceptions to this:

1) Muslims that work together and live together in a community for extended periods may indeed have a focused vote. The population of Muslims centered around the Ford manufacturing plants in Michigan may represent one such community.

2) Muslims who are stellar lawyers, businessmen, doctors, scientists or writers who pursue goals that may appeal to non-Muslims may do well in political elections. For example, Sadiq Khan, a Muslim of Pakistani heritage, was elected mayor of London in 2016 because Londoners thought he was the best candidate for the job.

It may be counterintuitive that Sunni Islam in America is a religion not protected by state laws and subsidies but may become more vibrant and responsive to its followers than in a country dominated by Islam. Its current diversity of organizations, structures, and goals more accurately represents and caters to the multitudes of Muslim immigrants than do the highly structured, monopolistic Christian churches that serve their Christian constituencies. Ironically, Muslim followers benefit from living in a free-market society.

Chapter Summary
Democracy is not a form of government that most Muslims grow up with. Muslims grew up with the Greek classics as they conquered many of Alexander the Great's lands. Their caliphates did not employ Athenian ideals. While many Muslim immigrants are knowledgeable of democracy and may have even experienced it in countries such as India, Pakistan, Lebanon, Palestine, and Egypt, they have not experienced real liberal democracy as we practice in our country. Remember, Islam claims that laws made by men to rule men are sinful. However, if they can use such laws to implement sharia that restricts our rights and freedoms in favor of their religious values, God will look the other way.

Chapter 10

Growth & Market Share

This chapter reviews two concepts with which most businesspeople are familiar. They are the product life cycle (PLC) and the growth-share matrix. Both ideas together will help us evaluate how different religions react to current trends and what strategies might be employed to make faith more virile and robust to the consumer. Yes, I did use the word "consumer." According to Dictionary.com, a consumer is "one that consumes."[1] Another definition is "a person or organization that uses a commodity or service." We usually identify a consumer as a person or an organization that consumes a product or a service, but how do you devour enlightenment and salvation? It is a means to which people fill a need in their lives, much like those other needs on Maslow's Hierarchy of Needs.[y] In a fundamental sense, people are consumers of religion. They find or are born into a belief that they are attracted to, and they commit their time, their resources, and their allegiance. In this chapter, we will measure those people in terms of how fast a religion grows and how big the numbers of faithful are. These two variables will indicate how viable the faith is and what things people can do to improve their belief, as that is our purpose as a believer. In Matthew 28, verse 19, Christ said: "Therefore go and make disciples of all nations..."[2]

In 1957, a management consulting company, Booz Allen Hamilton, Inc., developed the product life cycle concept as we know it now.[3] The product life cycle (PLC) is a graphic that depicts any given product on two vectors; the vertical vector being sales or consumption, which are proxy variables for demand; the horizontal vector representing time periods. This concept acknowledges that all products share similar characteristics of growth, maturity, and decline. Marketing and operational strategies are employed to increase demand and reduce expenses. These tactics impact growing market share or, in the case here, increasing the number of believers.

A product life cycle has four stages that explain and show product demand over time. The four steps are 1) product introduction, 2) product demand growth, 3) product demand maturity, and 4) product demand decline. Booz Allen Hamilton came into play because they determined how to manipulate tactics and strategies in each stage. Product sales can be extended or reduced as needed, expenses minimized, and profits maximized. It was a business strategy, pure and simple. While the concept analyzes products and determines policies that prolong growth and maturity, the idea also applies to industries, brands, and even non-business ideas such as religion.

So perhaps religions can be treated as businesses, or at the least, they could use a business model to determine where it stands vis-á-vis with its competitors. Like many industries and brands, religions have a relatively long life cycle. Most religions are born of other faiths. Theologists have proposed the life cycle idea before, and we know that Christianity and Islam use marketing strategies to improve their acceptance among the public.[4] An exciting proposition by Rajiv Malhotra, an Indian-American humorist, suggested that the product that the three great Abrahamic religions (Judaism, Christianity, and Islam) are selling has two theological components:

1. God's love in paradise and
2. Insurance from eternal damnation in Hell.[5]

We can smile that God's salvation breaks down into a "product" that each religion can try to sell, as evidenced by the number of converts to any given religion. To use the product life cycle (PLC), the number of those converts can tell us in which stage of the PLC the religion is located.

Since the PLC begins with Stage 1, Product Introduction, let us hypothesize what an introduction would look like for Christianity and Islam:

Introduction Stage

Product presentation to the public for the first time is the initial stage. When introducing a new product, service, or concept, the market size is usually small. This stage has limited consumption, and incoming resources such as money do not fully replace outgoing expenditures. The focus is to build an audience for the product. Founders and leadership must look at distribution and promotion.

Introduction Stage – Christianity

Christianity had a long-running market promotion when, for 1,500 years, the scriptures had been prophesying the coming of a savior.[6] Jesus Christ is considered the founder of the Church following his crucifixion by the Roman and Jewish authorities in ca. 30 CE. He had a dozen disciples and many other friends and supporters who were regarded as followers – perhaps up to 500 people. Almost two decades later, Paul, as "sales and marketing director," visited churches, wrote marketing treatises (13 epistles in the New Testament), and opened the religion to non-Jews (new markets). He conducted site visits, jaw-boned critics, and did what was needed to make the religion consumer-friendly (faith, not good works, was the key). The formative years of Christianity began with the ministry of Jesus (ca. 27-30 CE) and lasted until the death of the last of the Twelve Apostles (ca. 100 CE) and the completion of the key scriptures.

This religion, unlike many others, is based on missionary work. Christians took on critical responsibilities much like today's Red Cross, where they provided food for the hungry and medical help for the sick. Christian theology also had its problems, however. It did not tolerate the Roman Empire's polytheistic gods and consequently suffered the Empire's wrath. Roman emperors Caligula and Nero, from the first century, were notorious for persecuting Christians. Persecution seemed to make the apostles work harder. The book of Acts provides a detailed eyewitness account of the early Church's birth and growth and the spread of the gospels immediately after the resurrection of Jesus.

There is no hard-demographic data to support absolute numbers measuring the growth of Christianity, but fortunately, several scholars have posted their estimates based on different modeling techniques. The University of Virginia's emeritus professor of history, Robert Louis Wilken, estimates that in AD 100, there were fewer than 10,000 Christians in the Roman Empire.[7] As we prepare a graph of the Christianity PLC, I will use the figure of 10,000 as the base from which to start Stage 2. As it would turn out, this would be more than enough to get the religion started. Christianity had a long introduction phase (about 70 years).

Introduction Stage – Islam

Muslims contend that Muhammad's arrival was prophesied in the Bible some 2,000 years before the event. While Muhammad was born in 570, it was not until 610 that he begins receiving messages from God (Allah) through the angel Gabriel. Over the next 22 years, Muhammad not only continued to receive directives from God, but he also preached against polytheism, recruited advocates, fought battles against unbelievers, and directed his armies to do his bidding. Muslim converts shared booty from the spoils of war. There was a hefty price to pay for those who do not convert. Resistors of the faith were either killed, forced into slavery, or became second-class citizens. The spread of Islam was fast and fiery. All eligible males wanted to be part of Muhammad's army because of the potential to win spoils of war and, of course, admittance to paradise at the end of their lives. By the time of Muhammad's death in 632 CE, most of the indigenous people of the Arabian Peninsula had converted to Islam, bringing closure to the "Introductory Stage."

We know that Muhammad rode with a force of 10,000 soldiers when he captured Mecca in 630 CE. While it is possible that by the time of Muhammad's death, several thousand converts were living in Saudi Arabia, there are no documented numbers or census records. As I did with the Christianity PLC, I will do with the Islamic PLC and start their graph at 10,000 adherents. Compared to Christianity, Islam's introductory phase was short (about 20 years).

Growth Stage

The growth stage will be when the product increasingly gains approval among customers, the industry, and the broader public. During this stage, product demand and users start to increase. This stage is where competition comes in and tries to take their piece of the pie. If growth is healthy for one organization, then the market will usually sustain two or more. The second and subsequent competitors will often offer different attributes, different flavors, various means of distribution, and multiple price schemes. The consumer usually has many choices, and the producer has a large market to sell its products.

Growth Stage – Christianity

The Growth Stage of Christianity can be seen to start in 100 CE and lasts until 400 CE. Apostles, influenced by the Holy Spirit, went forward and started churches, baptizing the poor in faith and healing the sick in body. Many charismatic speakers swayed people to convert. Jesus was an apocalyptic prophet – meaning that he preached that God would come soon to set up His kingdom on earth. Jesus' ministry foretold that God would defeat the armies of the world, and there would be a day of judgment for all people. Prospective converts wanted to be on the right side of history, and they committed to believing in the Lord Jesus Christ. The feeling of urgency was pervasive during these early years.

During this initial period, there was much diversity in theological doctrine as each church leader would interpret church theology according to his opinion. For example, some church leaders did not believe that Jesus was God but portrayed him as God's mortal son. Others thought that he was divine, not human. It would not be until 381 CE that the Holy Spirit was worshipped together with the Father and the Son, as the Trinity.[8] During this period, much of Christianity's doctrine evolved, and the essential details changed as the religion took shape.

While Roman Emperor Nero in 64 CE was the first to persecute Christians, general persecution of Christians throughout the Roman Empire began in 250 CE.[9] This latter date was the first systemic effort on the part of imperial authorities to force Christians to give up their beliefs and worship Roman gods. The attempt eventually failed as there are just too many Christians in the Empire to intimidate. In 312 CE, the Roman Emperor Constantine had a dream that he saw the cross and soon won a great battle.[10] Christianity soon became legitimate and, within a century, replaced the polytheistic gods as the state religion of the Roman Empire.

Many things happened in the period from 300 to 325 CE that cemented Christianity's base as a legitimate religion. In 301 CE, Armenia, a Roman Empire province, became the first territory outside the Middle East to adopt Christianity.[11] It wasn't until 324 CE that Emperor Constantine declared himself sole ruler of the Roman Empire, upon which he hosted the Nicene Council in 325 CE to ensure conformity of the religion.

Peter the Apostle was considered the first Pope of Christ's church, and from the time of his martyrdom in 67 CE, till 400 CE, the Catholic Church slowly became a robust organization that guided the course of Christianity. As the church became institutionalized, there were still charismatic and free preaching missionaries traveling across the countryside, converting pagans and polytheistic communities. Being a state-sponsored church did not hurt the organization's growth, and like any good organization, having authority and resources was a means of ministering to the masses. A bureaucracy evolved administered by local priests, regional bishops, and a holy vicar.

Analyzing the membership numbers, by the year 200 CE, the number of Christians was up to 200,000, and by the year 300, just five generations later, the number is estimated to be 6 million.[12] The most accurate figures available for the next century came from different modeling techniques that forecast the number of Christians for the year 350 CE to be between 16 and 34 million.[13] Since there are no exact numbers to work from, the estimate used is 20 million Christian adherents in AD 400. Graph 1 below shows 10,000 Christians in AD 100, 200,000 Christians in 200, 6 million Christians in 300, and 20 million Christians in 400. The Introductory Stage ended in AD 100, and the Growth Stage ended in 400. Over this period of 300 years, the annualized growth rate was 2.57 percent.[z] During this same period, the world population grew only 0.01 percent per year, so this was indeed an active growth phase for the religion.

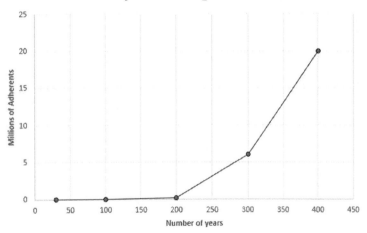

Graph 1

Growth Stage – Islam

The process of estimating Islam's growth rate is identical to the Christian growth rate. Muhammad died in 632, but just two years earlier, he invaded Mecca with an army of 10,000. While it would be safe to say that his base at the time of his death in 632 was extensive, there are no documented numbers to rely on, so I will be conservative and start the Islamic Growth Stage with 10,000 adherents.

In the first century after Muhammad died, the new Caliphs and their followers advanced their conquests into Egypt, Palestine, North Africa, Spain, Armenia, and Asia Minor (Turkey). In the next 300 years, the Caliphs set siege to Constantinople (the Byzantine Empire's capital), captured parts of Central Asia, Syria, Iraq, Iran, southern Italy, India, and parts of eastern Europe.

Comparing the same period for Islam provides contrasting viewpoints. To be fair, the growth stage for Christianity measured 300 years after the Introductory period. The same criteria will measure the Islamic growth stage. There are two sources of population estimates used to determine Islamic populations for the first 300 years. One source of estimated Islamic population growth comes from Houssain Kettani, who projects the Islamic community as a percent of the world population.[14] He forecasted the Islamic community as 3 percent in 700 CE, 7 percent in 800 CE, and 11 percent in 900 CE. Using the U.S. Census Bureau's Historical Estimates of World Population as the base, Islam's growth in its early years looks very robust, as portrayed by the solid line in Graph 2 below.[15] Kettani's population estimate at the end of three centuries is slightly less than 26 million but substantially higher than where the Christian population was at the same time. A compound annual growth calculator computes the yearly growth at 2.97 percent, a little higher than the Christian growth rate.

However, there is another source located on the Internet. On the Wikipedia webpage, "Timeline of seventh-century Muslim history," it states under the year 700 CE, "By the end of this century, the global Muslim population had grown to 1 percent of the total."[16] The corresponding Webpages for the eighth-century and ninth-century show similar percentages: 2 percent for 800 CE,[17] and 3 percent for 900 CE.[18] The dotted line in Graph 2 below represents a muted growth as presented in Wikipedia.[19] This second estimate of Islamic growth yields a 2.47 percent growth rate per annum, a little lower than Christianity's growth rate. In both cases, world population growth during this period is .046 percent. The actual growth phase of Islam is probably between these two estimates. There is no way to know existing membership, but from these forecasts, Islam and Christianity had different Introduction Stages and different Growth Stages as well.

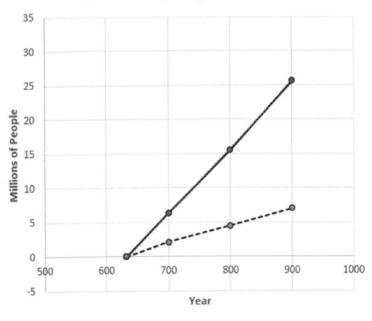

Graph 2

These two graphs represent each religion's growth, as measured in millions of people. Christianity had a long incubation period (70 years), whereas Islam came out of the cradle going gangbusters. Once each religion entered the Growth Stage, there was high demand, as witnessed by the membership rate that each group claimed. The two beliefs are different in that Christianity is mainly rooted in the religious sphere, whereas Islam embraces the political, economic, tribal, *and* spiritual. Christianity grew significantly from proselytizing and missionary work, while Islam depended on conquest and proselytizing.

Maturity Stage

The third stage of the PLC can be quite a difficult time for product managers. Within the first two stages, organizations try to build a marketplace and generate demand for their services to attain as large a market share as practical. Nevertheless, throughout the Maturity Stage, the main target for many businesses will be keeping their share of the market in the face of several different challenges. In the Maturity Stage, demand levels off, market share stabilizes, and competitors increase. During this stage, organizations look for innovative ways to make their product more appealing to the user to maintain and perhaps even increase their market share. To ensure that a product has as long a life as possible, it is often necessary to restructure the product to meet new needs as the user base changes. In a mature market, there is much competition. The best way to meet and beat that competition is to innovate and differentiate by offering a product with many different attributes that can meet many other people's needs.

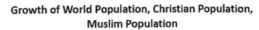

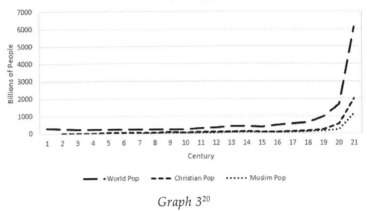

Graph 3[20]

Maturity Stage – Christianity

If we look at Graph 3 above, we can estimate the period from 401 to 1800 as the Maturity Stage for Christianity. In absolute numbers, the religion grew from 20 million people to 204 million people in 1,400 years.[21] While that seems a lot, the compound annual growth rate is just 0.17 percent. Ironically, that growth rate is still about 50 percent faster than the growth rate for the world population (0.11 percent) during the same period. In other words, Christianity was growing steadily faster than the world population.

In a mature phase, management begins to look for ways to grow the product. Distribution is important. For a religion to increase its membership, missionaries must build churches and congregations where the people are. During this period, orthodox Christianity centered in Rome and Constantinople, Alexandria, Antioch, and throughout the Roman and Byzantine Empire begins to push outwards through Europe, Asia, and North Africa. Church leaders in Russia, Serbia, Romania, Bulgaria, and throughout the Middle East and Central Asia established other orthodox churches. In a mature stage, it is common for the product to become innovative. The Reformation movement in fifteenth-century Europe opened the door for Protestant diversity. Christian membership expanded to all kinds of denominational Christians, i.e., Baptists, Methodists, Lutherans, Quakers, Amish, Pentecostal, etc. From the looks of it, Christianity is a slow-growing organizational behemoth.

One sign of maturity is the evolution of the religion into thousands of variations, each different from the others but still serving a sliver of the population. For example, the Catholic Church only has 53 percent of the world's Christians under its banner; Protestantism has 38 percent of the membership, and minority denominations have the rest.[22] This time frame of 401 to 1,800 allows Christianity to meet the characteristics of a mature product because of a) all of the different Christian brands that have emerged; b) there is only slight growth in the total market share of religions in the world's population; and c) there is an increased use of marketing tools to promote churches and Biblical content. These changes indicate a market presence trying to find innovative ways to make an old product more appealing. As our society fragments into more and more differentiated groups, there is pressure to water down the doctrine, especially for fringe groups. For example, probably less than 5 percent of the U.S. population is LGBTQ. Still, their leverage in getting major church denominations to accept LGBTQ clergy and doctrine is way beyond their reach.[23] This need to appeal to a fringe market is a sign of a mature product.

Maturity Stage – Islam

Looking at a similar period for the Islamic religion, 900 to 1800 CE would be compatible. That period recognizes two historical trends that brought Islam peace and security but only for a while. First, the Golden Age of Islam is recognized as being from the eighth century to the thirteenth century. Many outstanding achievements in medicine, the arts, mathematics, law, and literature took place. Second, the Ottoman Empire had reached its zenith in the late fifteenth century under Suleyman the Magnificent. While still formidable in the eighteenth century, the Ottoman Empire was losing ground to Western nations like Britain, Spain, and Portugal. Looking at Graph 3 above, Islam would also appear to be in a mature stage. Using Kettani's estimates of Islamic population growth, where Islam was estimated to have 26 million adherents in 900 CE and 126 million in 1800, the annual compound growth rate is 0.18 percent, which is slightly faster than the global population growth rate (0.17 percent) during this time frame.[24] For the most part, Islam was growing at the same rate as the world's population, which is indicative of a mature stage. Another characteristic of a mature market is an excess of competition. Islam has evolved into several different variations, each touting that they represent Muhammad's teachings. Most non-Muslims are familiar with the Sunni and the Shi'a sects of Islam. Other Islamic sects are the Alawi, the Sufi, the Wahhabi, the Korani, and the Ahmadiyya. During this maturity period, Islam has not reached the point of a significant number of adherents splitting away from its main branch as the Catholic Church experienced during the Reformation. In contemporary terms, Sunni Islam is the dominant sect globally at 85 percent.[25]

It is worth mentioning that Muhammad's teachings were against any innovation pertaining to doctrine. This orthodox faith will not fray at the edges as Christianity has, as it is blasphemous to change things without reason. See the section on Innovation in Chapter 4.

Aberrations in the PLC

It is not unusual for irregularities to occur in a product life cycle. Shifts in consumer demand or changes in raw materials can sometimes enhance or decrease the ability to produce and supply a market or for that market to afford the product. A similar change has taken place in the growth of the consumer market. The human population has expanded exponentially because of scientific and management techniques affecting sanitation, education, agriculture, and genetics. As parts of the community seek out spiritual faith, both Islam and Christianity link to this growth.

You can see this aberration in global population growth in Graph 3 and below in Graph 4. Graph 4 shows what has happened just in the last two hundred years.

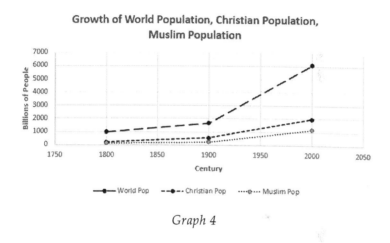

Graph 4

Based on the long view of the last two centuries, we see in Graph 4 that Christianity is growing as fast, if not slightly faster, than Islam. Both religions are linked to the growth of the world population but at different rates of growth. Christianity's annual compound growth for the last 200 years is 1.14 percent versus Islam's annual growth rate of 1.12 percent. As we will see in the demographic section in Chapter 12, Christian believers are older, with fewer offspring, and since they tend to live in more developed Western countries, their lifespan is longer. Today, the Christianity population increases about 65 million individuals yearly because of religious conversion and birth rates while losing 27.4 million people annually to factors such as religious apostasy, death, and immigration. Most of the net growth in Christianity is in Africa, Latin America, and Asia.[26]

Islamic adherents are younger, have more offspring but live primarily in third-world countries with lower life spans. Both religions together represent about half the world's population, which leaves room for much growth.

Decline Stage

The last product life cycle stage is the Decline Stage, which, as might be expected, is often the beginning of the end for a product. A fall in demand characterizes the Decline Stage. Adherents will typically stop using this product in favor of something newer and better, and there is generally not much a product manager can do to prevent this. For example, the decline of Christianity is an ongoing trend in Europe, Oceania, and Canada.[27] Immigration into Europe is mainly from the Middle East and North Africa, where the immigrants are primarily young Muslims. These immigrants replace the Christian base in Europe, where the residents are growing old and dying off. In Oceania, Christianity has declined due to secularization, and in Canada, immigration and the growth of agnosticism have taken hold. Neither Islam nor Christianity is in the Decline Stage from a worldwide perspective; however, these regions like Europe, Oceania, and Canada show that Christianity is in jeopardy. The last three Catholic Popes have recognized this trend and have urged the church to adapt to their changing audience. Popes St. John Paul II, Benedict XVI, and Francis have pushed "to clarify and reaffirm traditional teachings in response to liberalizing tendencies within the church and wider society."[28]

In conclusion, the PLC for the world's two largest religions is going strong. Several population projections are predicting Islam to be the world's largest religion by 2050. For several reasons, this outcome remains doubtful, however. In the last decade, Islamic growth has been strong, but that can change as economic situations improve. Suppose Islamic countries develop a sizeable middle class. In that case, population growth will fall off as parents determine that raising multiple children is a costly endeavor at the expense of substantial fringe benefits. Islam represents a more socialist and traditional form of community. Christianity often exhibits societies with better lifestyles, accompanied by individual freedoms and competitive markets. One depicts the quality of life, and the other, just a living.

The Growth-Share Matrix

In 1970, the Boston Consulting Group created the growth-share matrix to help corporations analyze their product lines.[29] The process used a two-vector array that ranked the different products by growth and market share. Growth indicates how attractive the product (in our case, the religion) is appealing to the population. If the rate of expansion is higher than the competition, then that specific faith has some advantage that causes people to become adherents. For example, as we stated earlier, the birth rate in Islamic families is higher than in Christian families, which gives Islam an inherent advantage in the amount of growth. The other vector, market share, measures adherents' competitive size that uses and accepts the religion. The actual term should be "relative market share," as it compares to other religions. Relative market share indicates that higher economies of scale and experience result in higher market penetration (missionaries, in this context) and higher conversion rates. In business, the goal would be increased cash flow, but in religion, the goal is to save souls by converting people to your religion. Looking at these two attributes (product growth and market share) allows management to judge any given product's viability compared to competitive products.

Major Religions of the World	2000 Adherents (Millions)	2013 Adherents (Millions)	2013 Market Share	CAGR 2000-2013
Buddhism	452	510	7.1%	0.93%
Chinese Folk Religion	432	433	6.0%	0.02%
Christianity	1,987	2,355	32.7%	1.32%
Hinduism	822	982	13.6%	1.38%
Islam	1,292	1,635	22.7%	1.83%
Judaism	14	15	0.2%	0.53%
Sikhism	20	25	0.3%	1.73%
Total World Population	6,143	7,210	100.0%	1.21%

Table 1[aa]

Growth Rate Ranking

Earlier, we analyzed the product life cycle as it applies to religions. Our data for the growth-share matrix in Table 1 includes seven significant religions of the world. The average growth of these seven influential religions between 2000 and 2013 was 1.3 percent compounded annually, which is slightly higher than the global population compounded annual growth rate (CAGR) of 1.2 percent during this period. Since the fastest growing religion is Islam at 1.8 percent per annum, I will make our matrix in Diagram 2 capable of handling up to 2.0 percent growth. I will use 1.0 percent as our midpoint; we automatically assume that the fastest growing religions would be above the 1.0 percent line, and the laggards would be below, as displayed in Table 2.

Fastest Growing Religions		Slowest Growing Religions	
Islam	1.83%	Buddhism	0.93%
Sikhism	1.73%	Judaism	0.53%
Hinduism	1.38%	Chinese Folk	0.02%
Christianity	1.32%		

Table 2: Fasted and Slowest Growing Religions

Market Share Ranking

Market share is a metric used to measure the consumers' preference for a product over other similar products. If there are

100 people in a sample – 20 people are Christians, and 15 people are Muslims – the sample's market share would be 20 percent Christians and 15 percent Muslims. In our case, the base we are using was the world's population in 2013. The world's population in 2013 was 7.21 billion people. Of that total, 2.355 billion people identify as Christian, which is a 32.7 percent market share. Table 3 below displays the market share for each religion. The religion with the largest market share is Christianity, at 32.7 percent. Diagram 2 will accommodate up to 40 percent market share with the halfway point at 20 percent. Religions with less than 20 percent market share fall into the Smaller Market Share Religions category. The breakdown looks like this:

Religions with Market Share > 20%		Religions with Market Share < 20%	
Christianity	32.7%	Hinduism	13.6%
Islam	22.7%	Buddhism	7.1%
		Chinese Folk	6.0%
		Sikhism	0.3%
		Judaism	0.2%

Table 3

Using the Market Share Ranking in collaboration with the Growth Rate Ranking, we have a matrix with four quadrants as shown in Diagram 1. The four quadrants are as follows:

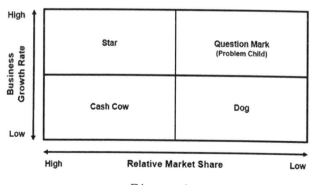

The Product Growth-Share Matrix

Diagram 1

Question Marks

This quadrant is sometimes referred to as a "problem child" because of the opportunities and problems that go with it. The product here has a relatively high growth rate (a plus) but a minuscule market share (a minus); thus, it is a Question Mark. Question Marks can be seen as the religions that require much closer investigation. People are attracted to these religions hence the stable growth rate. However, these religions do not have a sizeable congregational base. For some reason, people do not stay with the faith, or it is a new religion and is taking time to build up a base. It is a Question Mark as to whether the religion will succeed or fail. These, therefore, hold a low market share in a fast-growing market consuming many resources. It is questionable whether they have sustainability. They have the potential to gain market share, but if they do not, they become irrelevant. They have something to offer, but whether they can market their ideology and increase the numbers of adherents is questionable. The religions of Hinduism and Sikhism fall into this category. These religions are growing fast but have a small sum of members compared to the more significant faiths and even the world population.

Stars

The quadrant where the religions have a relatively high growth rate and a high market share is a Star. Religions that fall into this category have access to resources, and their sustainability is assured. The fact that the market share is high indicates that they meet most people's needs in their region. Most of the people that join these religions end up staying. These religions have the resources to send out missionaries (market penetration). They can market their ideology to attract new converts from other religions (new markets) and are big enough to increase their mosques, temples, or churches. They can offer new products like religious schools and even offer incentives like scholarships or school lunch programs (new products) to draw new members. Marketing of ideology, additional new locations, charismatic speakers, etc., all play a part in this effort to grow the religion. Christianity and Islam fall into this category.

Dogs

The name of this next quadrant, "Dog," is not meant to reflect on the beliefs or even any business products that fall into this category. The term "Dog" is intended to reflect on products and services with a low growth rate and a small market share. The religions that fall into this quadrant are mostly ancient religions that appeal only to select populations. In our discussion, only three religions fall into this category: Judaism, Buddhism, and Chinese Folk Religion. Judaism originated around 2000 BC, with Abraham as the father of the Jewish people. Judaism only appeals to the Jewish sect; thus, the growth and market share waxes and wanes with the Jewish population. In China, the Communist Party has tried to remove this aspect of organized religion in their country. The Chinese Folk Religion values have been trampled upon, which has eliminated most growth from this religion. The present-day government of China has generally suppressed Chinese Folk Religion to promote "modern" values.[30] Buddhists have a lower birth rate than other religious groups and do not actively seek conversions or religious switching.[31]

A person might assume that religions assigned to this quadrant will soon pass on or become specialty denominations. While I do not think any of these religions will die out anytime soon, I believe they will become specialized religions that appeal only to a limited population.

Cash Cows

Just like "Dog" is a business description of a particular quadrant, the term "Cash Cow" has similar origins. Technically, a cash cow is a business that generates a steady return of profits that far exceeds the outlay of cash to maintain it. Organizations that fit that description fall into this quadrant. Here, we have religions with low growth but a significant market share as compared to other religions. Weak growth means that demand for the product has peaked, but many people still worship the faith's tenets. If Buddhism and Chinese Folk Religions had a more significant market share, they would have fallen into this quadrant. Both religions have notable population sizes that can generate substantial resources, but unless they use their donations and gifts to grow the faith, their organizations will wither. More than likely, both religions will trend downward in both growth and relative market share.

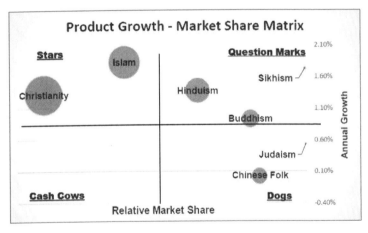

Diagram 2

Take-Away Conclusions

From the product life cycle, I think the last decade has shown that Islam is the largest, fastest-growing religion on the planet. It appeals to people who live in developing countries, where economic success is marginal, where education is biased towards the faith, where democracy has no supporting political institutions, and where most governments are socialist or authoritarian. The religion itself has a strong community affinity, so that it prospers here is no surprise. The doctrine provides balance to the injustices suffered by a population in turmoil. Higher fertility rates and an overall younger society are the critical parts of Islam's growth. From Diagram 2, it is evident that Islam has a substantial base, where the upper hierarchy has significant resources to contribute to the religion's success. These are the strategies that would make sense for Islam to follow:

- Adding new attributes and support services like schools, day-care services and facilities, charitable healthcare, and social services for families in poverty.
- Support a government that offers extensive social services and provides make-work jobs.
- Increase locations of mosques to cope with growing demand.
- Shift marketing messages from product awareness to product preference. In other words, explain to the consumers how Islam will fill the void in their life.
- Improve product quality. Put motivated people in locations where they will make a difference and use activists to get things done.
- Support a legal system that maintains strict religious laws such as sharia.
- Where necessary, either overtly or covertly, move resources to enhance and protect those ideas that will grow the faith.
- In countries with a democratic government, run for positions in the government.

Christianity appears to be a more mature religion; it appeals to older citizens with higher education levels, economic security, and democratic, free-market expectations. In some ways, Christianity was the progenitor of the Western work-ethic, and now it is perceived as part of that Western lifestyle. From looking at Diagram 2, it is evident that what Christianity has over Islam is the size of its base. The base can share financial resources and human resources that would overwhelm efforts by any other religion.

These are the strategies that would make sense for Christians to pursue:

- Product growth – It has been statistically proven that mission work grows liberal democracy.[32] Liberal democracy makes a community more stable and allows all people to work and live in communities that worship God. There are still many areas of the world that need missions. Mission work is one of the most critical functions that Christian institutions should pursue.
- Product modification – The Christian religion has messages of hope for all kinds of people, older adults, young people, families, invalids, etc. Preach the word that audiences need to hear. Christianity is the religion of liberal democracy and freedom and liberty. The temptation is to water down the doctrine to appeal to more people. Resist the temptation to change the faith to accommodate materialistic and lifestyle modifications. One problem that Western churches are resisting is the acceptance of homosexuality as it relates to religion. Islamic patrons do not have this problem; homosexuality is a sin. However, suppose a Western church accepts LGBTQ people into its clergy. If they send missionaries to areas with a Muslim population, their representatives will have a credibility problem and have difficulty recruiting adherents.

Side Note: The gay rights revolution is over 50 years old, starting with the 1969 Stonewall Riots in Greenwich

Village, New York. Since that time, most countries have legalized homosexuality. However, the death penalty still exists in 10 Islamic countries, mainly in the Middle East and Africa. Also, some 20 to 30 Islamic countries have made homosexuality a crime punishable by imprisonment. A recent example is the country of Brunei when "it recently introduced strict Islamic laws which made homosexual acts punishable by stoning to death."[33]

- Market Penetration – Christian churches are reliable in this realm: marketing techniques that include more locations, promotion, communication of church messages, and making it easy and convenient to attend services. The Bible makes for an excellent marketing presentation with hundreds of Biblical stories and parables. All these attributes work to drive market penetration, which is a definite advantage.
- Market modification – Send missionaries into new markets. Again, preach the message that meets the needs of the local community. Conversions from other religions are significant. Research shows that Christianity ranks first for religious conversions netting over each year some 2.7 million new Christians.[34]

None of these strategies are unique. In most cases, the specific religions are already following these paths. The purpose of this chapter was to explain why each religion is doing what it is doing. One final description of behavior that happens when a religion is in the mature stage is that large segments of religious adherents become "culturally" sacred, which means they don't subscribe to the fundamental truth any longer. Still, they do consider themselves a member of the religious community.[35] They come to church on Easter and Christmas, perhaps only because they want to make a good impression on their kids, or they think that only once or twice a year is enough to keep up their relationship with God.

Chapter Summary

When we look at Islam and Christianity through the Product Life Cycle's prism and the Growth-Share Matrix, their organizational behavior becomes realistic, like an essential service or an institution with benefits that people consume. While Christianity had a lengthier introduction period than Islam, Christianity's growth has matched Islam until the last few decades. Christianity is a more mature religion with a larger market share and a wealthier demographic than Islam. Undoubtedly, free-market economics has allowed Christianity to prosper. While Islam is growing, the quality of life found in most Muslim nations is marginal. Christianity has more resources than Islam, but the real driver for any religion is whether the leaders have the inspiration and the vision to make their faith an essential part of a person's spiritual needs.

End-of-Chapter Notes

y. "Maslow's Hierarchy of Needs is a motivational theory in psychology comprising a five-tier model of human needs, often depicted as hierarchical levels within a pyramid. From the bottom of the hierarchy upwards, the needs are physiological (food and clothing), safety (job security), love and belonging needs (friendship), esteem, and self-actualization. Needs lower down in the hierarchy must be satisfied before individuals can attend to needs higher up." Saul McLeod, "Maslow's Hierarchy of Needs," *Simple Psychology*, December 29, 2020, https://www.simplypsychology.org/maslow.html#gsc.tab=0

z. When using a compound annual growth rate (CAGR) calculator, you can plug in the beginning value (10,000) and the ending value (20,000,000) and the number of periods or years to be compounded (300 years).

aa. Source: The data above is based on the "Status of Global Mission, 2013, in the Context of A.D. 1800-2025" issued by Gordon-Conwell Theological Seminary, retrieved from http://christianityinview.com/downloads/ StatusOfGlobalMission.pdf. World population totals for 2000 and 2013 were taken from Worldometers, retrieved from https://www.worldometers.info/world-population/ world-population-by-year/

Chapter 11

Muslim-Jewish Enmity

One question that has intrigued me is, why is there a high level of discord between Muslim nations and Israel? This chapter examines the reasons that have caused this historic friction. The answer is not always apparent – though Israel's occupation of Palestine is, of course, the most obvious, at least since 1917. While this occupation of Palestine has been front and center, other incidents have added to this antipathy. I will explore the history of this enmity here.

Out of the 193 countries that are members of the United Nations, 26 nations don't recognize or keep diplomatic relations with Israel.[1] While some of these countries like Iran and Syria maintain a war footing against Israel, other countries like Indonesia and Pakistan keep their distance at the bequest of the Arab League, an association of 22 Arab Muslim countries in the Middle East. These 26 nations represent about 15 percent of the world's population, a significant proportion.[2]

Before the time of the Prophet Muhammad, numerous tribes of different ethnicities lived in Saudi Arabia. The land of Palestine, dating from Abraham's arrival in ca. 2000 BCE until the Ottoman Empire's expiration in the early twentieth century, was subject to constant invasion and occupation. To list some of the more well-known incursions, we can identify the Egyptians in the tenth century BCE, the Assyrians in the seventh and eighth centuries BCE, the Babylonians and the Persians in the sixth century BCE, followed by Alexander the Great in the fourth century BCE, and the Romans in the first century BCE. Each time a new empire marched into the area, Jews, Canaanites, Egyptians, and previous invaders involuntarily moved into the Arabian Desert. As the leader of a new monotheistic religious state, Muhammad had to deal with these different tribes in the desert. Most of the tribes had assimilated into the indigenous polytheistic culture, but the Jews were different; they were already monotheistic. Archaeological evidence shows that scribes produced copies of the Torah during the 1000 BCE to 500 BCE period. The Jewish people were well into practicing their customs and religious rituals at this time.[3]

Muhammad fled from Mecca in 622. By then, Gabriel's revelation of the Qur'an was about 60 percent complete, and it went against the polytheism of Muhammad's tribe, the Quraysh. Simultaneously, the tribes of Medina – a city-state about 300 miles to the north of Mecca – asked him to set up a tribal council to allow all area tribes to get involved in their community's governance. In Mecca, Muhammad's dealings with Jews and Christians had led him to believe that they were kindred souls, and he labeled them "People of the Book." However, in Medina, his relationship with the Jews was different. As he set about trying to implement a religion built on the necessary foundations of Judaism, the Jewish people became suspect. They would have none of this uncorroborated theology, rejecting Muhammad's message and overtures. Once it was clear the Jews would not accept him, Muhammad began to minimize or eliminate the Jewish influence. He shifted the direction of prayer from Jerusalem to Mecca, made Friday the special day of worship instead of Saturday, and renounced Jewish dietary laws (kosher preparation in favor of halal).

Numerous verses against the Jews and the Christians suddenly appeared in the Qur'an. As the Qur'an is believed to be the direct word of Allah, it was therefore perceived that Allah, through the angel Gabriel and Muhammad, was warning Muslims and Jews. The following verse is one of the more revealing: "O ye who believe! Take not the Jews and the Christians for friends. They are friends one to another. He among you who taketh them for friends is (one) of them" (5:51).[4]

In 627, the hatred became tangible. Muhammad defended and won the Battle of the Trench in Medina against his home tribe from Mecca. The Jewish tribe of Medina, the Banu Qurayza, had stayed neutral instead of aiding and supporting Muhammad. After the battle, Muhammad sought to consolidate his power over all the tribes in Medina, and consequently, he accused the Banu Qurayza of failing to honor their alliance. After a month-long siege, the Banu Qurayza surrendered to Muhammad. Because of their neutrality, Muhammad ordered that between 600-800 Jewish captives be beheaded and their wives and children sold into slavery.[5]

Islamic tradition holds that the Jews were once God's chosen people, but he rejected them for refusing to accept his prophets, both Jesus and Muhammad. The Christians did not accept Muhammad, but the Jewish people rejected both Jesus and Muhammad.

In 638, Islamic armies captured Jerusalem from the Byzantine Empire. The Crusaders reconquered Jerusalem in 1099, but then in 1187, Saladin, the first sultan of Egypt and Syria, took it back.[6] It has been 1,383 years since 638 when the Muslims initially conquered Palestine. They had ruled it for all that time except for 159 years when the Crusaders occupied it and again since 1948 when the State of Israel was declared following the Arab-Israeli War. Muslims have ruled this land for over a millennium (approximately 1,151 years) and believe the land rightfully belongs to them. Muslims believe that Jerusalem, and indeed all of Palestine, belongs to them for five reasons:

1. The Jewish people have broken their covenants with God on numerous occasions with disastrous results. They wandered in the desert with Moses until the generation that had sinned died out. The Babylonians conquered them because of their infidelities. Even Jesus predicted that the nation of Israel would be sacked (which it was, by the Roman Empire in AD 70-73) due to it lacking the commitment to believe in God.

The Jewish people have failed to recognize God's prophets (Jesus and Muhammad) and abide by their rules and laws. The liberal democracy of Israel today creates laws forged by man, not God. The Jewish state's economic prosperity has resulted in the worship of money, banking exploitation (usury), and the idolization of religious tombs, churches, sacred sites, and material things other than God. According to the Muslims, the Jewish state practices blasphemy and idolatry, two forms of shirk that warrant their nation's destruction.

2. Muslims consider Palestine a sacred place and a *waqf*. A waqf is an "inalienable charitable endowment under Islamic law, which typically involves donating a building, plot of land, or other assets for Muslim religious or charitable purposes with no intention of reclaiming the assets."[7] Lands already conquered and occupied by Muslims and any territories ever gained in the past are regarded as sacred ground, endowed by Allah to the *ummah*, the Muslim people forever. If ever such a province is lost, all Muslims must work to regain it by jihad, if necessary.[8] The issue of Palestine takes this concept one step further; it was conquered in 638 and turned into a waqf.[bb] It would be like setting up a charity with a permanent foundation for funding in the Western world. Later under the British Mandate of Palestine in 1922, the waqf was defined as state property, with revenues guaranteed to charitable foundations.[9] In other words, the territory was conquered by the Muslims and turned into community property, with excess taxes and profits used for Muslim charities. Later, under early British rule, that purpose was validated.[cc]

3. The psychological impact of the State of Israel on Muslims is difficult to overestimate. All through Islamic history, Jews were docile dhimmis subject to Muslim rule. Over the last century, Judaism has subverted traditional religious hierarchies in the Middle East. In doing so, it also undermined the credibility of Islamic superiority over Judaism. The insecurity and anxiety

created by this situation hardened political postures. For Israel, making peace with Islamic nations is a diplomatic achievement. For Muslim countries, accepting Israel concedes the dominance of Judaism over Islam.[10]

4. Muslims believe they have more rights to Palestine because the land does not belong to the people who lived there first but to those who established Allah's laws. Allah created the ground, and he created people to worship him in the land and to authorize the religion, regulations, and rulings of Allah. Specifically, a passage from the Qur'an (7:128) says:

And Moses said unto his people: Seek help in Allah and endure. Lo! the earth is Allah's. He giveth it for an inheritance to whom He will. And lo! the sequel is for those who keep their duty (unto Him).[11]

5. The fifth reason is the sacred night journey to heaven made by Muhammad. He traveled from the Great Mosque in Mecca to the Temple Mount in Jerusalem and visited all the great prophets in a dream. The journey is briefly mentioned in the Qur'an (17:1) but is known primarily through the hadith. After the capture of Jerusalem in 638, Muslims built the Al Aqsa Mosque over the Dome of the Rock in 691. In addition to Muhammad's night journey to heaven, the Dome of the Rock is considered the site where Abraham offered to sacrifice Ishmael (see Chapter 3). Jerusalem is considered Islam's third most holy site, after Mecca and Medina. While the Al Aqsa Mosque and compound are under Muslim administration, it is subject to Jewish laws and regulations. Jews and Christians have limited access to visit and tour the Rock and other parts of the compound. Resident Muslims revile Jewish access to the mosque area. An unspoken concern is that the Al Aqsa Mosque exists on the Temple Mount where the Jews wish to build the Third Temple. Muslims are worried that the mosque

would be demolished for that purpose.

Side Note: Jewish history asserts that the Temple Mount in Jerusalem was also the site of the First Temple built by King Solomon in 957 BC and destroyed by the Babylonians in 586 BC. The second Jewish Temple was constructed in the exact location in 516 BC and destroyed by the Romans in AD 70. There is strong evidence of a Byzantine church at the site in the fifth and sixth centuries.[12] In AD 610, the Persians drove the Byzantine Empire out of the Middle East and gave the Jews control of Jerusalem, at which time they started to rebuild the Third Temple. Later the Persians revoked Jewish authority and gave the site to the Christians, who tore down the ongoing Jewish construction and turned the area into a garbage dump. This garbage dump was what the Muslim armies found when they conquered the city in AD 638.[13] A credible account from later centuries is that the Muslim army leader, Caliph 'Umar, was reluctantly led to the location by the Christian patriarch Sophronius where they found the sacred Rock covered with rubbish.[14]

There are other reasons for the animosity between Muslims and Jews, specifically in Palestine-Israel. During the 1948 Arab-Israeli War, approximately 720,000 Palestinian Arabs fled their homes and wound up in refugee camps in Lebanon, Jordan, and Syria.[15] The Israelis were victorious but only repatriated a small amount of these Palestinians. There were other wars as well in which the Jewish state claimed victory.[dd] Jewish tactics in fighting terrorism are also seen as brutal, causing a backlash in the Arab world and beyond.

Several Muslim nations such as Egypt, Jordan, and even Saudi Arabia have found that having political relations with Israel can improve security, trade, and economic opportunity.

Some Muslim countries like Iran and Syria cannot let go of historical and contemporary enmity. The issue of whose God has sovereignty in this land has created the overall schism.

Chapter Summary

From 638 until 1948, except for 159 years when the Crusaders occupied the Holy Land, Muslims have ruled Palestine. That is 1,151 years under Muslim rule. Before the First World War, the Ottoman Empire was big enough to have had a dominant role in international politics in the region. The Ottoman Empire collapsed after the First World War, and the Jewish people won their freedom for a homeland. Muslims are frustrated to see their religion become impotent and irrelevant in matters such as these. They object to the continued occupation of lands designated as theirs, such as the West Bank and Gaza. Ironically, the Palestinians do not protest occupation of their lands by Jordan, Syria and Egypt, only those lands occupied by Israel.

The literature on this topic lists several reasons why Muslims refuse to accept the State of Israel. A significant reason is that Muslims believe that the Jews have violated their covenants with God numerous times and continue to do as witnessed by the refusal to honor Jesus and Muhammad as prophets of God. Islam maintains that land lost must be recaptured through jihad, if necessary. This emotional backlash may have been the feeling when it occurred, but we are now two or three generations past, and the change to Jewish governance is possibly slowly accepted.

End-of-Chapter Notes

bb. When the land was conquered, the caliph at the time, 'Umar Ibn al-Khattab, was asked whether the land should be partitioned between the troops or left in the possession of its population. The decision was made that the land should remain in the hands of its owners but the control of the land ought to be endowed as a waqf in perpetuity for all generations of Muslims.

cc. International laws and declarations after the First World War later gave rise to Israel's legitimate claim of territorial possession. Prior to the First World War, the Ottoman Empire was the region's administrator, but siding with the Axis Powers caused the Turks to lose their regional territories: Palestine, Syria, Iraq, Western Arab Peninsula, etc.

dd. Jordan, Syria, and Egypt sequestered much of the land apportioned for an autonomous Palestine state under UN Resolution 181. Israel reacquired this land in several military conflicts and is slowly ceding it back to the Palestinians in return for their recognition for the right of Israel to peacefully coexist.

Chapter 12

Who are the Players?

Initially, this chapter was going to be about the demographics of the Muslim community. But that information, while interesting, does not tell me what I want to know. I want to know what unique characteristics Muslims possess. Some Muslims are highly participative, while others are not. Some people grow up as Muslims but are lukewarm in their belief systems, while their neighbors down the street become virulent jihadis. While you will find these degrees of intensity in any organization or institution, I refer to these different levels of belief and participation as aspects of being "players" in the game. So, what are the different types of players that make up the religion? We will break down the constituencies after we look at the demographics.

Muslim Demographics

For those readers who want to know the demographics, I will provide a short summation. Based on the Pew Research Center statistics compiled in 2015, there were 1.8 billion Muslims, a market share of 24.1 percent of the global population.[1] The article identifies two trends that cement Islam's place as the fastest-growing religion in the world. Those two trends are high fertility rates and young median age. Consider that the median age compared to a non-Muslim, anywhere in the world, is 8 to 10 years younger. The estimated number of children per woman for a Muslim versus a non-Muslim is 2.9 versus 2.7, respectively. As I explained in Chapter 5 about child brides, it is customary in many countries for Muslim men to take child brides as part of their "allowance" of four wives and then produce numerous offspring who can help work and take care of the family as the

218

parents grow old. A large family is a form of social security.

Some developing countries are experiencing falling fertility rates. The growth of commercially available birth control has played a significant role, but so has women's liberation, their presence in the workforce, and the higher costs of childcare and education. Iran is one such nation where the fertility rate has fallen. In 1969, the fertility rate was seven children per female. In 2015, it was between 1.6 and 1.8 children, a trend that equates, comparatively, to national suicide.[2] As it turns out, the Muslim demographic does have similarities to the Christian demographic. The fertility rate seems to be influenced heavily by a country's economic and technical development. Developing countries have lower standards of education, healthcare, and commerce.

Consequently, families in these developing countries have less wealth but more children to offset the impact of production technology. Some 75-100 years ago, my mother grew up in a family with eight siblings, and my father's family had five. I would suggest Western nations are no different from Muslim countries in terms of family development; we are perhaps a generation, maybe two, ahead in technology development and distribution. Simple demographics would not tell us who we are dealing with when studying Islam.

The Players

Different scholars classify Islamic adherents into just a few different levels of players. Players are the people who participate, who make things happen, and who work together with their peers. Some players are highly involved in their religion; they represent intense assimilation and will do anything to further its reach. Some players have characteristics like moderate Christians. They are open-minded and consider all the variables of what their religion offers versus what fits their needs. In the simplest terms, they are doing what it takes to meet their values, and that is what we need to study.

I have identified five different types of players in the hierarchy of the Islamic faith. These players represent groups of people, i.e., constituencies, and their position relative to other players and can be envisioned on a map as a series of circles and ellipses (Diagram 3: Constituencies). While each constituency is responsive to leaders in the broader audience of which it is a part, individual and charismatic leaders at each level shape and direct their followers.

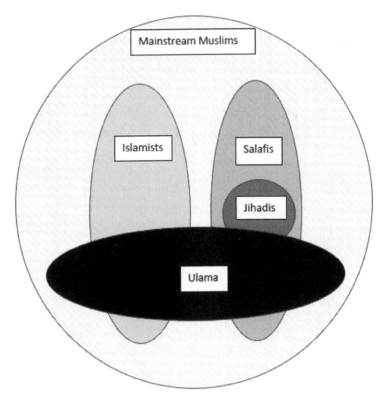

Diagram 3: Constituencies

Mainstream Muslims

Mainstream Muslims, both men and women, are the largest group of adherents; these are people who follow the Qur'an and the sunna of Muhammad. This category includes all branches of Islam, and it ranges from secularists to fundamentalists. This constituency is vast. A survey conducted by Pew Research on American Muslims finds them happy with their lives and moderate concerning many of the issues that have divided Muslims and Westerners worldwide.[3] Some views that mainstream American Muslims shared were that their communities were safe places to live; hard work pays off; about 80 percent of the diaspora reject Islamic extremism,[4] but most doubted the United States government and news media's trustworthiness. In comparison, mainstream Muslims in Middle Eastern countries are more sympathetic and agreeable with the accompanying violence against Israel.

Two issues are controversial to many Muslims: they tend to embrace big government and reject homosexuality. Big government is synonymous with a generous social safety net, and the anti-LGBTQ stance falls in line with teachings from the Qur'an (27:55). Mainstream Muslims go to weekly services as frequently, if not more, as their Christian counterparts, and one unique finding of mainstream Muslims is that only one-third of those sampled say that Islam is the one true faith that leads to eternal life.[5] While these descriptions primarily reflect Muslims in America, they could also reflect mainstream Muslims' views and values almost anywhere in the world. The mainstream Muslim is busy trying to earn a living, raise a family, and provide room and board for the charges in their custody. They depend on their religious leaders and their government officials to make their life easier with policies and dogma that fit their needs. The next stop is a quick look at how government and religion interact with mainstream Muslims.

Sunni Muslims (85 percent of adherents) do not have a defined hierarchy in their religion. The imam in their mosque is not part of a centralized network of leaders. Many years ago, they lived under a caliphate that dictated government policies and religious dogma. The caliphate's purpose was to provide the people with rules and laws that met Islamic theology criteria. If the caliphate afforded the proper exercise of religion and order, Sunnis abided by the caliphate's leadership even when they were foreign. When the last legitimate caliphate, the Ottoman Empire, dissolved in 1922 as it supported the Axis Powers in the First World War, there was no religious authority to fill the vacuum. The local governments in the Sunni-majority regions that were part of the Ottoman Empire had a lack of experience supplying the spiritual need that their constituents required. In other words, the local governments, while mostly secular, caused a rift between religion and governmental authority. Even today, a century later, most citizens in those countries ruled by the Ottomans languish under their country, city, or local governments because there is no religious leadership. The "Arab Spring" was a clear symptom of this problem. The Arab Spring was a series of anti-government protests, uprisings, and armed rebellions that spread across much of the Arab world in the early 2010s.

The Shi'a (approximately 15 percent of adherents) have a hierarchy in their belief system, a little like the Catholic Church but more comprehensive. Their Ayatollah not only rules on temporal issues but state decisions as well. In both cases, with no caliphate to provide religious doctrine, mainstream Muslims are dependent upon their governments for what little direction they provide in Muslim theology.

There is a caveat that affects both Sunni and Shiite constituencies. The government depends on the ulama, Muslim scholars, who determine whether a course of action or a decision to be made fits in with sharia. In Diagram 3 above, note that ulama can directly interact with each of the players. The ulama debate governmental policies as to whether they fit with the Qur'an, sunna, and consensus. For example, the Qur'an promises that for the poor and needy, their basic needs will be met (51:19). Thus, most Muslim governments provide generous social safety nets, inadvertently removing the incentives to look for immediate work.[6]

One more finding helps explain the dichotomy between the Islamist players and the Salafi and Jihadist players mentioned in the next section. A recent study by Koopmans et al. (2020) researched the violence that we recognize as linked to or caused by strong religious beliefs.[7] Global violence by groups can be found originating from all the major religions. The research from this study determined that the level of fundamentalist belief was a strong indicator of religious violence. A survey of over 4,000 Muslim respondents in seven countries across Europe, North America, the Middle East, and Africa found that 49 percent would be classified as fundamentalists. Two of the defining features of fundamentalism are the belief in the literal interpretation of scripture, and fundamentalists are more prone to violence in support of their views. When Muhammad says to kill the apostate in certain situations, the Muslim fundamentalist will kill the apostate. This research explains the clean break between the Salafis and Jihadists who fall into the fundamentalist camp and the nontraditional Islamists.

The Islamists

An Islamist is an Islamic political or social activist who wants Islamic law, sharia, to be the primary source of governance and cultural identity in a state.[8] For the most part, these players are more liberal than traditional Muslims working for both social reform and political reform in Muslim countries. Each Islamist group promotes Islam, and Islamic values differ widely from group to group, given their local circumstances. Many of these adherents belong to the Muslim Brotherhood or Brotherhood-inspired organizations willing to embrace new ideas such as technology to enhance the religion's traditional values. The main difference between a mainstream Muslim and an Islamist is the degree of passivity. Mainstream Muslims are occupationally focused and become passive to the ever-present needs of Islam. Islamists are activists or active in their religion, helping organizations that meet the community's needs.

Two forces have strained Islam, one being the radical imams who condemn mainstream believers as straying from Islam's core principles. The second is the introduction of Western ideas and concepts in law, politics, civics, and government. First, Islamists feel the need to modernize the educational and religious practices and challenge the puritan strand of Islam that dominates the Middle East. The political reformer Islamist prioritizes such issues as popular participation, institution-building, constitutionalism, and elections. The general theme behind Islamism is as follows:

- The rejection of terrorist activities in Muslim countries and the West except for Israel.
- The advocation of peaceful political participation.
- Rejecting the use of takfir or excommunication from the religion as a strategic lever.
- The acceptance of plurality and tolerance with other nonreligious groups to achieve group goals.
- The establishment of an Islamic state governed by sharia, using proselytization on the local level and legislation on the national level.
- Using hierarchical organizations to project power and conduct face-to-face interactions nationally.
- The manipulation of social networks such as mosques, charities, and organizational systems to generate public recognition and, ultimately, voter turnout.

While Islamists portray themselves as nonviolent and non-confrontational and willing to work within the system, there should be no illusions about the ideological commitments. The crux of the debate between Jihadists and Islamists is not over the ends, "but rather the means by which to realize the greater goal of Islamic governance throughout the Muslim world."[9]

The Salafis

Salaf, in Arabic, means "ancestor."[10] Salafism is a branch of Sunni Islam, and Salafis are pious Muslims who want to establish and govern Islamic states based solely on the Qur'an and the sunna of the Prophet as understood by the first generations of Muslims close to Muhammad. This movement is ideologically akin to the early Puritan movement in England as well as America. To purge their practice of modern influences, they try to emulate the founders of the faith – the Prophet Muhammad's contemporaries and the two generations that came after his death in AD 632. Young Salafis, for example, often dress in sandals and robes like those worn in seventh-century Arabia.

Several very significant and traumatic schisms, both theological and political, characterized early Muslim history. As a result, several competing religious and political doctrines emerged among Muslims, which posed problems for the religion's governance. One dominant theme that emerged was the desire to be like the first generations that surrounded Muhammad and his Companions – the epithet "Salafi" designates a pious person or possessing various kinds of noble characteristics and virtuous features reminiscent of the Prophet's time.

Side Note: According to the hadith, men should wear beards (see the hadith in Chapter 2, al-Bukhari, Volume 7, Hadith #781). Those most closely associated with beards are the Salafis. The leading case for beards in the hadith is linked explicitly to set the Muslims apart and distinguish them based on clothing and outward appearance from polytheists, Jews, and Christians. According to the sunna, the Companions carefully trimmed their beards, and Muhammad, himself, encouraged short or no mustaches.

With the rise of political Islam, the beard, especially a full beard in the Salafi tradition, is recognized as a sign of deep piety. In the terrorist organization known as the Islamic State, beards are mandatory. ISIS even added a prohibition on mocking the beard, using the Qur'an (9:65-66) to justify their rationale.[11] In 2014, the U.S. military released a new policy outlining how religious service members might apply for a waiver to wear a beard as a way of expressing religious views.[12]

The Salafist interpretation of Islamic doctrine tends to be literal and originalist. Salafism focuses on eliminating idolatry (*shirk*) and affirming God's Oneness (*tawhid*).[ee] Salafis see themselves as the only authentic Muslims, and they have distinct views and opinions about religion and politics:

- Salafis are religious, not political activists.
- Salafis avoid political or organizational allegiances because they divide the Muslim community and distract Islam's study.
- Salafis believe it is not permissible to revolt against a Muslim government.
- Salafis tend to see the concept of jihad in defensive terms – aiding Muslims under attack rather than waging war for aggressive purposes. Salafis and jihadis agree that any jihad can only be defensive, but they have radically different notions of what constitutes defense.[13]

Salafis reject association with organizations or people willing to compromise religious purity for political objectives. They refuse acceptance of more liberal and inclusive groups willing to recognize some good even in so-called "deviant" teachings. The "purists" categorically reject the Islamists for embracing members who contaminate the religion with discouraged practices (such as democracy or usury). Not only will they not communicate with them, but they also reject funding from any source that has deviant organizations among its grantees. Ironically, this implies that the most "radical" of the Salafis would be the most immune to jihadist teachings, while the "more moderate" Salafis may be open to jihadist overtures.

Salafism is the most conservative form of Islam. The movement developed in Egypt in the late 19th century as a response to Western European colonization. Even then, it had roots in the 18th-century Wahhabi movement that originated and thrives in Saudi Arabia, even today.[14]

Jihadis

Jihadis, "holy warriors," are some of today's most prominent terrorists.[ff] These players can be part of the broader Salafi Movement, but note, most Salafis are not jihadis. Jihadi-Salafism is a unique ideological combination in Sunni Islam. It involves an international network of scholars, websites, media outlets, and, most recently, vast numbers of social media supporters.[gg]

Two streams of Islamic thought contributed to the emergence of the jihadi school in the latter part of the twentieth century. The first stream of thought was Salafism; a Sunni theological movement concerned with purifying the faith. The second school of thought caused an adverse reaction among the militant Salafis, and that was the Muslim Brotherhood, which originated in Egypt in 1928. The Muslim Brotherhood, which still wanted sharia and all its trappings, was a political movement that worked through civil activism to develop an Islamic constituency. The Muslim Brotherhood evolved in reaction to Western concepts such as democracy and political parties. It was willing to use tolerance and subjectivity in dealing with "quasi" Muslim governments and movements. That was unacceptable to the jihadist movement.

Side Note: The hatred between Iran and Saudi Arabia began when Wahhabism evolved in the eighteenth century. Salafis hate Shiites (the dominant sect in Iran) because they practice idolatry, such as the worship of saints, shrines, tombs of prominent clerics, and the excessive reverence of some of the Prophet Muhammad's family. Salafis consider the Shiites as apostates and deserters of the religion. Conflicts escalated in 1792 when Saudi Wahhabi forces attacked the Shiites in eastern Arabia. Later in 1802, they sacked the shrine and city of Karbala, Iraq. In 1927, the Saudis sought to convert or expel Shi'a clerics forcibly.[15] Even today, the conflict still simmers, with the U.S. Trump administration in 2017, at the behest of the Saudi government, putting trade sanctions on the Iranian government.

Jihadis need a totalitarian system of government in which the Qur'an and hadiths are the governing parameters. Anyone who does not share their understanding of Islam will be declared an apostate. If one wants to know what a jihadi state will look like, contemplate the Taliban or ISIS's self-proclaimed caliphate – some examples of organizations that jihadis consider legitimately Islamic.

The key points to recognize about jihadis are as follows:

- Unity of thought – no pluralism and no democracy.
- Unadulterated sharia in every country in the Middle East.
- The violence they do to their people and governments are 1) necessary, 2) religiously sanctioned, and 3) the fault of the West, Israel, and apostate regimes.
- They see their fight as a conflict between Islam and the apostate West. Apostate countries dominate Islamic

states, and only the jihadis can break through.

- Finally, Middle East countries are weak; they do not have the political will to remove tyrants or reform their societies.

Side Note: While the Taliban is considered the type of Islamic state that Jihadis would emulate, their leader, Mawlawi Hibatullah Akhundzada, is not regarded as qualified to be a caliph. So, what are the qualifications to be a caliph?

- "To qualify for the caliphate, a person has to be an adult male of the tribe of Quraysh (Muhammad's tribe), of good character, free from mental and physical defects, with administrative ability, knowledge of the Qur'an and hadith, and the courage to defend the territory of Islam."[16]
- How did Hibatullah Akhundzada fall short of the qualifications? First, he was not of the Quraysh tribe. Second, the caliph must espouse proper Salafi theology, not the Hanafi School of Law's interpretation of the law.[17]

Jihadis lose credibility among mainstream Muslims when they attack innocent citizens, damage the sources of a nation's wealth such as tourism or oil, kill other Muslims and declare other Muslims as apostates. Criticism from influential religious leaders in the ulama is particularly damaging to their cause, as is criticism from former jihadis and prominent current jihadis. Denunciation from these sources can damage their ability to recruit fighters and funding; thus, a renegade terrorist unit can find itself alone in the field with no resources and no cooperation from other like-minded jihadis.

The Ulama

The ulama (also spelled ulema) are the religious scholars of Islam. This category includes muftis, sheiks, and imams. More than any of the other players, these scholars impact economic, social, and political change. Of course, governments can also bring about change, but they do so by providing incentives or restrictions, i.e., through coercion. In contrast, the ulama has authority through the prestige of their influence, and this is usually more profound and longer lasting than when a government forces compliance.

Islam is a comprehensive lifestyle, whether on a public or private level, individual or communal, political, civil, or economic. Most of the day-to-day decisions in a Muslim's life are predetermined, but some are not. Take democracy, for example. Should a Muslim citizen vote in an upcoming election? A religious scholar with the Islamist philosophy would first scour the Qur'an, the hadith, and consensus opinions to find reasons to support the act of voting. A religious scholar with Salafist leanings would do the same and find reasons not to participate in the election. The scholar's prestige and importance are hidden values that can sway the indecisive person. Because every act requires religious justification, organizations, governments, and even terrorist groups have their staff of ulama. One issue that is mentioned frequently about the more famous and influential religious scholars is that they are given a great deal of respect by their followers, so much so that their followers and students blindly follow them without considering the sources of Islam directly.[18]

Islam stresses the direct connection between the individual believer and God; the ulama are not Islam's equivalent of priests. They have obtained a role in Islamic society that is far more comprehensive than that of Christian priests. One might view the ulama from the Western point of view of adversarial law. For example, Palestinian suicide bombings raised questions of religious legitimacy. The *mufti* (head of the ulama) in Saudi Arabia said, "such attacks are not a part of the jihad, and I fear that they are just suicides, plain and simple," and concluded from this that suicide bombings are illegal in Islam.[19] One Muslim Brotherhood leader, also a religious scholar, rebutted this *fatwa* (a legal ruling) and justified the bombings, calling them "martyrdom operations."

In general, the ulama's position strengthens or weakens, depending on a particular government's mindset toward Islam. They flourish in locations like Iran, Afghanistan, and Sudan – countries strictly governed by Islamic principles. The influence that the ulama has is in direct proportion to Islam's use as a governing philosophy. These scholars devote their lives to the study of the Qur'an and sunna, the two primary sources of sharia. Members of the ulama are experts in religious doctrine. Regarded as the keepers of Islam by mainstream Muslims, the ulama interpret and administer sharia law. This acknowledgment, in turn, gives them many roles to play; their advice is sought on every issue, from the proper way to keep a kitchen to the rules of warfare. Absolutely nothing is beyond the range of the Qur'an; thus, for this reason, no subject matter is beyond their reach.

Side Note: Assuming the fatwa issued is in an orthodox Islamic country, a fatwa can have the force of law. So, what does it take for a religious scholar to be able to issue such a ruling?[20] The main criteria are:

1. To issue a fatwa, one must have all the learning requirements. The scholar must know everything in the Qur'an and sunna plus any rulings by consensus and analogy that might relate to the issue at hand. Quranic verses cannot be "cherry-picked" that present one side of a controversy.

2. The scholar must have mastery of the Arabic language. Arabic is the language of the Qur'an. Translations distort meanings, and it is possible that in the conversion, the content changes.

3. The scholar cannot ignore established Islamic sciences and oversimplify sharia. Interpretation of the law focuses on either the verdicts of consensus or analogy versus the Qur'an and sunna. The scholar must envelop both for an influential fatwa.

4. It is acceptable for scholars to have differing opinions, except concerning knowledge of orthodox Islam, which all Muslims must know.

5. Fatwas must have some realistic outcome.

These are the main points that the ulama must follow to issue fatwas. It is not everyone who can become a scholar, and a fatwa from a renowned scholar always carries more weight than one from an unknown scholar.

The ulama has no formal legislative role, so their power is exercised in two ways: they exert influence over public opinion and legitimize (or not) the ruler's authority. They can usually be found in a mosque, although they are not always the imam, or they may represent some religious school or organization. The ulama is particularly in demand where Islam intersects with the modern world. Western technology and thought have become increasingly secular, and as many Muslims would say, "decadent." Many Muslims turn to the ulama as guides through the minefield of modern (Western) life.

Many governments, organizations, and movements maintain a large staff of ulama whom they can consult with to get their actions approved. When needed, the government or the terrorist group can get one of their religious scholars to issue a "fatwa" that endorses their efforts. A fatwa has the effect of legitimizing an activity or behavior by finding godly examples in the Qur'an or sunna and making a case for justification. The caliphate tightly controlled the ulama, making it unlikely that two fatwas would be issued nullifying each other. However, with each Muslim nation having equal sovereignty, it was to be expected that the Palestinians would find an ulama to issue a fatwa nullifying the Saudi fatwa against suicide bombing.

Here is an example of how the ulama can affect free-market competition. A British supermarket chain, Sainsbury's, opened 11 stores in Cairo in 1999. Local grocers, feeling the pinch of business rivalry, petitioned their ulama for assistance. The clerics granted a fatwa condemning shopping at the stores. Unfounded rumors that the supermarket chain was Jewish-owned and donated significant amounts of money to Zionist causes accompanied the fatwa. Senior store executives issued vehement denials but to no avail. Shoppers boycotted the stores, and the supermarket chain pulled out, taking a loss of $100 million.[21]

One important role these religious scholars dominate is determining whether a product or service is halal (permissible or lawful) for the Muslim consumer to use. In the technologically driven West, many products and practices are not halal. Still, with slight changes in their preparation or process or a difference in the ingredients, the product can be made halal or sharia compliant. It is the ulama that evaluates the merchandise and judges them permissible or not.

"Halal" is an Arabic term that means "lawful or permissible." Initially, halal pertained to food products, mainly meat. Some foods and food preparation are not permitted because it affects the quality and nutrition of the food.

Halal does not just pertain to food products. Other products that need to be pronounced halal are cosmetics, personal care products, and pharmaceuticals. Let's take cosmetics for one example. The ingredients for a tube of lipstick may meet halal certification, but the product's end use may not meet Islamic expectations of integrity and self-respect. If the product's advertisement is for healthcare, like the brand Chapstick that protects lips from being cracked, the product might be acceptable to Muslim consumers.

Another example is in pharmaceuticals. In many instances, Muslims have refused to take COVID-19 vaccines. It seems that several of the vaccines use pork-derived gelatin as a stabilizer in their storage and transport phase. On the surface, it would seem this product would not be halal. Several ulama initially came out against the vaccine, but numerous ulama rightly judged that the virus was the more significant threat and supported the vaccine's use, even though it used pork derivatives in its preparation. There are other vaccines for measles, polio, diphtheria, and meningitis, to name a few, that use this protocol. Also, other necessary medicines have side effects that cause addiction, abortions, and birth control that are not halal. Still, their acceptance would lead to a higher quality of life.

"Sharia-compliant" usually refers to taking a product that does not meet sharia guidelines and changing it so that it does. Modifying a product's ingredients, or the process of preparation, or how the product is used can sometimes meet the standards imposed by sharia. It then becomes sharia compliant. Most frequently, this term is used in the financial industry, but it can be used for other products and other industries as well. In the Qur'an and hadith, practices that are haram are usury, ambiguity in contracts, gambling, games of chance, speculation, financial derivatives, fraud, bribery, the use of false weights and standards, taking others' property unlawfully, and transactions on prohibited things.

There is much confusion as to what is permissible and what is not. That is what the ulama are for; to research the Qur'an, hadith, the sunna, and any laws of consensus to pronounce a product or service as halal or haram.

It may be strange to the Western mindset, but the ulama are

crucial in decision-making in a Muslim-dominated organization. The more religious an Islamic country is, the more power the ulama have. Any Western operation doing business in a Muslim country should consider engaging a religious scholar as a consultant to advise religious rulings on its behalf.

Chapter Summary

If an outside observer of Islam stood back and looked, they would notice a well-defined organizational structure. Just like any organization, some categories are primed to do specific duties. It is no surprise to see this effect in Muslim countries either. Mainstream Muslims function as worker bees to keep the economy rolling. Islamists are the progressives always seeking better ways to get something done, and the Salafis are the fundamentalists that like things the way their ancestors did. Jihadists represent those who believe that force must be used to protect and spread Muhammad's message. Interacting with each level of the organization are the religious scholars, the ulama, who make themselves available to interpret sharia as it applies to everyday decisions. The ulama must evaluate each new development that requires a decision for their interpretation. Their analysis and explanations keep companies, organizations, and even countries from violating sharia.

End-of-Chapter Notes

ee.   Shirk and tawhid are covered in Chapter 4.

ff.   The use of "jihadi" to designate Salafis of a militant stripe is controversial. Jihad has positive connotations in Islam and those who fight to further the cause think of themselves as "holy warriors." The term was used in the Arab media by Iyad Al-Baghdadi, "Salafi, Jihadis, Takfir: Demystifying Militant Islamism in Syria." January 15, 2013.

gg.   Out of 1.8 billion Muslims, one estimate places the number of Jihadis between 100,000 and 230,000 across almost 70 countries. See Seth Jones, Charles Vallee, Danika Newlee, Nicholas Harrington, Clayton Sharb, and Hannah Byrne, "The Evolution of the Salafi-Jihadist Threat: Current and Future Challenges from the Islamic State, Al-Qaeda, and Other Groups," *Center for Strategic and International Studies*, November 2018, pp. 7-9.

Chapter 13

Where is Islam Headed?

Let me share a selfish secret with you – I wrote this book for myself. There were many things I did not understand about Islam, and this opportunity to research specific issues about the religion also illuminated my understanding of Christianity. So, what causes the enmity between the Arabs and the Jewish people? How can one branch of Islam legitimately kill adherents from other sects of Islam? What is sharia, and how does sharia finance affect international trade? Is Islam the religion of peace? There were a lot of whys, whats, and hows that I investigated. My aim is for the chapters in this book to provide a rationale why Islam functions the way it does. My research also provided me with an incentive to look at my religion. What I found was not so good, but it was interesting. Before my research, I found the Bible an uninteresting history book. Now, I see it as a sourcebook that helps explains the history behind many aspects of Islam. While I am still a Christian, I see my religion's flaws much more clearly than before. That will be a topic for another time. For now, let me hypothesize where I see Islam trending.

So, what could go wrong (for Islam, that is)

Usually, when one sees a comment like that, it implies a lighthearted hint that many things could go wrong with the current situation. I propose that we do not take for granted that Islam will be the future's dominant religion. Western values are under attack because of a changing world, but so are those of Islam. Four situations are poised to change the Islamic faith as we move forward in the future.

1. The growth of Islam is not assured.

Pundits predict that Islam will overtake Christianity in the number of adherents sometime within the next 30-50 years. The youth of Muslim populations and the fertility of their family units are the basis of their growth projections. A family unit composed of a patriarch with several young wives could propagate their growth beyond expectations. However, there are two reasons why I do not believe that will happen.

First, looking at world population growth, some credible organizations backed by the United Nations' funding suggest that the world population will plateau by 2050-60.[1] Climate change and environmental disorders are acknowledged as culprits causing famines, food shortages, and resource depletion. These problems will hit the poorer nations much worse than those with capital resources and technology to bail them out. As painful as it sounds, several Muslim countries fall into that category. The UN estimates 100 to 200 million people are facing crisis levels of starvation or worse.[2]

Second, there are no developed Islamic countries like the United States, Japan, or Germany in terms of economic development. However, there *are* numerous emerging countries like Iran, Jordan, and Turkey. An emerging country is one with a high level of economic growth, usually through industrialization. Different sources designate anywhere from 45 to 50 Islamic states as emerging countries.[hh] Of all Islamic countries, the World Bank estimates 25 percent have per capita incomes that put their populations in the middle-class bracket or better.[3] This middle-income designation includes countries like Iran, Iraq, Jordan, Turkey, and Saudi Arabia.

I am going with this argument because many Islamic countries have tasted the bitter fruit of capitalism. They are working hard to modernize their countries, and with modernization, women become emancipated; children cease to become a form of social security, and childbearing statistics shrink. As we experienced this shrinkage in the West where, over two generations, families have shrunk from having 10-15 family members to two to four, it could feasibly happen throughout the Muslim world as more countries move from developing country status to emerging country status.

2. Radical Islamic extremism is losing what little bit of empathy it had with mainstream Muslims and worldwide citizens.

After the Second World War, the Nuremberg Trials administered the penalties for war crimes committed by 24 Nazi officials.[4] The Nazi officials argued they had followed their superiors' orders and acted under their value system's framework as perpetuated by the Nazi Party. Under normal conditions, the "superior order's defense" does not hold up. Usually, a soldier, who commits atrocities at the behest of his superior, should know better because the organization would not condone such activity. However, the argument was different in Germany's case – Adolph Hitler was the leader of the Nazi Party, but Friedrich Nietzsche shaped its ideology.[5]

Nietzsche, a German philosopher of the late nineteenth century, wrote that Christianity and Judaism were responsible for Western cultural weakness.[6] Nietzsche's books, *The Anti-Christ, Beyond Good and Evil, Thus Spoke Zarathustra*, and *The Will to Power*, all suggested he favored the concept of eugenics and the idea of breeding a master race. The theories of Social Darwinism had primed Nietzsche's ideology expounded in the late nineteenth century in the United States and Western Europe. This ideology was one of the concepts that justified the slaughter and extermination of the Jews and the mentally and physically disabled.[7] Nietzsche's philosophy was responsible for crafting Nazi policy to form the idea of Aryan supremacy. Much, if not all, of the dogma of the Nazi Party celebrated Nietzsche's philosophy and adopted it as its own.

The defense of many Nazis on trial at Nuremberg was that their superiors' orders were in line with their values and legal system. It was, therefore, acceptable to follow their directions. However, the court's rulings found that the atrocities were so brutal that "what is utterly immoral cannot be law."[8] When laws and morals separate, society must follow morals, or it will surely fall. As the Prophet Isaiah lamented as he prophesied the fall of Israel to the Babylonians (Isaiah 5:20):

Woe to those who call evil good and good evil,
Who put darkness for light and light for darkness,
Who put bitter for sweet and sweet for bitter?[9]

Now, take this example from Nuremberg and place it alongside radical Islam. Islam teaches that the Prophet Muhammad is the best example of moral behavior for humanity (33:21). Sunna, and their supporting hadiths, supplement the Qur'an as a total philosophy of Islam. If we look at Muhammad's biography, there are stories where he ordered several individuals' deaths for writing poetry against him.[10] If we bring this forward to today, we look at terrorist activities where similar actions occur for the same reasons. For example, terrorists killed 12 people at the magazine *Charlie Hebdo* in 2015 for ridiculing the Islamic faith.[11]

Under Islam's auspices, Muhammad commands his followers to kill for reasons that we in the Western world would see no justification. They have their superior, Muhammad, and they have their philosophy, the Qur'an, and sunna. The Nazis had theirs as well. At some point, non-radical Muslims and the ulama will recognize what the Nuremberg jurists declared, "what is utterly immoral cannot be law."

3. The religious values of Islam will lose the war of ideas. A quasi-capitalist religion cannot compete with, much

less defeat a religion comprised of free will and tolerance for free markets.

I made the case in Chapter 8 that Islam is a religion that embraces free markets but restricts society with limited speech, no freedom of religion, and onerous financial obligations. Islam endorses private ownership, hard work, and a free market. It also supports a distributive mindset where capital is not accumulated but disbursed for the community's needs. We also recognize that Muslims are paranoid about outsiders that criticize or mock the faith or its founder. Muslims use religious tactics to eliminate competition (Chapter 12) and define their community as subservient to the Qur'an and hadith (Chapter 9). Islamic countries find it convenient to ignore democratic institutions that protect individual freedoms because they believe God can make better decisions than men. Many Islamic majority countries treat Christian and Jewish residents as second-class citizens. What we can conclude is that there is no individual freedom of speech or action under Islam. Capitalism with liberal democracy is the most efficient means of resource allocation, and liberal democracy is a direct result of Christianity.[12] When liberal democracy is restricted, capitalism loses its effectiveness as a resource allocator.

Free-market economies function well in the allocation of resources. Consumer freedom allows the invisible hand of the marketplace to determine which products make it and which ones do not. Ideas are part of that free-market mentality. Theories are susceptible to testing, criticism, and accountability – even assumptions about religion. Christianity was subject to opinion, and the Reformation was the result. If Islam, or any religion, cannot take the criticism, it must be a weak religion that its adherents are afraid to hold up to the light.

Christianity is the religion of free-market economies and individual rights. When the efficient allocation of resources couples with new ideas and concepts that meet people's needs, the community is the beneficiary of such a religion. While Islam may be a religion that comes from God, it does not have the checks and balances that have emerged in the Christian community.

4. Unless sharia opens its doors to critical thinking and reasoning, its laws and society will remain feudal and underdeveloped. They will have no hope for a better place in the future.

Critical thinking defined here is the "process of constructing thoughts, views, and legal stands via evaluation, comparison, analysis, and synthesis of the available source materials."[13] Islamic scholars can make passionate cases that stir the heart and motivate the faithful, but Christian theologians are taught to approach any subject with more analysis, using a systems approach that includes deductive and inductive approaches. Even the Bible tells us to "test everything. Hold on to the good" (1 Thessalonians 5:21). Most Western philosophers are familiar with the "Socratic" method of critical thinking. Asking questions is the Socratic method of learning, and his way of discourse was to probe a subject to find holes or weaknesses in the framework. Ardent Muslims will vow that their religion is open to critical thinking. But that is not the case as evidenced by these two analogies: 1) Muslim jurists, by and large, still cling to laws made through the traditional culture of the past for use and application in the present day. 2) Most Muslim schools focus on rote memorization of the Qur'an and discourage independent thinking. People from Islamic cultures generally assess truth through lines of authority, not individual reasoning. Early Islam's authoritative nature and the relatively high illiteracy rates in modern Muslim societies require oral didactics grounded in authority structures. When the Ottoman Empire was dismantled, the ulama became the obvious disperser of authority. Of course, individuals engage in critical reasoning in Muslim countries, but it is relatively less valued and less prevalent than in the West.[14]

There were two periods when Muslims used critical thinking to develop their civilization. When Muhammad died in the seventh century, he left little organization on how laws were to be decided upon and enforced. The use of critical thinking developed a corpus of jurisprudence from which to govern the community. Second, during the Islamic Golden Age, which dated from the eighth century to the thirteenth century, scholars made strides in math, algebra, astronomy, medicine, literature, technology, and architecture.[15] But then the door was shut. It is no coincidence that Islam's geographical spread reached its zenith toward the end of this period.

In accepting critical thinking, Muslims must deal with two dimensions: faith and rationality. Adherents do not see the conflict between the two, but the literalism of Islam restrains critical thinking.[16] Islamic cultures tend to establish state leaders and religious scholars as authorities, whereas Western culture's authority is reason itself. Critical thinking questions everything, including God's righteousness, but Islam does not tolerate this. When authority is derived from the position rather than reason, the act of questioning leadership is dangerous because it has the potential to upset the system.[17] Muslims do not query God's actions or the interpretations of his laws because it is seen as questioning leadership.

Consequently, in Islamic countries, governing rulers and religious scholars maintain that questioning God's activities is to be an apostate. When authority is derived from reason, questions are expected because critical examination sharpens and legitimizes the very basis of authority. The result is that Muslims have gotten themselves into a big box of quicksand.

National leaders and religious scholars will not be of much help in this matter, either. For the ulama, their power is knowledge of the holy texts. Critical thinking means to question their decisions on a topic. If their writings, lectures, or fatwas are questionable, their credibility is also. Leaders do not want mainstream Muslims to question their authority or their actions. They can lose power and influence in that manner. That explains their lack of democratic institutions. Muslim leaders maintain that democracy is not as good as God's law, but more than once, it was apparent that a Muslim leader was not so right with God.

Chapter Summary

Muslims have a religious ideology that once represented the state-of-the-art precepts that showed the way to heaven. Their driving force is not what it was before. In the religion's early years, this fit their lifestyle and their customs. Fourteen centuries later, lifestyles have changed, but their belief system has not. While you would think that the doorway to heaven would always be the same throughout eternity, the political, social, and religious environment has changed. Islam has not changed, creating tensions not only with Western countries but also between Islamic nations. Muslims have become stereotyped with established patterns of behavior that I cover in this book. If they want to become all that they can be, they must not only become tolerant of others with pluralistic visions but force themselves to change as well.

End-of-Chapter Notes

hh. According to the Pew Research Center, in 2015 there were 50 Muslim-majority countries. Worldatlas.com identified 45 Islamic countries (April 2017).

Reference Notes

Preface

1. Dictionary.com (n.d.), "mechanics." Retrieved January 9, 2021, from https://www.dictionary.com/browse/mechanics

Introduction

1. A. Bakalian and M. Bozorgmehr, *Backlash 9/11* (Oakland, CA: University of California Press, 2009), 40.

2. Eric Schmitt, "In Battle to Defang ISIS, U.S. Targets Its Psychology," *The New York Times*, December 28, 2014.

3. E.M. Caner and E.F. Caner, *Unveiling Islam* (Grand Rapids, MI: Kregel Publications, 2009), 203.

4. Amy Zegart, "Insider Threats and Organizational Root Causes: The 2009 Fort Hood Terrorist Attack," *The U.S. Army War College Quarterly, Parameters* 45, no. 2 (2015): 42.

5. Costas Panagopoulos, "The Polls-Trends: Arab and Muslim Americans and Islam in the aftermath of 9/11," *Public Opinion Quarterly* 70, no. 4 (2006): 608-624.

6. Andrew C. McCarthy, "Islam – Facts or Dreams?" *Imprimis* 45, no. 2 (2016): 2.

7. "Sharifa Alkhateeb – Muslim educator shares ultimate goal of Muslim education in America." Accessed March 12, 2018, from https://www.c-span.org/video/?c4673227/user-clip-sharifa-alkhateeb-muslim-director-shares-ultimate-goal-muslim-education-america

8. Brian Dodwell, Daniel Milton, and Don Rassler, "The Caliphate's Global Workforce: An Inside Look at the Islamic State's Foreign Fighter Paper Trail," Combating Terrorism Center at West Point, April 2016, 18-19.

9. International Crisis Group, "Indonesia Backgrounder: Why Salafism and Terrorism Mostly Don't Mix," *Asia Report #83*. Published September 13, 2004.

10. Jacob Zenn, "The Terrorist Calculus in Kidnapping Girls in Nigeria: Cases from Chibok and Dapchi," *CTC Sentinel* 4, no. 3 (2018): 4.

11. T.A. Walton, "Eyes of the Ospreys: An Analysis of RAF Coastal Command's Operational Research Section in Counter-U-Boat Operations," *International Journal of Naval History* 12, no. 3 (2015): https://www.ijnhonline.org/eyes-of-the-ospreys-an-analysis-of-raf-coastal-commands-operational-research-section-in-counter-u-boat-operations/

12. Max Weber, *The Protestant Ethic and the "Spirit" of Capitalism* (New York: Scribner, 1958).

13. Robert D. Woodberry, "The Missionary Roots of Liberal Democracy," *American Political Science Review* 106 (2), May 2012, 244-274.

14. *Farlex Dictionary of Idioms,* s.v.v. "spinning in his grave." Accessed July 21, 2019, https://idioms.thefreedictionary.com/spinning+in+his+grave

15. Denise A. Spellberg, *Thomas Jefferson's Qur'an* (New York: Vintage, 2013), 92.

16. Ibid., 230.

17. Ibid., 235.

18. UShistory, "The Declaration of Independence" (n.d.), https://www.ushistory.org/declaration/document/

19. Spellberg, *Thomas Jefferson's Qur'an*, 236.

Chapter 1

1. Texas A&M University, "6,000 years ago, the Sahara Desert was tropical, so what happened?" *ScienceDaily* (November 30, 2016), www.sciencedaily.com/releases/2016/11/161130141053.htm

2. D. Drummond, *Holy Land, Whose Land?* 2nd ed. (Terre Haute, Indiana: Fairhurst Press, 2004).

3. James Henry Breasted, "Earliest Man, the Orient, Greece,

and Rome," in *Outlines of European History,* ed. James Harvey Robinson, James Henry Breasted and Charles A. Beard (Boston: Ginn, 1914), 56-57.

4. *New International Version Archaeological Study Bible,* "Introduction to Genesis" (Grand Rapids, Michigan: Zondervan, 2005), 2.

5. Amy-Jill Levine, *The Old Testament Course Guidebook* (Chantilly, VA: The Great Courses, 2001), 18.

6. Roger Atwood, "Egypt's Final Redoubt in Canaan," *Archaeology,* July/August 2017, 26-33.

7. Matt Rosenberg, "Largest Cities Throughout History," *ThoughtCo.com.* Last updated July 12, 2018, https://www.thoughtco.com/largest-cities-throughout-history-4068071

8. Ian Morris, "The Dawn of a New Dark Age," *Stratfor.* Last updated July 13, 2016, https://worldview.stratfor.com/article/dawn-new-dark-age

9. Robert P. Maloney, "Usury and Restrictions on Interest-Taking in the Ancient Near East," *The Catholic Biblical Quarterly* 36, no. 1 (1974): 1-20.

10. Timeanddate.com, "Distance from Los Angeles to..." Last updated January 30, 2020, https://www.timeanddate.com/worldclock/distances.html?n=137

11. Richard T. Ritenbaugh, "Bible verses about Way of the Land of the Philistines," *BibleTools.* Last updated January 30, 2020, https://www.bibletools.org/index.cfm/fuseaction/Topical.show/RTD/CGG/ID/7531/Way-of-Land-of-Philistines.htm

12. Bible History online, "The Journeys of Abraham." Last updated January 30, 2020, https://www.bible-history.com/maps/6-abrahams-journeys.html

13. *New International Version Archaeological Study Bible,* 2005.

14. Levine, *The Old Testament Course Guidebook,* 46.

15. *New International Version Archaeological Study Bible,* "Cultural and Historical Notes" and "Archaeological Sites"

(Grand Rapids, MI: Zondervan, 2005), 36 & 52.

16. Sir Sayyid Aḥmad Khān, *A Series of Essays on the Life of Mohammad: and Subjects Subsidiary Thereto* (London: Trübner & Co., 1870), 74-76.

17. Muhammad Marmaduke Pickthall, *The Meaning of The Glorious Koran: An Explanatory Translation* (New York: Alfred A. Knopf, 1930). Consulted online at "Quran Archive – Texts and Studies on the Quran," http://quran-archive.org/explorer/marmaduke-pickthall/1930

18. *Encyclopedia Britannica*, s.v. "Kaaba," accessed January 30, 2020, https://www.britannica.com/topic/Kaaba-shrine-Mecca-Saudi-Arabia

19. Don Jaide, "Shiva Ji, The Black Dreadlock God of India," *Rasta Livewire*. Last updated April 26, 2009, https://www.africaresource.com/rasta/sesostris-the-great-the-egyptian-hercules/shiva-ji-the-black-skinned-dread-locks-god-of-india-the-black-gods-of-india-by-sodhi-ram-dhan-sant-gurdev-hinduism/

20. Martin Armstrong, "Why Was Jesus Crucified?" *Armstrong Economics*. Last accessed December 28, 2017, https://www.armstrongeconomics.com/international-news/rule-of-law/why-was-jesus-crucified/

21. C.C. Wylie and J.R. Naiden, "The Image which Fell Down from Jupiter," *Popular Astronomy*, vol. 44 (1936): 514.

22. *New International Version Archaeological Study Bible*, 2005.

23. Rafat Amari, *Islam: In Light of History* (Prospect Heights, IL: Religion Research Institute, 2004).

24. Ziauddin Sardar, *Mecca: The Sacred City* (New York: Bloomsbury, 2014), 346-47.

25. Pickthall, *The Meaning of The Glorious Koran: An Explanatory Translation*.

26. Ibid.

27. *New International Version Archaeological Study Bible*, "Introduction to Exodus" (Grand Rapids, MI: Zondervan,

2005), 84.

28. *New International Version Cultural Backgrounds Study Bible,* "Literacy" (Grand Rapids, MI: Zondervan, 2016), 140.

29. Ibid., 141.

30. Bart Ehrman, *The New Testament* (Chantilly, VA: The Great Courses, 2000), 101.

31. Clara Moskowitz, "Bible Possibly Written Centuries Earlier, Text Suggests." *Live Science,* January 15, 2010, https://www.livescience.com/8008-bible-possibly-written-centuries-earlier-text-suggests.html

32. Ehrman, *The New Testament,* 137.

33. Mark Allan Powell, *Introducing the New Testament: A Historical, Literary, and Theological Survey,* 2nd ed. (Ada, MI: Baker Academic, 2018).

34. *New International Version Archaeological Study Bible,* 2005.

35. Shahid Bin Waheed (n.d.), Who is the Prophet of Deuteronomy 18:18? http://www.answering-christianity.com/deut1818_rebuttal.htm

36. Joseph P. Gudel, "To Every Muslim an Answer," *Christian Research Journal,* Winter, 1986, 18-25.

37. *New International Version Archaeological Study Bible,* 2005.

38. Islam 101(2006), www.islam101.com/hajj/baca.htm

39. *New International Version Archaeological Study Bible,* 2005.

40. Ibn Ishaq, *The Life of Muhammad,* trans. A. Guillaume (Oxford: Oxford University Press, 1980), 106.

41. *New International Version Archaeological Study Bible,* 2005.

42. Abdu'l-Ahad Dawud, *Muhammad in the Bible,* 5th ed. (Kuwait City: Ministry of Awqaf & Islamic Affairs, 1995), 157.

43. *New International Version Archaeological Study Bible,* 2005.

44. Ibid.

45. Ibid.

46. Ibid.

Chapter 2

1. Denise A. Spellberg, *Thomas Jefferson's Qur'an* (New York: Vintage Books, 2013), 26.

2. Ibid.

3. Dorothy Drummond, *Holy Land, Whose Land?* (Terre Haute, IN: Fairhurst Press, 2004), 165.

4. Bill Warner, "Kafir," *Center for the Study of Political Islam* (n.d.), https://www.cspii.org/education/articles/kafir/

5. Drummond, *Holy Land, Whose Land?* 166-167.

6. Muhammad Marmaduke Pickthall, *The Meaning of The Glorious Koran: An Explanatory Translation* (New York: Alfred A. Knopf, 1930). Consulted online at "Quran Archive – Texts and Studies on the Quran," http://quran-archive.org/explorer/marmaduke-pickthall/1930

7. *Religions*, "Shahadah: the statement of faith." Last updated August 23, 2009, https://www.bbc.co.uk/religion/religions/islam/practices/shahadah.shtml

8. Vincenzo Oliveti, "The House of Islam," in *The Muslim 500: 2016*, ed. S. Abadallah Schleifer (Amman, Jordan: The Royal Islamic Strategic Studies Centre, 2015), 22.

9. *New International Version Archaeological Study Bible*, 2005.

10. Frank Lothar Hossfeld and Erich Zenger, Klaus Baltzer (ed.), *Psalms 3: A Commentary on Psalms 101-150, trans.* Linda M. Maloney (Minneapolis: Fortress Press, 2011), 293-294.

11. Wikipedia, "Dating the Bible," May 3, 2020, https://en.wikipedia.org/wiki/Dating_the_Bible

12. E.M. Caner and E.F. Caner, *Unveiling Islam* (Grand Rapids, MI: Kregel Publications, 2009), 83.

13. Pickthall, *The Meaning of The Glorious Koran: An Explanatory Translation*.

14. Ibid.

15. Mohammad Taqi Usmani, Rafiq Abdur Rehman (ed.), *An Approach to the Qur'anic sciences*, trans. Mohammed Swaleh

Siddiqui (Birmingham: Darul Ish'at, 2000), 191-6.

16. Reza Aslan, "How to Read the Quran," *Slate*, November 20, 2008, www.slate.com/articles/arts/books/2008/11/how_ to_read_the_quran.html

17. Samuel M. Zwemer, "Translations of the Koran," *The Moslem World*, July 1915, 246.

18. Umbreen Javaid, "Religious Militant Extremism: Repercussions for Pakistan," *Political Studies* 1, no. 17, June 30, 2010: 53-62, http://pu.edu.pk/images/journal/ pols/Currentissue-pdf/Religious%20Militant%20 Extremism%5B1%5D.pdf

19. Vir Narain, "Bamiyan and the 'triumph' of education: the growth of the Islamic fundamentalist madrassa system of education in South Asia and some political consequences," *Humanist in Canada*, no. 139 (2001): 10-11. *Gale Academic OneFile* (accessed December 3, 2019), https://link.gale.com/ apps/doc/A30495053/AONE?u=anon~8626b5f0&sid=googl eScholar&xid=5321804f.

20. Ahmed Rashid, *Taliban* (New York: I.B. Tauris, 2000), 23.

21. "The Battle of the Books: The Bible v the Koran," *The Economist*, December 19, 2007, www.economist.com/ node/10311317/

22. Pickthall, *The Meaning of The Glorious Koran: An Explanatory Translation*.

23. Aslan, "How to Read the Quran," *Slate*, November 20, 2008, https://www.slate.com/articles/arts/books/2008/11/ how_to_read_the_quran.html

24. Spellberg, *Thomas Jefferson's Qur'an*, 85.

25. "Scripture Access Statistics," Wycliffe Global Alliance, 2018. Retrieved from https://www.wycliffe.sg/news/2018stats

26. Ali B. Ali-Dinar (ed.), "Quran Translated into 114 Languages," University of Pennsylvania – African Studies Center, 1993, http://www.africa.upenn.edu/Publications/ Quran_Translated_13255.html

27. StackExchange, "What does Islam say about reading the Quran in a language other than Arabic?" (2019), https://islam.stackexchange.com/questions/406/what-does-islam-say-about-reading-the-quran-in-a-language-other-than-arabic

28. Zwemer, "Translations of the Koran," 258.

29. Jewel Hossain Jalil, "The Qur'an: A legal Source?" *Academia* (n.d.), https://www.academia.edu/10731304/The_Qur%CA%BE%C4%81n_A_legal_source

30. Issam Eido, "The Sunnah," *The Encyclopedia of Islamic Bioethics*, July 11, 2019, www.oxfordislamicstudies.com/article/opr/t9002/e0314

31. Ibid.

32. Pickthall, *The Meaning of The Glorious Koran: An Explanatory Translation*.

33. Muhammad Mustafa Azami, *Studies in Hadith Methodology and Literature* (Oak Brook, IL: American Trust Publications, 1977), 1.

34. Munir Ba'Albaki, *Al-Mawrid: A Modern English-Arabic Dictionary*, 7th ed. (Beirut, Lebanon: Dar Ilm Lilmalayin, 1995), 854.

35. N. Ahmad, *Qur'anic and Non-Qur'anic Islam*, 2nd ed. (New York: Vanguard, 1997).

36. Bill Musk, *The Unseen Face of Islam* (London: Monarch, 1989), 277.

37. Muhammad Muhsin Khan, *The Translation of the Meanings of Summarized Sahih Al-Bukhari* (Riyadh, Saudi Arabia: Maktaba Dar-us-Salam, 1996), 949.

38. Muhammad Muhsin Khan, *The Translation of the Meanings of Summarized Sahih Al-Bukhari* (Riyadh, Saudi Arabia: Maktaba Dar-us-Salam, 1996), 949.

39. Bart Ehrman, *Lost Scriptures: Books That Did Not Make It into the New Testament* (Oxford: Oxford University Press, 2003), 19-20.

40. Essam Ayyad, "Early Transmission of Hadith: Incentives and Challenges," *Journal of Islamic and Human Advanced Research* 3, no. 11 (2013): 762-782.

41. Pickthall, *The Meaning of The Glorious Koran: An Explanatory Translation*.

42. Giulio Meotti, "Covering Up Our Culture to Avoid Giving Offense," *The Gatestone Institute*, June 16, 2019, https://www.gatestoneinstitute.org/14363/covering-up-culture

43. Karen Armstrong, *Islam: A Short History* (New York: Random House, 2002), 11.

44. Vocabulary.com., s.v. "abrogation," accessed July 21, 2019, https://www.vocabulary.com/dictionary/abrogation

45. Mike Scruggs, "Is Islam a Religion of Peace and Tolerance?" *The Tribune Papers*, November 26, 2013, http://www.thetribunepapers.com/2013/11/26/is-islam-a-religion-of-peace-and-tolerance/

46. Ahmad ibn al Naqib al Misri, *Umdat al-Salik (Reliance of the Traveller: A Classic Manual of Islamic Sacred Law)*, trans. Nuh Ha Mim Keller (Beltsville, MD: Amana Publications, 1994), 199.

47. Norman L. Geisler and Abdul Saleeb, *Answering Islam* (Grand Rapids, MI: Baker Books, 2002), 98.

48. Pickthall, *The Meaning of The Glorious Koran: An Explanatory Translation*.

49. Anis A. Shorrosh, *Islam Revealed* (Nashville: Thomas Nelson, 1988), 163.

50. Mohammad Hashim Kamali, *Principles of Islamic Jurisprudence*, 3rd ed. (Cambridge, UK: The Islamic Texts Society, 2003).

51. Justin Parrott, "Jihad in Islam: Just-War Theory in the Quran and Sunnah," Yaqeen Institute of Islamic Research, October 16, 2016, https://yaqeeninstitute.org/justin-parrott/jihad-as-defense-just-war-theory-in-the-quran-and-sunnah/#.Xji6xCNMGUk

52. *New International Version Archaeological Study Bible*, 2005.

53. Ibid.

54. Spellberg, *Thomas Jefferson's Qur'an*, x.

55. Josh Magness, "New Muslim congresswoman to be sworn in with Thomas Jefferson's centuries-old Quran," *McClatchy*, January 3, 2019, www.mcclatchydc.com/news/politics-government/article223866655.html

56. Ibid.

57. Spellberg, *Thomas Jefferson's Qur'an*, 85.

58. Ibid., 92.

59. Ibid., 230.

Chapter 3

1. Sahih al-Bukhari, Volume 9, Book 84:57-58, https://www.sahih-bukhari.com/Pages/Bukhari_9_84.php

2. Maurice Bucaille, *The Bible, the Qur'an and Science*, trans. Pannell and Bucaille (Paris: Seghers, 1983), 120-21.

3. *New International Version Archaeological Study Bible*, 2005.

4. Samuel M. Zwemer, *The Moslem Doctrine of God* (New York: American Tract Society, 1905), 34.

5. Muhammad Marmaduke Pickthall, *The Meaning of The Glorious Koran: An Explanatory Translation* (New York: Alfred A. Knopf, 1930). Consulted online at "Quran Archive – Texts and Studies on the Quran," http://quran-archive.org/explorer/marmaduke-pickthall/1930

6. N.L. Geisler and A. Saleeb, *Answering Islam*, 2nd ed. (Grand Rapids, MI: Baker Books, 2002), 145.

7. *New International Version Archaeological Study Bible*, 2005.

8. Bart Ehrman, "Scope," *The New Testament* (Chantilly, VA: The Great Courses, 2000), 3.

9. Amy-Jill Levine, *The Old Testament Course Guidebook* (Chantilly, VA: The Great Courses, 2001), 19.

10. Ehrman, "Scope," *The New Testament*, 130.

11. Nabeel Qureshi, *Seeking Allah, Finding Jesus* (Zondervan,

2014), 181.

12. Ibid., 131.
13. Ibid., 133.
14. Ibid., 34.
15. Ibid., 5.
16. *New International Version Archaeological Study Bible*, 2005.
17. Ibid.
18. Merriam-Webster, s.v. "allegory," https://www.merriam-webster.com/dictionary/allegory
19. S. Marc Cohen, "The Allegory of the Cave," *Philosophy 320*, 2006, https://faculty.washington.edu/smcohen/320/index.html
20. Ehrman, "Scope," *The New Testament*, 32.
21. "Jesus vs. Paul," *Doctrine.org*, 2019, https://doctrine.org/jesus-vs-paul
22. Ehrman, "Scope," *The New Testament*, 134.
23. Geisler and Saleeb, *Answering Islam*, 213.
24. Pickthall, *The Meaning of The Glorious Koran: An Explanatory Translation*.
25. Geisler and Saleeb, *Answering Islam*, 55.
26. Ibid., 47.
27. Badru Kateregga and David Shenk, *Islam and Christianity* (Grand Rapids: William B. Eerdmans Publishing, 1980), 35.
28. Pickthall, *The Meaning of The Glorious Koran: An Explanatory Translation*.
29. Ibid.
30. Ibid.
31. "Break the Cross," *Dabiq*, no. 15, 2016, 55.
32. Valerie Tarico, Chapter 2, "Christian Belief through the Lens of Cognitive Science," in John W. Loftus, ed., *The Christian Delusion: Why Faith Fails* (Amherst, NY: Prometheus Books, 2010), 49.
33. Nicholas Rathod, "The Founding Fathers' Religious Wisdom," *Center for American Progress*, January 8, 2008,

https://www.americanprogress.org/issues/religion/news/2008/01/08/3794/the-founding-fathers-religious-wisdom/

34. Jesus-Islam.org, "Why did the Christians hide the gospel of Barnabas?" (n.d.), http://www.jesus-islam.org/questions/pourquoi-les-chretiens-ont-ils-cache-levangile-de-barnabas/

35. Matt Perman, "What is the Doctrine of the Trinity?" January 23, 2006, https://www.desiringgod.org/articles/what-is-the-doctrine-of-the-trinity

36. Ray Pritchard, "God in Three Persons: A Doctrine We Barely Understand" (2019), https://www.christianity.com/god/trinity/god-in-three-persons-a-doctrine-we-barely-understand-11634405.html

37. Pickthall, *The Meaning of The Glorious Koran: An Explanatory Translation.*

38. Ibid.

39. Ibid.

40. *Britannica Encyclopedia of World Religions*, s.v. "Trinity" (Chicago: Encyclopedia Britannica, 2006).

41. E.M. Caner and E.F. Caner, *Unveiling Islam* (Grand Rapids, MI: Kregel Publications, 2009), 205.

42. Kateregga and Shenk, *Islam and Christianity*, 101.

43. Geisler and Saleeb, *Answering Islam*, 37.

44. Crystalinks, "Jinn." Accessed February 5, 2019, www.crystalinks.com/jinn.html

45. Pickthall, *The Meaning of The Glorious Koran: An Explanatory Translation.*

46. The Religion of Islam, "The World of the Jinn" (2019), www.islamreligion.com/articles/669/viewall/world-of-jinn/

47. Riz Virk, "Religion and the Simulation Hypothesis, Part 1: Is God An AI?" HackerNoon.com, April 4, 2019, https://hackernoon.com/religion-and-the-simulation-hypothesis-is-god-an-ai-part-i-e2ac001cale

48. Pickthall, *The Meaning of The Glorious Koran: An Explanatory*

Translation.

Chapter 4

1. Bill Warner, "Kafir," Center for the Study of Political Islam, accessed July 21, 2019, www.cspii.org/education/articles/kafir/

2. Abby Ohlheiser, "There Are 13 Countries Where Atheism Is Punishable by Death." *The Wire*, December 10, 2013, https://www.theatlantic.com/international/archive/2013/12/13-countries-where-atheism-punishable-death/355961/

3. Muhammad Marmaduke Pickthall, *The Meaning of The Glorious Koran: An Explanatory Translation* (New York: Alfred A. Knopf, 1930). Consulted online at "Quran Archive – Texts and Studies on the Quran," http://quran-archive.org/explorer/marmaduke-pickthall/1930

4. E.W. Lane, *An Arabic-English Lexicon* (London: Williams & Norgate, 1863), http://www.tyndalearchive.com/TABS/Lane/

5. Nabeel Qureshi, *Seeking Allah, Finding Jesus* (Zondervan, 2014), 208.

6. Pickthall, *The Meaning of The Glorious Koran: An Explanatory Translation.*

7. Kareem Shaheen, "Syria: Isis releases footages of Palmyra ruins intact and 'will not destroy them,'" *The Guardian*, May 27, 2015, https://www.theguardian.com/world/2015/may/27/isis-releases-footage-of-palmyra-ruins-intact

8. *New International Version Archaeological Study Bible*, 2005.

9. Ibid.

10. Pickthall, *The Meaning of The Glorious Koran: An Explanatory Translation.*

11. Daniel Burke, "Why images of Mohammed offend Muslims," CNN, May 4, 2015, https://www.cnn.com/2015/05/04/living/islam-prophet-images/index.html

12. Denise A. Spellberg, *Thomas Jefferson's Qur'an* (New York: Vintage, 2013), 31-33.

13. Adrian Morgan, "Voltaire's 'Mahomet': Still Controversial After All These Years [incl. Tariq Ramadan]," *Campus Watch*, August 31, 2010, https://www.meforum.org/campus-watch/17748/voltaire-mahomet-still-controversial-after-all

14. Matt Soniak, "How a Mohammad Statue Ended up at the Supreme Court," *MentalFloss*, January 11, 2008, https://mentalfloss.com/article/17802/how-mohammad-statue-ended-supreme-court

15. "Courtroom Friezes: South and North Walls," Office of the Curator, Supreme Court of the United States, May 8, 2003, www.supremecourt.gov/about/northandsouthwalls.pdf

16. Jennifer Tanabe, *New World Encyclopedia*, s.v. "Iconoclasm," accessed November 26, 2018, www.newworldencyclopedia.org/p/index.php?title=Iconoclasm&oldid=1016022

17. Sarah Stone, "Erased from History – Hatshepsut, The Bearded Female King of Egypt," July 10, 2015, TodayIFoundOut.com, http://www.todayifoundout.com/index.php/2015/07/hatshepsut-female-king-egypt-wore-fake-beard/

18. *New International Version Archaeological Study Bible*, 2005.

19. Cyril Mango, "Historical Introduction," in *Iconoclasm*, Anthony Bryer & Judith Herrin, eds. (Birmingham: Centre for Byzantine Studies, University of Birmingham, 1977), 1-6.

20. Jennifer Tanabe, *New World Encyclopedia*, s.v. "Iconoclasm," accessed November 26, 2019, www.newworldencyclopedia.org/p/index.php?title=Iconoclasm&oldid=1016022

21. Ibid.

22. Ibid.

23. *New International Version Archaeological Study Bible*, 2005.

24. Ibid.

25. Ibid.

26. Denis MacEoin, "European Court of Human Rights Blasphemy Laws: Where a Word Out of Place Can Cost

Your Life," *The Gatestone Institute*, December 14, 2018, https://www.gatestoneinstitute.org/13377/european-court-human-rights-blasphemy-laws

27. James Orr, General Editor, *International Standard Bible Encyclopedia*, s.v. "Apostasy" (1915), https://www.biblestudytools.com/dictionary/Apostasy/

28. *The Economist*, "The Battle of the Books," December 19, 2007, www.economist.com/node/10311317/

29. Kate Lyons, Garry Blight, "Where in the World is the worst place to be a Christian?" *The Guardian*, July 27, 2015, https://www.theguardian.com/world/ng-interactive/2015/jul/27/where-in-the-world-is-it-worst-place-to-be-a-christian

30. James Orr, General Editor, *International Standard Bible Encyclopedia*, s.v. "Heresy," 1915, https://www.biblestudytools.com/dictionary/heresy/

31. MacEoin, "European Court of Human Rights Blasphemy Laws: Where a Word Out of Place Can Cost Your Life."

32. Cole Bunzel, "The Islamic State's Mufti on Trial: The Saga of the 'Silsila 'Ilmiyya,'" *CTC Sentinel* 11, no. 9 (2018): 14-17.

33. R. Green, "Dispute Over Takfir Rocks Islamic State," *The Middle East Media Research Institute*, August 4, 2017, https://www.memri.org/reports/dispute-over-takfir-rocks-islamic-state

34. Sebastian Gorka, *Defeating Jihad* (Washington, DC: Regnery Publishing, 2016), 75.

35. "What is Innovation and Who is an Innovator?" *Dar Al-Ifta* (2019), http://www.dar-alifta.org/Foreign/ViewArticle.aspx?ID=5909&CategoryID=5

36. Sahih Muslim, "The Book of Judicial Decisions," *1718a, Book 30, Hadith 23,* https://sunnah.com/muslim/30/23

37. Qureshi, *Seeking Allah, Finding Jesus*, 116.

38. "Full speech of King Salman at the end of President Trump's visit," *Arab News*, May 22, 2017, http://www.

arabnews.com/node/1102971/saudi-arabia

39. Mark Durie, "Is Islam a Religion of Peace?" *Middle East Forum*, December 16, 2015, https://www.meforum.org/5715/islam-religion-of-peace

40. Ibid.

41. Gardiner Harris, "Obama in Mosque Visit, Denounces Anti-Muslim Bias," *The New York Times*, February 3, 2016, www.nytimes.com/2016/02/04/us/politics/obama-muslims-baltimore-mosque.html

42. Spellberg, *Thomas Jefferson's Qur'an*, 114.

43. Pickthall, *The Meaning of The Glorious Koran: An Explanatory Translation*.

Chapter 5

1. Pew Research Center, "Chapter 6: Interfaith Relations." April 30, 2013, https://www.pewforum.org/2013/04/30/the-worlds-muslims-religion-politics-society-interfaith-relations/

2. Muhammad Marmaduke Pickthall, *The Meaning of The Glorious Koran: An Explanatory Translation* (New York: Alfred A. Knopf, 1930). Consulted online at "Quran Archive – Texts and Studies on the Quran," http://quran-archive.org/explorer/marmaduke-pickthall/1930

3. Sultan M. Munadi and Christine Hauser, "Afghan Convert to Christianity Is Released, Officials Say," *The New York Times*, March 28, 2006, https://www.nytimes.com/2006/03/28/world/asia/afghan-convert-to-christianity-is-released-officials-say.html

4. *Refugee Review Tribunal*, November 23, 2006, https://www.refworld.org/pdfid/4b6fe128d.pdf

5. Bart Ehrman, *How Jesus Became God* (Chantilly, VA: The Great Courses, 2014), 146.

6. Pickthall, *The Meaning of The Glorious Koran: An Explanatory Translation*.

7. Ibid.
8. BBC, "Abortion," September 7, 2009, https://www.bbc.co.uk/religion/religions/islam/islamethics/abortion_1.shtml
9. Ibid.
10. Muhammad Muhsin Khan, *The Translation of the Meanings of Summarized Sahih Al-Bukhari* (Riyadh, Saudi Arabia: Maktaba Dar-us-Salam, 1996), 949.
11. *New International Version Archaeological Study Bible,* 2005.
12. Phyllis Chesler, "Worldwide Trends in Honor Killings," *Middle East Quarterly* 17, no. 2 (2010): 3-11.
13. For example, see *The New York Times,* July 9, 2010, June 4, 2011; *The Washington Post,* November 22, 2008.
14. Phyllis Chesler and Nathan Bloom, "Hindu vs. Muslim Honor Killings," *Middle East Quarterly* 19, no. 3 (2012): 43-52.
15. Pickthall, *The Meaning of The Glorious Koran: An Explanatory Translation.*
16. Chesler, "Worldwide Trends in Honor Killings," 3-11.
17. *New International Version Archaeological Study Bible,* 2005.
18. Brittany Allen and Katy Miller, "Physical Development in Girls: What to Expect During Puberty," HealthyChildren.org, June 4, 2019, https://www.healthychildren.org/English/ages-stages/gradeschool/puberty/Pages/Physical-Development-Girls-What-to-Expect.aspx
19. Rebecca S. Brown, "A Legacy of Destruction: King John & Isabella of Angouleme," June 7, 2017, https://rebeccastarrbrown.com/2017/06/07/a-legacy-of-destruction-king-john-isabella-of-angouleme/
20. Cecily J. Hilsdale, "Constructing a Byzantine 'Augusta:' A Greek Book for a French Bride," in *The Art Bulletin* 87, no. 3 (2005): 458-483.
21. Jeffrey Hamilton, *The Plantagenets: History of a Dynasty* (New York: Continuum, 2010).
22. *Catholic Encyclopedia,* s.v.v. "The Blessed Virgin Mary,"

by A. Maas (New York: Robert Appleton Company, 1912). Accessed December 22, 2019, from New Advent: http://www.newadvent.org/cathen/15464b.htm

23. Edilberto Loaiza, Sr. and Sylvia Wong, "Marrying Too Young," *United Nations Population Fund*, 2012, 45. https://www.unfpa.org/sites/default/files/pub-pdf/MarryingTooYoung.pdf

24. *WorldAtlas*, "South Asia: Constituent Countries and Their Populations and Economies" (2019), https://www.worldatlas.com/articles/the-population-and-economy-of-the-south-asian-countries.html

25. Loaiza, Sr. and Wong, "Marrying Too Young," 6.

26. Ibid., 12.

27. Ibid., 11.

28. Amy North, "Drought Drop Out and Early Marriage: Feeling the Effects of Climate Change in East Africa," *Equals*, issue 24, February 2010, http://www.e4conference.org/wp-content/uploads/2010/02/Equals24.pdf

29. R.K. Murthy, "Review of Sexual and Reproductive Health and Rights in the Context of Disasters in Asia," *Asian Pacific Resource and Research Centre for Women* (Chennai: Arrow, 2009).

30. Juliette Myers and Rowan Harvey, "Breaking Vows: Early and Forced Marriage and Girls' Education," *Plan International*, June 2011, 9.

31. Eric Winkel, "Aisha Bint Abi Bakr," Alexander Wain and Mohammad H. Kamali, ed. *The Architects of Islamic Civilization* (Selangor, Malaysia: Pelanduk Publications, 2017), 19-25.

32. Fox News, "ISIS throws man off roof for being gay; mob pelts corpse with rocks," December 6, 2016, https://www.foxnews.com/world/isis-throws-man-off-roof-for-being-gay-mob-pelts-corpse-with-rocks

33. *New International Version Archaeological Study Bible*, 2005.

34. Ibid.

35. Ibid.

36. Greg Koukl, "What was the Sin of Sodom and Gomorrah?" March 8, 2013, https://www.str.org/articles/what-was-the-sin-of-sodom-and-gomorrah#.XZvijWZOmUk

37. Pew Research Center, "The Global Divide on Homosexuality," June 4, 2013, https://www.pewresearch.org/global/2013/06/04/the-global-divide-on-homosexuality/

38. Jonathan A.C. Brown, "Muslim Scholar on How Islam Really Views Homosexuality," *Variety*, June 30, 2015, https://variety.com/2015/voices/opinion/islam-gay-marriage-beliefs-muslim-religion-1201531047/

39. Pickthall, *The Meaning of The Glorious Koran: An Explanatory Translation*.

40. Asma Lamrabet, "Is 'Stoning' the Punishment for Adultery in Islam?" November 2016, http://www.asma-lamrabet.com/articles/is-stoning-the-punishment-for-adultery-in-islam/

41. Brown, "Muslim Scholar on How Islam Really Views Homosexuality," *Variety*, June 30, 2015, https://variety.com/2015/voices/opinion/islam-gay-marriage-beliefs-muslim-religion-1201531047/

42. A.L., "How homosexuality became a crime in the Middle East," *The Economist*, June 6, 2018, https://www.economist.com/open-future/2018/06/06/how-homosexuality-became-a-crime-in-the-middle-east

43. Ibid.

44. F.E. Peters, *The Children of Abraham* (Princeton, NJ: Princeton University Press, 2004), 64.

45. Ibid.

46. A. Scheiber, "The Origins of 'Obadyah, the Norman Proselyte," *Journal of Jewish Studies* 5, no. 37 (1954).

47. Holocaust Memorial Center, "Holocaust Badges" (2019), https://www.holocaustcenter.org/visit/library-archive/

holocaust-badges/

48. *New World Encyclopedia*, s.v. "Dhimmi" (2017), https://www.newworldencyclopedia.org/entry/Dhimmi

49. H. Patrick Glenn, *Legal Traditions of the World* (Oxford: Oxford University Press, 2007), 219.

50. *World History Encyclopedia*, s.v.v. "The Early Christianization of Armenia," by Mark Cartwright, March 22, 2018, https://www.worldhistory.org/article/801/the-early-christianization-of-armenia/

51. Hagop Barsoumian, "The Eastern Question and the Tanzimat Era," in Richard G. Hovannisian, ed., *The Armenian People from Ancient to Modern Times, II: Foreign Dominion to Statehood: The Fifteenth Century to the Twentieth Century* (New York: St. Martin's, 1997), 175-201.

52. History.com Editors, "Armenian Genocide," June 6, 2019, *History*, https://www.history.com/topics/world-war-i/armenian-genocide

53. Taner Akçam, *A Shameful Act: The Armenian Genocide and the Question of Turkish Responsibility* (New York: Metropolitan Books, 2006), 1-93.

54. Henry Morgenthau, *Ambassador Morgenthau's Story* (Detroit: Wayne State University, 2003), 112.

55. Ibid., 113.

56. Ibid., 221, 224.

57. National Society of Defense, *A Universal Proclamation to All the People of Islam*, The Seat of the Caliphate, The Ottoman Empire (Muta'at al Hairayet, 1333/1915), trans. American Agency and Consulate, Cairo, in U.S. State Department document 867.4016/57, March 10, 1915. (Author's note: while 1915 is the Common Era year, 1333 is the year in the Islamic calendar.)

58. Morgenthau, *Ambassador Morgenthau's Story*, 208-209.

59. John G. Heidenrich, *How to Prevent Genocide: A Guide for Policymakers, Scholars, and the Concerned Citizen* (Santa

Barbara: Greenwood Publishing Group, 2001), 5.

60. Sara Cohan, "A Brief History of the Armenian Genocide," *Social Education* 69, no. 6 (2005): 333-337, https://genocideeducation.org/wp-content/uploads/2014/08/A-Brief-History-of-the-Armenian-Genocide.pdf

Chapter 6

1. George Sale, *The Koran: Commonly Called the Alcoran of Mohammed* (London: L. Hawes, W. Clarke, R. Collins, and T. Wilcox, 1734).

2. Denise A. Spellberg, *Thomas Jefferson's Qur'an* (New York: Vintage, 2013), 83.

3. Wikipedia, "List of countries by population in 1700," 2020, https://en.wikipedia.org/wiki/List_of_countries_by_population_in_1700

4. Spellberg, *Thomas Jefferson's Qur'an*, 236.

5. "Individual Differences in Perception," in *Encyclopedia of Perception,* by Bruce E. Goldstein (Thousand Oaks, CA: SAGE Publications, 2010), 492.

6. R. Landau, *Islam and the Arabs* (London: George Allen and Unwin Ltd., 1958), 141.

7. Muhammad Marmaduke Pickthall, *The Meaning of The Glorious Koran: An Explanatory Translation* (New York: Alfred A. Knopf, 1930). Consulted online at "Quran Archive – Texts and Studies on the Quran," http://quran-archive.org/explorer/marmaduke-pickthall/1930

8. Ibid.

9. *UK Essays*, "The Four Main Sources of Islamic Law Religion Essay," November 2018, https://www.ukessays.com/essays/religion/the-four-main-sources-of-islamic-law-religion-essay.php?vref=1

10. M.H. Kamali, *Principles of Islamic Jurisprudence*, 3rd ed. (Cambridge: Islamic Texts Society, 2005), 26-27.

11. N.J. Coulson, *A History of Islamic Law* (Edinburgh University

Press, 1964), 11-12.

12. Javaid Rehman and Aibek Ahmedov, "Islamic Law of Obligatory Alms (Zakat)," in Shaheen Mansoor, ed., *Sources of Islamic Law* (London: UK Center for Legal Education, 2011), 20.

13. Ibid., 31.

14. Michael Mumisa, "Sharia law and the death penalty: Would abolition of the death penalty be unfaithful to the message of Islam?" *Penal Reform International*, 2015, 9.

15. Onder Bakircioglu, "The Principal Sources of Islamic Law," in Tallyn Gray, ed., *Islam and International Criminal Law and Justice* (Brussels: Torkel Opsahl Academic EPublisher, 2018), https://www.legal-tools.org/doc/0528c5/pdf/

16. Irshad Abdal-Haqq, "Islamic Law: An Overview of its Origins and Elements," in Hisham M. Ramadan, ed., *Understanding Islamic Law: From Classical to Contemporary* (Oxford: AltaMira Press, 2006), 21.

17. Rehman and Ahmedov, *Sources of Islamic Law*, 17.

18. Ahmad ibn Naqib al Misri, *Umdat al-Salik* (*Reliance of the Traveller: A Classic Manual of Islamic Sacred Law*), trans. Nuh Ha Mim Keller (Beltsville, MD: Amana Publications, 1994).

19. Rehman and Ahmedov, *Sources of Islamic Law*, 46.

20. Cole Bunzel, "From Paper State to Caliphate: The Ideology of the Islamic State," Center for Middle East Policy at Brookings, March 2015, 33.

21. Rehman and Ahmedov, *Sources of Islamic Law*, 46.

22. Ibid., 47.

23. Ibid., 48.

24. Abdul Hakim al-Matroudi, *The Hanbali School of Law and Ibn Taymiyyah* (New York: Routledge, 1999), 7.

25. International Crisis Group, "Indonesia Backgrounder: Why Salafism and Terror Mostly Don't Mix," *Asia Report #83*, September 13, 2004, 3.

26. Norman Anderson, *Islamic Law in the Modern World* (New

York: New York University Press, 1959).

27. Mumisa, "Sharia law and the death penalty: Would abolition of the death penalty be unfaithful to the message of Islam?" 11.

28. ZeroHedge, "Khashoggi's Children 'Pardon' Father's Killers, Which Means All Could Get Off Free," May 22, 2020, https://www.zerohedge.com/geopolitical/khashoggis-children-pardon-fathers-killers-which-means-everyone-could-get-free

29. Mohammad Hashim Kamali, "Strictly from the Quranic Perspective," *The New Straits*, April 25, 2009.

30. Mike Mount, "Khalid Sheikh Mohammed: I beheaded American reporter," CNN.com, March 1, 2019.

31. ABC News, "Headless bodies found in mass graves in IS Syrian stronghold thought to be those of sex slaves." Retrieved March 1, 2019, https://www.abc.net.au/news/2019-03-01/is-mass-grave-yazidi-sex-slave-islamic-state-syria-baghouz/10862994

32. 1P5 Staff, "Is the Practice of Beheading Justified in Islam?" One Peter Five, July 27, 2016, https://onepeterfive.com/practice-beheading-justified-islam/

33. Pickthall, *The Meaning of The Glorious Koran: An Explanatory Translation*.

34. Ibid.

35. 1P5 Staff, "Is the Practice of Beheading Justified in Islam?"

36. Ibid.

37. Jewish History 620-629 (2015), "627 April, Massacre of the Banu Qurayza" (2015), http://www.jewishhistory.org.il/history.php?startyear=620&endyear=629

38. 1P5 Staff, "Is the Practice of Beheading Justified in Islam?"

39. Charles H. Dyer and Mark Tobey, *The Isis Crisis* (Chicago: Moody Publishers, 2015), 75.

40. Talia Shadwell, "Six young couples flogged in front of crowd for 'having sex outside marriage,'" *The Mirror*,

March 5, 2019, https://www.mirror.co.uk/news/world-news/six-young-couples-flogged-front-14090286

41. Max Rodenbeck, "How She Wants to Modify Muslims," review of *Heretic: Why Islam Needs a Reformation Now* by Ayaan Hirsi Ali, *New York Review of Books,* LXII (19): 36, December 3, 2015.

42. Rod Nordland, "In Bold Display, Taliban Orders Stoning Deaths," *The New York Times*, August 16, 2010, http://www.nytimes.com/2010/08/17/world/asia/17stoning.html

43. Kathryn Seifert, "Death by Stoning: Why Is This Sickening Punishment Legal?" *Psychology Today*, February 18, 2014, https://www.psychologytoday.com/us/blog/stop-the-cycle/201402/death-stoning-why-is-sickening-punishment-legal

44. Wikipedia, "Capital and corporal punishment in Judaism," 2020, https://en.wikipedia.org/wiki/Capital_and_corporal_punishment_in_Judaism#cite_note-Jewishvirtuallibrary.org_Capital_Punishment-13

45. Paul L. Maier, *Pontius Pilate* (Wheaton, IL: Tyndale House Publishers, 1973), 213-236.

46. Cornell Law School, "Death Penalty Database" (2019), https://deathpenaltyworldwide.org/project/death-penalty-database/

47. Southern Poverty Law Center, "Anti-Sharia law bills in the United States," February 5, 2018, https://www.splcenter.org/hatewatch/2018/02/05/anti-sharia-law-bills-united-states

48. American Bar Association, "Resolution Adopted by the House of Delegates," August 8-9, 2011, https://www.philadelphiabar.org/WebObjects/PBAReadOnly.woa/Contents/WebServerResources/CMSResources/ABA_resolution.pdf

49. Andrea Elliott, "David Yerushalmi, the Man Behind the Anti-Shariah Movement," *The New York Times*, July 31,

2011, https://www.nytimes.com/2011/07/31/us/31shariah. html

50. Kevin M. Schultz, *Tri-Faith America: How Catholics and Jews Held Postwar America to Its Protestant Promise* (New York: Oxford University Press, 2011), 23.

51. Sadakat Kadri, *Heaven on Earth: A Journey Through Shari'a Law from the Deserts of Ancient Arabia* (New York: Macmillan, 2012), 279.

52. Lionel Beehner, "Religious Conversion and Sharia Law," *Council on Foreign Relations*, June 6, 2007, https://www.cfr. org/backgrounder/religious-conversion-and-sharia-law

53. Christopher R. Lepore, "Asserting State Sovereignty over National Communities of Islam in the United States and Britain: Sharia Courts as a Tool of Muslim Accommodation and Integration," *Washington University Global Studies Law Review* 11, no. 3 (2012): 672.

Chapter 7

1. Olivia B. Waxman, "The First Africans in Virginia Landed in 1619," *Time*, August 20, 2019, https://time.com/5653369/august-1619-jamestown-history/

2. Hakim Adi, "Africa and the Transatlantic Slave Trade," *BBC History*, 2014, http://www.bbc.co.uk/history/british/abolition/africa_article_01.shtml

3. Crystal Ponti, "America's History of Slavery Began Long Before Jamestown," *History*, August 26, 2019, https://www.history.com/news/american-slavery-before-jamestown-1619

4. *Encyclopedia Britannica*, s.v.v. "Transatlantic slave trade," by Thomas Lewis, September 7, 2018, https://www.britannica.com/topic/transatlantic-slave-trade

5. Wikipedia, "Timeline of 8th-century Muslim history," 2019, https://en.wikipedia.org/wiki/Timeline_of_8th-century_Muslim_history

6. The New York Public Library, "In Motion: The African-American Migration Experience," 2005, http://www.inmotionaame.org/migrations/topic.cfm@migration=1&topic=2.html

7. Michael A. Gomez, *Black Crescent: The Experience and Legacy of African Muslims in the Americas* (New York: Cambridge University Press, 2005), 143-200.

8. Hakim Adi, "Africa and the Transatlantic Slave Trade," *BBC History*, 2014, http://www.bbc.co.uk/history/british/abolition/africa_article_01.shtml

9. Ibid.

10. Ibid.

11. Jane I. Smith, *Islam in America* (New York: Columbia University Press, 1999), 51-53.

12. Sarah Cwiek, "What explains Michigan's large Arab American community?" Michigan Radio, July 9, 2014, https://www.michiganradio.org/post/what-explains-michigans-large-arab-american-community#stream/0

13. Joy Mohammed, "How Henry Ford's Dream Pitted Blacks Against Muslims in Urban Michigan," April 14, 2017, https://wearyourvoicemag.com/race/henry-ford-blacks-muslims

14. Besheer Mohamed, "New Estimates Show U.S. Muslim Population Continues to Grow," Pew Research Center, January 3, 2018, https://www.pewresearch.org/fact-tank/2018/01/03/new-estimates-show-u-s-muslim-population-continues-to-grow/

15. *Oxford Research Encyclopedia of Religion*, s.v.v. "African American Islam," by Herbert Berg, September 2015, https://oxfordre.com/religion/view/10.1093/acrefore/9780199340378.001.0001/acrefore-9780199340378-e-9?rskey=EiLXwx&result=1

16. Edward E. Curtis, IV, "Five Myths about Mosques in America," *Washington Post*, August 29, 2010, https://www.washingtonpost.com/wp-dyn/content/article/2010/08/26/

AR2010082605510.html

17. Sherman A. Jackson, *Islam and the Blackamerican: Looking Toward the Third Resurrection* (Oxford: Oxford University Press, 2005), 44.

18. Patrick D. Bowen, "Abdul Hamid Suleiman and the Origins of the Moorish Science Temple," *Journal of Race, Ethnicity, and Religion* 2 (2011), 1-54.

19. *Oxford Research Encyclopedia of Religion*, s.v.v. "African American Islam," by Herbert Berg, September 3, 2015, https://oxfordre.com/religion/search?siteToSearch=religion&q=African+American+islam&searchBtn=Search&isQuickSearch=true

20. Ibid.

21. *Encyclopedia Britannica, Inc.*, s.v.v. "Nation of Islam," November 19, 2019, www.britannica.com/topic/Nation-of-Islam

22. Southern Poverty Law Center, "Nation of Islam," 2019, https://www.splcenter.org/fighting-hate/extremist-files/group/nation-islam

23. Ariel Zilber, "Lessons in Leadership: An appreciation of Malcolm X," *The Jerusalem Post*, February 29, 2016, https://www.jpost.com/Opinion/Lessons-in-leadership-An-appreciation-of-Malcolm-X-446482

24. David Kenneth, "What Does 'X' Stand for in the Nation of Islam?" September 29, 2017, https://classroom.synonym.com/what-does-x-stand-for-in-the-nation-of-islam-12086893.html

25. Ask MetaFilter, "On the history of the use of 'X' as a surname stand-in in the Nation of Islam," 2009, https://ask.metafilter.com/131876/On-the-history-of-the-use-of-X-as-a-surname-standin-in-the-Nation-of-Islam

26. *Oxford Research Encyclopedia of Religion*, s.v.v. "African American Islam."

27. Joe Carter, "9 Things You Should Know About the

Nation of Islam," September 13, 2017, https://www.thegospelcoalition.org/article/9-things-you-should-know-about-the-nation-of-islam/

28. Neil MacFarquhar, "Nation of Islam at a Crossroad as Leader Exits," *The New York Times*, February 26, 2007, www.nytimes.com/2007/02/26/us/26farrakhan.html

29. John Esposito, *What Everyone Needs to Know About Islam* (New York: Oxford University Press, 2002), 53.

Chapter 8

1. Maxime Rodinson, *Islam and Capitalism*, trans. Brian Pearce (Austin: University of Texas Press, 1978), 17.

2. Muhammad Taqi Usmani, *An Introduction to Islamic Finance*, 14th ed. (Karachi: Maktaba Ma'ariful Qur'an, 2002).

3. K. Chaudhuri, *Trade and Civilisation in the Indian Ocean: An Economic History from the Rise of Islam to 1750* (Cambridge: Cambridge University Press, 1985).

4. The Picket Line, "Aristotle on Distributive Justice," October 14, 2009, https://sniggle.net/TPL/index5.php?entry=14Oct09

5. Khaliq Ahmad and Arif Hassan, "Distributive Justice: The Islamic Perspective," *Intellectual Discourse* 8 no. 2 (2000): 159-172.

6. Muhammad Marmaduke Pickthall, *The Meaning of The Glorious Koran: An Explanatory Translation* (New York: Alfred A. Knopf, 1930). Consulted online at "Quran Archive – Texts and Studies on the Quran," http://quran-archive.org/explorer/marmaduke-pickthall/1930

7. Khaliq Ahmad and Arif Hassan, *Intellectual Discourse*, 159-172.

8. Ibid.

9. Muhammad Sarwar, *al-Kafi, Volume 1 of 8*, 2nd ed. (New York: The Islamic Seminary Inc., 2015), 345.

10. I.A. Imtiazi (ed.), *Management of Zakah in Modern Muslim*

Society (Jeddah: Islamic Research Institute, 1989), 222.

11. Sam Westrop, "American Islamist Charity Openly Partners with Designated Terrorists," *Middle East Forum*, January 4, 2018, https://www.meforum.org/7144/american-islamist-charity-partners-with-terrorists

12. USLegal, s.v.v. "Commutative Justice Law and Legal Definition," 2019, https://definitions.uslegal.com/c/commutative-justice/

13. Mashood A. Baderin, *Issues in Islamic Law, Volume 2* (New York: Routledge, 2016), 268.

14. T. Kuran, "Institutional Causes of Underdevelopment in the Middle East: A Historical Perspective," in *Institutional Change and Economic Behavior*, ed. by J. Kornai, L. Matyas, and G. Roland (New York: Palgrave-Macmillan, 2008), 64, 76.

15. R. Ruston, "Does it matter what we do with our money?" *Priests & People*, May 1993, 171-177.

16. Most notable of these are 2:188; 2:274-280; 3:130; 4:29; 4:161; 9:34-35; 30:39.

17. Pickthall, *The Meaning of The Glorious Koran: An Explanatory Translation*.

18. Joshua Vincent, "Historical, Religious and Scholastic Prohibition of Usury: The Common Origins of Western and Islamic Financial Practices," *Law School Student Scholarship. 600*, May 1, 2014, https://scholarship.shu.edu/cgi/viewcontent.cgi?referer=https://www.google.com/&httpsredir=1&article=1600&context=student_scholarship

19. Robert P. Maloney, "Usury and Restrictions on Interest-Taking in the Ancient Near East," *The Catholic Biblical Quarterly* 36, no. 1 (1974): 1-20.

20. Wayne A.M. Visser and Alastair McIntosh, "A short review of the historical critique of usury," *Accounting, Business and Financial History* 8, no. 2 (1998): 175-189.

21. G.R. Driver and J.C. Miles (eds.), *The Babylonian Laws*

(Oxford: Clarendon Press, 1955), 175.

22. Maloney, "Usury and Restrictions on Interest-Taking in the Ancient Near East," 1-20.

23. Ibid.

24. Ibid.

25. Ibid.

26. Ibid.

27. Ljerka Cerovic, Stella Suljic Nikolaj, and Dario Maradin, "Comparative Analysis of Conventional and Islamic Banking: Importance of Market Regulation," *EKON. MISAO I PRAKSA DBK GOD* (XXVI), May 16, 2017, 241-263, https://pdfs.semanticscholar.org/309a/45ed77efb3d8a0e869b4c00cb1aaf251dcb8.pdf

28. Exodus 22:24-5; Leviticus 25:35-7; Deuteronomy 23:19-21; Proverbs 28:8; Psalms 15:5; Nehemiah 5:7 (*New International Version Archaeological Study Bible*, 2005).

29. *New International Version Archaeological Study Bible*, 2005.

30. Visser and McIntosh, "A short review of the historical critique of usury," 175-189.

31. *New International Version Archaeological Study Bible*, 2005.

32. Visser and McIntosh, "A short review of the historical critique of usury," 175-189.

33. Jennie Cohen, "History of the Knights Templar," *History*, September 3, 2018, https://www.history.com/news/who-were-the-knights-templar-2

34. Ruston, "Does it matter what we do with our money?" 171-177.

35. Plato, *The Dialogues of Plato*, trans. B. Jowett, in Five Volumes, 3rd edition (Oxford: Oxford University Press, 1892), 742.

36. Pope John Paul II, *Sollicitudo Rei Socialis* (London: Catholic Truth Society, 1989).

37. *Catholic Encyclopedia*, s.v. "Usury," by A. Vermeersch (New York: Robert Appleton Company, 1912), http://www.

newadvent.org/cathen/15235c.htm

38. A. Birnie, *The History and Ethics of Interest* (London: William Hodge, 1958).

39. R. Skidelsky, *John Maynard Keynes: The Economist as Savior, 1920-1937*, Volume 2 (London: Macmillan, 1992).

40. *New International Version Archaeological Study Bible*, 2005.

41. D.W. Pearce and R.K. Turner, *Economics of Natural Resources and the Environment* (London: Harvester Wheatsheaf, 1990).

42. H.F. Daly and J.B. Cobb, *For the Common Good* (London: Greenprint, 1990).

43. Alex Mayyasi, "Of Money and Morals," *Aeon,* July 7, 2017, https://aeon.co/essays/how-did-usury-stop-being-a-sin-and-become-respectable-finance

44. *The Oxford Dictionary of Islam*, s.v. "Haram," accessed July 21, 2019, http://www.oxfordislamicstudies.com/article/opr/t125/e808

45. Theodore Karasik, Frederic Wehrey, and Steven Strom, "Islamic Finance in a Global Context: Opportunities and Challenges," *Chicago Journal of International Law* 7, no. 2 (2007): 379, 381.

46. Ibid.

47. Zamir Iqbal and Abbas Mirakhor, *An Introduction to Islamic Finance Theory and Practice* (New York: John Wiley & Sons, 2007), 115.

48. Wikipedia, "List of African territories and states by date of colonization," January 29, 2021, https://en.wikipedia.org/wiki/List_of_African_territories_and_states_by_date_of_colonization

49. Cerovic, Nikolaj, and Maradin, "Comparative Analysis of Conventional and Islamic Banking: Importance of Market Regulation," 241-263.

50. S. Michalopoulos, A. Naghavi, and G. Prarolo, "Islam, Inequality and Pre-Industrial Comparative Development," *National Bureau of Economic Research*, August 2015, www.

nber.org/papers/w21506.pdf, 4.

51. Mustafa Akyol, "Is Islam a socialist religion?" *Hurriyet Daily News*, May 9, 2012, www.hurriyetdailynews.com/opinion/mustafa-akyol/is-islam-a-socialist-religion---20301

Chapter 9

1. Phillip Marcelo and Jeff Karoub, "Muslim candidates running in record numbers face backlash," *Associated Press*, July 16, 2018, https://apnews.com/article/62d762b7e25b49bc916d02f8d538a247

2. Ibid.

3. L. Pintak, J. Albright, Brian J. Bowe, S. Pasha et al. "#Islamophobia: Stoking Fear and Prejudice in the 2018 Midterms," *Social Science Research Council*, November 5, 2019, https://doi.org/10.35650/MD.2006.a.2019

4. Emgage, Washington, DC, 2020, www.millionmuslimvotes.com

5. Michael Gabriel Hernandez, "Groups say over half of Muslim candidates win US office," July 11, 2020, Anadolu Agency, https://www.aa.com.tr/en/americas/groups-say-over-half-of-muslim-candidates-win-us-office/2035090

6. Tim Challies, "At Least 5 Things Scripture Teaches Us About Governments," September 30, 2012, https://www.challies.com/articles/at-least-5-things-scripture-teaches-us-about-governments/

7. All passages in this section come from the *New International Version Cultural Backgrounds Study Bible*, 2016.

8. Art Lindsley, "What Does the Bible Say about the Role of Government?" January 17, 2018, https://tifwe.org/bible-role-of-government/

9. Charles H. Dyer and Mark Tobey, *The Isis Crisis* (Chicago: Moody Publishers, 2015), 114.

10. Samuel P. Huntington, *The Clash of Civilizations* (New York: Simon & Schuster, 1996), 209.

11. *English Oxford Living Dictionaries*, s.v.v. "Liberal democracy," 2019, https://en.oxforddictionaries.com/definition/liberal_d emocracy

12. Andrea Palpant Dilley, "The Surprising Discovery About Those Colonialist, Proselytizing Missionaries," *Christianity Today*, January/February 2014, www.christianitytoday. com/ct/2014/january-february/world-missionaries-made. html

13. Ayatollah Khomeini, "The Form of Islamic Government," 1977, https://www.al-islam.org/islamic-government-governance-of-jurist-imam-khomeini/form-islamic-government

14. UShistory.org, "The Declaration of Independence," July 4, 1776, http://www.ushistory.org/declaration/document/

15. Shadi Hamid, Peter Mandaville, and William McCants, "How America Changed Its Approach to Political Islam," *The Atlantic*, October 4, 2017, https://www.theatlantic.com/international/archive/2017/10/america-political-islam/541287/

16. Ibid.

17. Nathan J. Brown, Amr Hamzawy, and Marina Ottaway, "Islamist Movements and the Democratic Process in the Arab World: Exploring the Gray Zones," *Carnegie Papers*, #67, 17, March 2006, https://carnegieendowment.org/files/cp_67_grayzones_final.pdf

18. Human Rights Watch, *World Report 2020, 2021*, https://www.hrw.org/world-report/2020#

19. *Senate report 104-158*, "Congressional Term Limits." October 17, 1995, https://www.govinfo.gov/content/pkg/CRPT-104srpt158/html/CRPT-104srpt158.htm

20. Freedom House, *Freedom in the World 2019*, 2020, https://freedomhouse.org/report/freedom-world/2019/democracy-retreat

21. Saif Khalid and Saqib Sarker, "Bangladesh election makes mockery of democracy: BNP's Alamgir," *Al Jazeera*, December 31, 2018, https://www.aljazeera.com/

news/2018/12/bangladesh-election-mockery-democracy-bnp-chief-alamgir-181231183622220.html

22. Freedom House, *Freedom in the World 2019*, 2020, https://freedomhouse.org/report/freedom-world/2019/democracy-retreat

23. *The Oxford Dictionary of Islam,* s.v. "Secularism," by John L. Esposito, ed. (Oxford: Oxford University Press, 2014).

24. Thomas L. Friedman, "The First Law of Petropolitics," *Foreign Policy*, May/June 2006, 28-36.

25. U. Shavit, "The Lesser of Two Evils: Islamic Law and the Emergence of a Broad Agreement on Muslim Participation in Western Political Systems," *Contemporary Islam* 8, no. 3 (2013): 239-259.

26. Denise A. Spellberg, *Thomas Jefferson's Qur'an* (New York: Vintage, 2013), 81.

27. Ariel Edwards-Levy, "Newt Gingrich: I'd Support a Muslim Running for President Only if They'd Commit to 'Give Up Sharia,'" *Huffington Post*, January 17, 2012.

28. Andrew Bostom, "Shi'ite Iran's Genocidal Jew Hatred (Part 3)" (blog), July 20, 2008, https://www.andrewbostom.org/2008/07/390/

29. Pew Research Center, "Muslim Americans: No Signs of Growth in Alienation or Support for Extremism," August 30, 2011, https://www.people-press.org/2011/08/30/muslim-americans-no-signs-of-growth-in-alienation-or-support-for-extremism/

30. Dom Calicchio, "Ilhan Omar's GOP challenger tweets 'I am an American' after Omar describes herself 6 other ways," Fox News, February 26, 2020, https://www.foxnews.com/politics/ilhan-omars-gop-challenger-tweets-i-am-an-american-after-omar-describes-herself-6-other-ways

31. Human Rights Watch, *World Report 2020, 2021,* https://www.hrw.org/world-report/2020#

32. D. Greenberg, M. Najle, O. Bola, and R.P. Jones, "Fifty

Years After Stonewall: Widespread Support for LGBT Issues – Findings from American Values," *Atlas 2018*. Public Religion Research Institute, March 26, 2019, https://www.prri.org/research/fifty-years-after-stonewall-widespread-support-for-lgbt-issues-findings-from-american-values-atlas-2018/

33. Pickthall, *The Meaning of The Glorious Koran: An Explanatory Translation*.

34. William Gawthrop, "Islam's Tools of Penetration," *CIFA Working Brief*, slides 6, 7, 15, April 19, 2007.

35. Tariq Alhomayed, "The Political Activist Yusuf al Qaradawi," *Asharq Al-awsat*, January 21, 2010.

36. Yusuf Al-Qaradawi, "Why is secularism incompatible with Islam?" *Saudi Gazette*, June 11, 2010.

37. Carolyn Warner, *Confessions of an Interest Group: The Catholic Church and Political Parties in Europe* (Princeton: Princeton University Press, 2000).

38. Carolyn M. Warner and Manfred W. Wenner, "Religion and the Political Organization of Muslims in Europe," *Perspectives on Politics* 4 no. 3 (2006): 457-479.

Chapter 10

1. Dictionary.com, s.v. "Consumer," 2019, https://www.dictionary.com/browse/consumer

2. *New International Version Archaeological Study Bible*, 2005.

3. Emma Rudeck, "A Brief History of Product Lifecycle Management," Concurrent Engineering blog, March 6, 2014, https://www.concurrent-engineering.co.uk/Blog/bid/100180/A-Brief-History-of-Product-Lifecycle-Management

4. *The Economist*, "The Battle of the Books," December 19, 2007, www.economist.com/node/10311317/

5. Rajiv Malhotra, "A Business Model of Religion – 1," 2001, rajivmalhotra.com/library/business-model-religion-1/

6. See Deuteronomy 18:18-20.

7. R.L. Wilken, *The First Thousand Years: A Global History of Christianity* (New Haven: Yale University Press, 2012), 65-66.

8. P.J. Heather and John Matthews, *Goths in the Fourth Century* (Liverpool: Liverpool University Press, 1991), 136.

9. Wilken, *The First Thousand Years: A Global History of Christianity*, 65.

10. Christianity in View, "Timeline of Christian History," 2016, http://christianityinview.com/timeline.html

11. Armenia, "Armenia: The First Christian Country," 2019, https://armenia.travel/en/armenia/first-christian-country

12. Wilken, *The First Thousand Years: A Global History of Christianity*, 65-66.

13. W.A. Dreyer, "The amazing growth of the early church," *HTS Teologiese Studies/Theological Studies* 68, no. 1 (2012), doi:10.4102/hts.v68i1.1268.

14. Houssain Kettani, *The World Muslim Population, History & Prospect* (Liverpool: Research Publishing Services, 2014).

15. United States Census Bureau, *Historical Estimates of World Population*, 2018, https://www.census.gov/data/tables/time-series/demo/international-programs/historical-est-world pop.html

16. Wikipedia, "Timeline of 7th-century Muslim history," 2019, https://en.wikipedia.org/wiki/Timeline_of_7th-century_Muslim_history

17. Wikipedia, "Timeline of 8th-century Muslim history," 2019, https://en.wikipedia.org/wiki/Timeline_of_8th-century_Muslim_history

18. Wikipedia, "Timeline of 9th-century Muslim history," 2019, https://en.wikipedia.org/wiki/Timeline_of_9th-century_Muslim_history

19. Wikipedia, "Timeline of 10th-century Muslim history," 2019, https://en.wikipedia.org/wiki/Timeline_of_10th-century_Muslim_history

20. World Population is based on data from the United States

Census Bureau, Historical Estimates of World Population, retrieved from https://www.census.gov/data/tables/time-series/demo/international-programs/historical-est-worldpop.html; Muslim Population is based on data from Kettani, Houssain, *The World Muslim Population, History & Prospect* (Research Publishing Services, 2014); Christian Population is based on data from several different sources: Debra Albaugh (2014), *In Our Image: The History and Mystery In Our Look at Life*, preview mini-book, Lulu.com and the Gordon-Conwell Theological Seminary, 2013.

21. Gordon-Conwell Theological Seminary, "Status of Global Mission 2013," 2013, https://www.gordonconwell.edu/center-for-global-christianity/christianity-in-global-context/

22. Agenzia Fides, "Catholic Church Statistics 2016," Zenit, October 24, 2016, https://zenit.org/articles/catholic-church-statistics-2016/

23. "LGBT Demographic Data Interactive," The Williams Institute, UCLA School of Law, January 2019, https://williamsinstitute.law.ucla.edu/visualization/lgbt-stats/?topic=LGBT#about-the-data

24. Kettani, *The World Muslim Population, History & Prospect*.

25. Wildolive, "Different branches of Islam," October 5, 2016, http://www.wildolive.co.uk/islam_denominations.htm

26. Lewis Ray Rambo and Charles E. Farhadian (eds.), *The Oxford Handbook of Religious Conversion* (Oxford: Oxford University Press, 2014), 59.

27. Gina Bellofatto and Todd M. Johnson, "Key Findings of Christianity in its Global Context, 1970-2020," *International Bulletin of Mission Research* 37 (2013): 157-164.

28. Francis X. Rocca, "Pope Francis, in Christmas Message, Says Church Must Adapt to Post-Christian West," *The Wall Street Journal*, December 21, 2019.

29. Bruce D. Henderson, "The Product Portfolio," BCG Henderson Institute, January 1, 1970, https://www.bcg.

com/publications/1970/strategy-the-product-portfolio

30. Richard Madsen, "The Upsurge of Religion in China," *Journal of Democracy* 21, no. 4 (October 2010): 64-65.

31. Kelsey Jo Starr, "5 facts about Buddhists around the world," Pew Research Center, April 5, 2019, https://www.pewresearch.org/fact-tank/2019/04/05/5-facts-about-buddhists-around-the-world/

32. Robert D. Woodberry, "The Missionary Roots of Liberal Democracy," *American Political Science Review* (106) 2 (May 2012): 244-274.

33. ZeroHedge, "Still Stonewall'd: Mapping the Legal Status of Homosexuality Worldwide," June 30, 2019, https://www.thestreet.com/phildavis/news/still-stonewall-d-mapping-the-legal-status-of-homosexuality-worldwide

34. David B. Barrett, George Thomas Kurian, Todd M. Johnson (eds.), *World Christian Encyclopedia* (Oxford University Press, 2001), 360, https://en.wikipedia.org/wiki/List_of_converts_to_Christianity

35. Shawn's Odyssey, "The lifecycle of religions," November 28, 2016, http://shawnsodyssey.net/the-lifecycle-of-religions/

Chapter 11

1. Wikipedia, "International recognition of Israel," 2020, https://en.wikipedia.org/wiki/International_recognition_of_Israel

2. Worldometer, "Countries in the world by population (2021)," https://www.worldometers.info/world-population/population-by-country

3. Clara Moskowitz, "Bible Possibly Written Centuries Earlier, Text Suggests," *Live Science*, January 15, 2010, https://www.livescience.com/8008-bible-possibly-written-centuries-earlier-text-suggests.html

4. Muhammad Marmaduke Pickthall, *The Meaning of The Glorious Koran: An Explanatory Translation* (New York:

Alfred A. Knopf, 1930). Consulted online at "Quran Archive – Texts and Studies on the Quran," http://quran-archive.org/explorer/marmaduke-pickthall/1930

5. Jewish History, "Massacre of the Banu Qurayza," April 27, 2015, http://www.jewishhistory.org.il/history.php?startyear=620&endyear=629

6. J.M. Arlandson, "Islam's belated militant and mystical claim on Jerusalem," Answering Islam (n.d.), https://www.answering-islam.org/Authors/Arlandson/jerusalem.htm

7. Awqaf SA, "What is Waqf" (2019), https://awqafsa.org.za/what-is-waqf/

8. Center for Security Policy, *Shariah: the Threat to America* (Washington, DC: Center for Security Policy Press, 2010), 91.

9. The Anglo-American Committee of Inquiry, *A Survey of Palestine* (Jerusalem: British Mandate Government of Palestine, 1946), 226-228.

10. Rafael Castro, "The Deep Reason Muslim World Hates Zionism," *Ynet News*, September 8, 2017, https://www.ynetnews.com/articles/0,7340,L-5025906,00.html

11. Pickthall, *The Meaning of The Glorious Koran: An Explanatory Translation*.

12. Etgar Lefkovits, "Was the Aksa Mosque built over the remains of a Byzantine church?" *Jerusalem Post*, November 16, 2008, https://www.jpost.com/Israel/Was-the-Aksa-Mosque-built-over-the-remains-of-a-Byzantine-church

13. Ghada Karmi, Jerusalem Today: *What Future for the Peace Process?* (Reading, UK: Garnet & Ithaca Press, 1997), 116.

14. F.E. Peters, *Jerusalem* (Princeton: Princeton University Press, 1985), 186-192.

15. Benny Morris, *Righteous Victims: A History of the Zionist-Arab Conflict,* 1881-2001, 1st ed. (New York: Vintage Books, 2001), 252-258.

Chapter 12

1. Michael Lipka and Conrad Hackett, "Why Muslims are the world's fastest-growing religious group," Pew Research Center, April 6, 2017, https://www.pewresearch.org/fact-tank/2017/04/06/why-muslims-are-the-worlds-fastest-growing-religious-group/

2. David P. Goldman, "Why Iran is obsessed with Jews (hint: same as Hitler)," *Asia Times*, August 3, 2015, https://asiatimes.com/2015/08/why-iran-is-obsessed-with-jews-hint-same-as-hitler/

3. Tom Rosentiel, "Muslim Americans: Middle Class and Mostly Mainstream," Pew Research Center, May 22, 2007, https://www.pewresearch.org/2007/05/22/muslim-americans-middle-class-and-mostly-mainstream/

4. Pew Research Center, "Muslim Americans: No Signs of Growth in Alienation or Support for Extremism," August 30, 2011, https://www.people-press.org/2011/08/30/muslim-americans-no-signs-of-growth-in-alienation-or-support-for-extremism/

5. Ibid.

6. *Stratfor*, "Youth Unemployment: The Middle East's Ticking Time Bomb," February 28, 2018, https://worldview.stratfor.com/article/youth-unemployment-middle-east-teen-jobless

7. Ruud Koopmans, Eylem Kanol, and Dietlind Stolle, "Scriptural legitimation and the mobilization of support for religious violence: experimental evidence across three religions and seven countries," *Journal of Ethnic and Migration Studies* 47 (7), 2021, 1498-1516.

8. Shadi Hamid and Rashid Dar, "Islamism, Salafism, and Jihadism: A primer," Brookings, July 15, 2016, https://www.brookings.edu/blog/markaz/2016/07/15/islamism-salafism-and-jihadism-a-primer/

9. Lydia Khalil, "Al-Qaeda & the Muslim Brotherhood: United

by Strategy, Divided by Tactics," *Terrorism Monitor* 4, no. 6 (2006), accessed January 18, 2019, https://jamestown.org/program/al-qaeda-the-muslim-brotherhood-united-by-strategy-divided-by-tactics/

10. Andrea Elliott, "The Jihadist Next Door," *The New York Times*, January 27, 2010.

11. Bruce Fudge, "The Beards of the Ancestors: from the Prophet's Companions to the 'Islamic State,'" in *Barbe et Barbus*, ed. Youri Volokhine (New York: Peter Lang, 2019).

12. Hope Hodge Seck, "Air Force Grants Beard Waiver to Muslim Airman," *Military.com*, November 20, 2018, https://www.military.com/kitup/2018/11/20/air-force-grants-first-beard-waiver-muslim-airman.html#.W_XI2IytvbA.twitter

13. International Crisis Group, "Indonesia Backgrounder: Why Salafism and Terrorism Mostly Don't Mix," September 13, 2004, *Asia Report* #83, i.

14. Cole Bunzel, "From Paper State to Caliphate: The Ideology of the Islamic State," Center for Middle East Policy at Brookings, March 2015.

15. Ibid.

16. Encyclopedia.com, s.v. "Caliph," by G. Makdisi, accessed December 26, 2019, https://www.encyclopedia.com/philosophy-and-religion/islam/islam/caliph

17. Bunzel, "From Paper State to Caliphate: The Ideology of the Islamic State," 33.

18. Quintan Wiktorowicz, "Anatomy of the Salafi Movement," *Studies in Conflict and Terrorism* 29 (2006): 207-239.

19. Shaul Mishal and Avraham Sela, *The Palestinian Hamas: Vision, Violence, and Coexistence* (New York: Columbia University Press, 2000), 109.

20. Arnold Yasin Mol, "Denouncing Terrorism in the West: English Publications of Anti-terrorism Fatwa's as Western Islamic Discourse with an analysis of the 'Open Letter to Baghdadi' (longread)," Zenodo, 2016, http://doi.org/10.5281/

zenodo.259595

21. BBC News, "Sainsbury's pulls out of Egypt," April 9, 2001, http://news.bbc.co.uk/2/hi/business/1268099.stm

Chapter 13

1. Rick Gladstone, "World Population Could Peak Decades Ahead of U.N. Forecast, Study Asserts," July 14, 2020, *The New York Times*, https://www.nytimes.com/2020/07/14/world/americas/global-population-trends.html

2. UN News, "As famines of 'biblical proportion' loom, Security Council urged to 'act fast,'" April 21, 2020, https://news.un.org/en/story/2020/04/1062272

3. The World Bank, "Data" (n.d.), https://datahelpdesk.worldbank.org/knowledgebase/articles/906519

4. Wolfgang Merkel and Sonja Grimm, *War and Democratization: Legality, Legitimacy and Effectiveness* (Routledge, 2013), 122.

5. Johnny M. Sakr, "The Philosophical Correlation Between Nazi Fascist Ideology and Radical Islamic Theology and Jurisprudential Thought," *Western Australian Jurist* 8 (2012): 311-397.

6. Jacob Golomb, *Nietzsche and Jewish Culture* (Routledge, 2003), 94.

7. Richard Bulliet, Pamela Crossley, and Daniel Headrick, *The Earth and Its Peoples: A Global History* (Cengage Learning, 2010), vol 2: 816.

8. H.L.A. Hart, "Positivism and the Separation of Law and Morals," *Harvard Law Review* 71, no. 4 (1958): 593-629.

9. *New International Version Archaeological Study Bible*, 2005.

10. William Muir, *The Life of Mahomet* (Smith, Elder and Co., 1861), 130-133.

11. Adam Withnall and John Lichfield, "Charlie Hebdo shooting: At least 12 killed as shots fired at satirical magazine's Paris office," *The Independent*, London, January 14, 2014.

12. Robert D. Woodberry, "The Missionary Roots of Liberal

Democracy," *American Political Science Review* 106 (2), May 2012, 244-274.

13. Sayed Sikander Shah Haneef and Mek Wok Mahmud, "Critical Thinking in Islamic Law: The Search for Strategies," *Shariah Journal* 18, no. 1 (2010) 67-90.

14. Nabeel Qureshi, *Seeking Allah, Finding Jesus* (Zondervan, 2014), 79.

15. Arshad Khan, *Islam, Muslims, and America: Understanding the Basis of Their Conflict* (New York: Algora Publishing, 2003), 19.

16. Tariq Ramadan, "Critical Thinking for Muslims," Citizen of an Idiocracy, 2016, https://adnanramin.wordpress. com/2015/12/31/critical-thinking-for-muslims/

17. Qureshi, *Seeking Allah, Finding Jesus*, 108.

O-BOOKS

SPIRITUALITY

O is a symbol of the world, of oneness and unity; this eye represents knowledge and insight. We publish titles on general spirituality and living a spiritual life. We aim to inform and help you on your own journey in this life.
If you have enjoyed this book, why not tell other readers by posting a review on your preferred book site?

Recent bestsellers from O-Books are:

Heart of Tantric Sex
Diana Richardson
Revealing Eastern secrets of deep love and intimacy to Western couples.
Paperback: 978-1-90381-637-0 ebook: 978-1-84694-637-0

Crystal Prescriptions
The A-Z guide to over 1,200 symptoms and their healing crystals
Judy Hall
The first in the popular series of eight books, this handy little guide is packed as tight as a pill-bottle with crystal remedies for ailments.
Paperback: 978-1-90504-740-6 ebook: 978-1-84694-629-5

Your Simple Path
Find Happiness in every step
Ian Tucker
A guide to helping us reconnect with what is really important in our lives.
Paperback: 978-1-78279-349-6 ebook: 978-1-78279-348-9

365 Days of Wisdom
Daily Messages To Inspire You Through The Year
Dadi Janki
Daily messages which cool the mind, warm the heart and guide you along your journey.
Paperback: 978-1-84694-863-3 ebook: 978-1-84694-864-0

Body of Wisdom
Women's Spiritual Power and How it Serves
Hilary Hart
Bringing together the dreams and experiences of women across the world with today's most visionary spiritual teachers.
Paperback: 978-1-78099-696-7 ebook: 978-1-78099-695-0

Dying to Be Free
From Enforced Secrecy to Near Death to True Transformation
Hannah Robinson
After an unexpected accident and near-death experience, Hannah Robinson found herself radically transforming her life, while a remarkable new insight altered her relationship with her father, a practising Catholic priest.
Paperback: 978-1-78535-254-6 ebook: 978-1-78535-255-3

The Ecology of the Soul

A Manual of Peace, Power and Personal Growth for Real People
in the Real World
Aidan Walker
Balance your own inner Ecology of the Soul to regain your
natural state of peace, power and wellbeing.
Paperback: 978-1-78279-850-7 ebook: 978-1-78279-849-1

Not I, Not other than I

The Life and Teachings of Russel Williams
Steve Taylor, Russel Williams
The miraculous life and inspiring teachings of one of the World's
greatest living Sages.
Paperback: 978-1-78279-729-6 ebook: 978-1-78279-728-9

On the Other Side of Love

A woman's unconventional journey towards wisdom
Muriel Maufroy
When life has lost all meaning, what do you do?
Paperback: 978-1-78535-281-2 ebook: 978-1-78535-282-9

Practicing A Course In Miracles

A translation of the Workbook in plain language, with
mentor's notes
Elizabeth A. Cronkhite
The practical second and third volumes of The Plain-Language
A Course In Miracles.
Paperback: 978-1-84694-403-1 ebook: 978-1-78099-072-9

Quantum Bliss
The Quantum Mechanics of Happiness, Abundance, and Health
George S. Mentz
Quantum Bliss is the breakthrough summary of success and spirituality secrets that customers have been waiting for.
Paperback: 978-1-78535-203-4 ebook: 978-1-78535-204-1

The Upside Down Mountain
Mags MacKean
A must-read for anyone weary of chasing success and happiness – one woman's inspirational journey swapping the uphill slog for the downhill slope.
Paperback: 978-1-78535-171-6 ebook: 978-1-78535-172-3

Your Personal Tuning Fork
The Endocrine System
Deborah Bates
Discover your body's health secret, the endocrine system, and 'twang' your way to sustainable health!
Paperback: 978-1-84694-503-8 ebook: 978-1-78099-697-4

Readers of ebooks can buy or view any of these bestsellers by clicking on the live link in the title. Most titles are published in paperback and as an ebook. Paperbacks are available in traditional bookshops. Both print and ebook formats are available online.
Find more titles and sign up to our readers' newsletter at http://www.johnhuntpublishing.com/mind-body-spirit
Follow us on Facebook at https://www.facebook.com/OBooks/ and Twitter at https://twitter.com/obooks